# Penal Discipline, Reformatory Projects and the English Prison Commission 1895–1939

# Penal Discipline, Reformatory Projects and the English Prison Commission 1895–1939

W. J. Forsythe

University of Exeter Press

*To Patricia and Nuala*

*With Love*

First published in 1990 by
University of Exeter Press
Reed Hall
Streatham Drive
Exeter   EX4 4QR
UK

Typeset by Kestrel Data, Exeter
Printed in the UK by Short Run Press Ltd, Exeter

**British Library Cataloguing in Publication Data**
Forsythe, W. J. (William James)
    Penal discipline, reformatory projects and the English
    Prison Commission 1895–1939.
    1. England. Prisons, history
    I. Title
    365.942

    ISBN 0-85989-344-8

# Contents

# Acknowledgements

I want to record my gratitude to the following people and institutions for the help they gave me in researching and writing this book.

The British Academy and the University of Exeter for funding the research upon which this book is based and the University of Exeter for allowing me the research leave necessary to undertake the work.

Sir John Ruggles-Brise for allowing me to visit Sir Evelyn Ruggles-Brise's family home and to see the private papers of Sir Evelyn: also for the immense kindness he and his staff showed me.

Peter English, Head of the Law Department of Exeter University, for his encouragement of and interest in this study.

The Home Office.

The staff at the Public Record Office, Kew.

The Postgraduate Medical Centre library, Wonford Hospital, Exeter.

The University of Exeter Library and especially Heather Eva of the inter-library loan section there.

The staff of the Bodleian Library, Oxford.

Lastly my wife Patricia, who typed and arranged the entire text.

# Abbreviations in References

| | |
|---|---|
| RCP | Reports of the Commissioners of Prisons |
| RCP and DCP | Reports of the Commissioners of Prisons and Directors of Convict Prisons |
| RDCP | Reports of the Directors of Convict Prisons |
| PRO | Public Record Office. [Kew] |
| BMJ | British Medical Journal |
| PP | Parliamentary Papers |
| ECRO | Essex County Records Office |
| PC | Prison Commission |
| HO | Home Office |
| Parl.Deb. | Parliamentary Debates |
| obs | Observations |
| cut. | Cutting of a newspaper stored in Public Record Office file |

# Introduction

There has recently been much debate about changing ideology and practice in the nineteenth and early twentieth century English prison system. The tone of this debate was initially set by Michel Foucault[1] and Michael Ignatieff[2] in the 1970s. Foucault and Ignatieff emphasised different aspects but the tenor of their thesis was that a remarkable and highly significant change occurred in prisons in France and Britain between 1775 and 1850. As Ignatieff subsequently explained,[3] he and Foucault argued that the prisons of this era took shape as the infliction of public pain upon the body gave way to the prevalence of punishment in a new panoptic bureaucratised institution, operating according to formally defined rules and the tenets of the human sciences, the penitentiary as a new type of punishment which made credible the claim that penal punishment was deterrent, reformatory and humane. Foucault and Ignatieff were sceptical of claims to progressive improvement made on behalf of these institutions and saw them as places which camouflaged the relentless cross fertilisation of structures of power and control with the human sciences beneath grand claims of benevolence and progress.

For Foucault and Ignatieff the period during which this revolution was accomplished was one of around seventy years after 1775. Certainly there were different emphases between them. Foucault, for example, pointed to the growth of rationalistic symmetrical and inter connected modes of quarantining criminality and of routinising the behaviour of the poor whilst Ignatieff remarked on the control of the lower by the higher classes and the disciplining of dissidents. In this he implicated the theology underpinning the evangelical emphasis on the sin of the prisoner, the need for atonement through suffering and the universal availability of divine grace to all who penitently kneeled at the gates of Christ's kingdom.

It is worth dwelling for a moment upon this apparent difference between Foucault and Ignatieff. There is a question as to the degree to which Ignatieff in fact differed from Foucault in regard to Ignatieff's emphasis on the genuine reformatory endeavour which he attributed to John Howard, the late eighteenth century prison explorer, and his early nineteenth century successors. Certainly Ignatieff made clear Howard's passionate commitment to the Christian notion of universal human value and the possibility of redemption and pointed up the problematic nature of penal projects to reconcile deterrence, reformation and humanitarianism. Yet in the event his argument was that a system of little less than totalitarian terror was created in the early nineteenth century prison system and that the newly emergent industrialising middle classes used this system to indoctrinate or terrorise all who did not exhibit the docility, deference and obedience required of them in the new era.[4] Subsequently he even came to doubt the genuiness of Howard's own enthusiasm for the reformatory potential of separate cellular confinement.[5] However, in his original thesis Ignatieff argued that the real function of reformatory projects in prisons in the late eighteenth and early nineteenth centuries was less to emphasise the value of all in the eyes of God than to assure those who held power, wealth and knowledge of their rectitude and continuance in these things so that the class based structure of society remained intact. As he remarked: 'the reformers did extend the state's obligation to prisoners, but not on the basis of full recognition of their rights as human beings. Their right to decent treatment remained conditional on their willingness to re-enter the moral consensus . . . the language of "police" not "humanity".'[6]

Both Foucault and Ignatieff made clear that they saw these prisons, which were claimed to be founded upon reconditioning of human attitude and behaviour and spiritual redemption, as origins of a modern era of penality, intrusive into the human mind, positivistic in its obsession with maps of the criminal personality, secretively tyrannical in its hidden administrative judgements, segregative and expansionary. Foucault, in particular, viewed the claims of the prison to be based upon concepts of universal value and reconciliation between prisoner and society as a sham for the prison was a place in which occurred a tyrannical segregation in which the artificial discourses of the human sciences served and were served by the structures of power.

This disturbing analysis of the ancestry of the modern prison came to be known as 'revisionist' because it dramatically revised earlier cheering notions of modern penality as progressive improvement. It was not long before revisionism itself had its critics who argued that the picture of great grey monolithic prisons, mechanically ordered by rigidly stratified staff under the watchful eyes of inspectors, governors, chaplains dedicated to the new intellectual disciplines underpinning the conversion or reconditioning of prisoners, was in fact inaccurate. So, for example, Margaret DeLacy[7] and Janet Saunders[8] argued that what actually happened in prisons in Lancashire and Warwickshire in the nineteenth century was often different from the claims of enthusiasts in London about new forms of prison discipline and depended upon a complex interplay between local power groups as much as the requirements of the State. Indeed DeLacy questioned whether the separate system, under which prisoners were isolated in their separate cells and submitted to education, training and evangelisation, was fully operated in most prisons. In other words, the argument ran, Foucault and Ignatieff mistook the rhetoric of the State for actual administrative practice.

This argument has, in its turn, been met with the thesis that of course rhetoric and practice were not the same.[9] Nonetheless, the prisons of mid-Victorian England were almost all entirely different from those which were explored by John Howard in the late eighteenth century.[10] Although their administration varied from area to area, it was argued that there should be no doubt that the system as a whole was characterised by an emphasis on predictable and routine administrative practice, a tendency towards educational and spiritual reformatory projects intended to change attitude and conduct, rigid segregation of types of prisoner from each other (men from women, misdemeanants from felons for example), division of staff into stratified grades and an emphasis on evangelicalism and associationist psychology as the basis of reformatory methods. If, like Ignatieff, one compared the prisons of the late eighteenth century and those of the mid nineteenth the change was unmistakable. Even the small borough prisons which survived were quite unlike those described by John Howard.[11]

The debate has recently become more wide ranging in that it has been extended to encompass the later nineteenth and early twentieth centuries. Radzinowicz and Hood[12] unambiguously argued that revisionists were mistaken in placing the origin of the modern English penal system in the context of a remarkable expansion of carceral subjugation and normalising treatment. In fact, they claimed, the influence of the human sciences was never such as to alter the fundamental dependence of English penality upon the classical principles of limited deterrence and uniformity of treatment. They urged that in the late nineteenth and early twentieth centuries the prison system in fact diminished in size and impact. So they remarked in the conclusion of their recent analysis: 'some penal historians have made much of the widespread use of "mass imprisonment", of the spreading tentacles of the "carceral archipelago" in the nineteenth century. But this view cannot be said to be confirmed by later Victorian and Edwardian experience. What we witness is rather a mass movement away from reliance on incarceration and a growing distrust of the "asylum theory".'[13]

To Radzinowicz and Hood the Foucaultian street-cleaning operation, by which great numbers of deviants were institutionalised and quarantined, was not borne out by the facts. Furthermore, they persuasively argued that the penal system was cautious of new human scientific knowledges such as neo Darwinian Lombrosian positivism or the English eugenics movement of the early twentieth century. Penal institutions, it seemed, preferred to base their operation on an altogether more traditional view of the prisoner as morally culpable, responsible and reformable rather than as biologically and characteristically flawed.

Their account appeared around the same time as the widely acclaimed account by David Garland *Punishment and Welfare*.[14] Garland's argument was the opposite. He argued that Foucault's dating of the processes of categorisation, normalisation and classification between 1775 and 1850 was wrong. In fact, he said, the Victorian penal system depended predominently upon classical notions of judicially calibrated punishment of rational offenders who were believed to have made culpable decisions to commit crimes and were deterred and punished strictly on that basis. The real upset to classical measured publicly defined deterrent punishment occurred between 1895 and 1914. Then the new positivistic criminologies and the discourses of eugenics cross-fertilised with the structures of power to produce a new type of penality which treated and managed deviants on the basis of their character type or propensities. To Garland therefore there was a second wave of change after the total institutional revolution described by Foucault and dated by him between 1775 and 1850 and it was this second wave of change which was particularly significant in laying the foundations of modern penality. Institutions were themselves differentiated to service and control the various groups delineated by science. However, new types of non custodial assessment, intervention and disposal arose, such as community-based supervision, which were resonant to a new era of welfarist control and intrusion. Positivism had thus become a central intellectual support of the new penality and systematically emphasised the functions of quarantine, segregation, individualisation and differentiation which, according to Garland, Foucault had misdated. Furthermore the struggle of middle-class professional groups to gain power and influence was a significant aspect of the history of the creation of the new (and abiding) penality.

So between 1895 and 1914 Garland emphasised the new eugenic and criminological sciences which tended to draw heavily from Darwinian and Social Darwinian modes of analysis. Under the influence of those who advocated them numerous proposals for new kinds of disposal were advocated, many of which were implemented—colonies for vagrants, sterilization of deviants, preventive detention for habitual criminals, containment of mentally defective people, psychological assessment techniques and so forth. Henceforth the offender would be allocated on the basis of propensity, character and need to one or more of an increasing number of disposals founded on the discourses of the human sciences.

To Foucault, and to a lesser extent other revisionists reformation of the attitude and conduct of prisoners constituted a field of activity for intellectuals, professionals and functionaries who proposed theories and applied the methods which sprang from those theories. The deepest purpose of the reformatory disciplinary project was, despite the rhetoric of reformation, not to reduce numbers of criminals but rather to strengthen and expand mechanisms of carceral and more general means of social/penal control. So, the notions of, say, conciliation between prisoners and society, environmental or biological influences upon human behaviour, moral example and close engagement between staff and prisoner, individualisation of training or treatment to suit assessed propensity, indeterminacy of sentence, all of which lay at the heart of reformatory discourses, in fact served to justify more extensive uses of incarceration, segregation or at least control of social deviants.

Furthermore to revisionists reformatory discourses served to underpin the mechanisms of power in that they delineated the distinction between deviancy and normality. Indeed Foucault especially pointed out that such awesome structures as penitentiaries and the compelling discourses which gave birth to them taught the mass of the people to see the necessity, humanity and justice of such modes of objectifying, segregating and disciplining deviants altogether unaware that by this continuing human scientific discursive definition and redefinition the boundaries between normality and abnormality became more fluid. These boundaries were thus subject to somewhat capricious rearrangement although the underlying tendency was to widen the definition of what could legitimately be seen as deviancy and hence to justify an expanding network of policing, judicial, welfare and carceral institutions as well as a remarkable increase of powers and personnel necessary to service them.

There can be little doubt that the work of Foucault in particular and revisionists in general has deeply compromised or even discredited the reformatory endeavour in prisons. Given the current critical situation in British prisons it is essential to re-examine this particular aspect of their history in order to understand whether Foucault was right that it was merely a convenient way of extending carceral subjugation or whether the disinterested idealism which was claimed by its advocates was a significant part of prison discipline, more than mere rhetoric to justify further control.To modern eyes the evangelical chaplains, athletic Christian borstal housemasters, gentlemanly prison govenors and self-assured prison commissioners who appear hereafter may seem to represent a type of paternalism which has now passed into history. Nevertheless, these officials claimed that they were representing a very important belief about human value and potential in their work and repeated this claim at international congresses, in official reports, in newspapers and eventually in radio broadcasts. The legitimacy of that claim and the problematic nature of the projects which arose from it are the subject matter of this book.

## NOTES

1. M. Foucault, *Discipline and Punish: The Birth of the Prison* (Penguin 1979).
2. M. Ignatieff, *A Just Measure of Pain: The Penitentiary in the Industrial Revolution* (MacMillan 1978).
3. M. Ignatieff, 'State, Civil Society and Total Institutions', in S. Cohen and A. Scull (eds) *Social Control and the State* (Robertson 1983): 75-105.
4. Ignatieff, *A Just Measure of Pain.*
5. M. Ignatieff, review of Sean McConville *History of English Prison Administration, Times Literary Supplement:* 23 Oct. 1981. 1230 col. c.
6. Ignatieff, *A Just Measure of Pain:* 211, 214.
7. M. Delacy, 'Grinding Men Good: Lancashire's Prisons at Mid Century' in V. Bailey (ed) *Policy and Punishment in Nineteenth-Century Britain* (Croom Helm 1981). M.Delacy, *Prison Reform in Lancashire 1700-1850* (Manchester University Press 1986).
8. J. Saunders, 'Institutionalised Offenders: A Study of the Victorian Institution with Special Reference to Warwickshire' (PhD thesis, University of Warwick, 1983).
9. W. J. Forsythe, *The Reform of Prisoners 1830-1900* (Croom Helm 1987).
10. J. Howard, *The State of the Prisons* (1777).
11. W. J. Forsythe, *A System of Discipline. Exeter Borough Prison 1819-1863* (University of Exeter Press 1983).
12. L. Radzinowicz and R. Hood, *A History of English Criminal Law and Its Administration,* Vol. 5, *The Emergence of Penal Policy* (Stevens and Sons 1986).
13. Ibid: 778.
14. D. Garland, *Punishment and Welfare* (Gower 1985).

# Chapter One

# The Transformation of Reformatory Theory
## 1820–1910

By 1820 there were two main approaches to the reformation of prisoners in England. These were the evangelical and associationist and each had a substantial effect upon the development of English prisons up to 1860. Thereafter the reformatory endeavour went into decline for the optimistic claim that the attitude and conduct of large numbers of prisoners could be changed by the methods deriving from those approaches was less widely believed.

Evangelicals emphasised that all members of society were heirs to God's grace, children of a loving deity. They accepted entirely that their society should be structured hierarchically[1] but called for a spiritual renaissance among all classes in order that by forging zealous missionary and charitable links between rich and poor all members of society would face up to the universal sinfulness of man[2] redeemable only by divine grace made available through Christ's sacrifice, a central tenet of evangelical theology. The established orders must therefore turn from 'ambition and worldly grandeur'[3] and engage in dynamic, solicitous charitable activity with the poor[4] who, like lost sheep, were straying from the paths of religion and goodness. The evangelical movement appeared to contemporaries to promise stability and security in a society widely believed to be threatened by crime, disorder and hedonism and evangelicals therefore achieved a very great influence on the formulation of programmes of social reform because they appeared to guarantee an effective missionary engagement with 'the labouring heathen'[5] in a society feared by large numbers of churchmen and others to be at the edge of 'class warfare' and disintegration.[6]

The evangelical version of prisoner reformation was of ardent chaplains exhorting, instructing and admonishing prisoners and of grave, zealous governors and staff exemplifying the Christian man. On the reformatory side therefore they wished the prison to be a moral/spiritual forcing house in which relationships would be characterised by sincerity, compassion, endeavour and ardent enthusiasm for Christian improvement in direct contrast to their belief that prisoners in unreformed prisons in fact contaminated one another with vice and crime, neglected by those who had their charge.

Between 1830 and 1850 there was advanced a model of prison discipline based upon this desire for moral and spiritual reclamation of the individual prisoner. Large numbers of prisons were rebuilt to apply this model which was known as the separate system. Prisons were therefore constructed with tiered corridors lined by cells radiating out from a central administrative block. The aim was to isolate prisoners from each other in separate cells, place them in separate cubicles in chapel, mask them whenever they moved from one part of the prison to another so as to prevent recognition believed to encourage fellowship amongst prisoners after their release.

It was intended by this method that prisoners so isolated would be forced in upon themselves and that they would hear at last the voices of conscience and religion. Chaplains and staff would instruct, admonish and exhort them, teach them to read and know scripture, show them the stumbling blocks of their own sin, train them in a trade and so forth. So, in place of reckless self-seeking criminality there would be created a humble repentant thirst for atonement with God through Christ, a true and permanent reformation of attitude and conduct.

The other notion which also depended upon an idea of reconstruction of environment in order to produce attitudinal and behavioural change was a more secular and in theory deterministic notion of conditioning of prisoners. Advanced most pointedly by Jeremy Bentham in the late eighteenth century, this reformatory thesis depended upon a view of human psychology which was widely argued and derived from eighteenth century philosophy. It was known as associationism and essentially the idea was that human attitude is founded upon experience, that the human mind seeks to repeat that which gives pleasure, to avoid that which gives pain. So, Bentham argued that the application of rewards and penalties within a prison was capable by such conditioning of reversing the inappropriate mental links between crime and pleasure established in the years before the criminal entered prison. Bentham assumed that crime and vice were fostered in early life by their association in the mind with pleasure because of deficient or inappropriate parental training and a failure of environmental influences during upbringing. Prison must therefore eradicate the faulty association by inflicting pain whilst erecting new attitudes by a regime which rewarded with privileges such things as industriousness, obedience and dutifulness and penalised their reverse. By conditioning therefore permanent psychological change—and hence reformation—might be brought about.[7]

Bentham advocated the establishment of a particular kind of prison which he called a Panopticon which in its pure form was not generally accepted. However the idea that rewards and punishments did have an influence on attitude and conduct was imported into the prison system during the period between 1835 and 1865 especially in the management of convicts sentenced either to long terms of transportation or its successor penal servitude. Consequently the idea that convicts work their way up through a series of stages with additional privileges and eventual release on licence was characteristic of the discipline of convicts and had roots in associationist assumptions. In addition evangelicalism and associationism were not necessarily incompatible ideas of reformation, but could be fused as with convicts who served their initial eighteen months (later reduced to nine) in separation before proceeding to the staged promotion system of the public works convict prisons such as Portland.

There was, of course, much discrepancy between the theory and practice of the systems which were based on these ideas. Between 1835 and 1865 elements of the ideas were fused together to produce idiosyncratic local arrangements, a mosaic of disciplinary methods drawing in one or more ways from these new theories. Despite this patchwork adaptation prison administration during the early Victorian era moved substantially towards the idea that by an appropriate regime the individual prisoner could be reformed and restored to his or her surrounding society. Clearly other considerations favoured the spread of these systems, for example that prisoners were easier to manage in separation, but the quest for successful reformatory techniques was one which occupied prison disciplinarians of the early Victorian era very greatly. Indeed the assumptions underlying evangelicalism and associationism generally commanded wide acceptance in early Victorian England.

These approaches depended upon the notion that behaviour patterns were the result of postnatal human experience whether a failure of educational, familial or ecclesiastical systems to teach Christian attitudes or the inappropriate conditioning to vicious or criminal behaviour by parents and peers. Therefore it followed that such attitude and conduct could be altered by bringing to bear new environmental influences upon the defective person. These optimistic expectations of improvement were thus lodged in an environmentalist analysis of cause and cure and this environmentalism prevailed over other analyses which asserted a more deep seated and unchangeable foundation of human conduct. So, for example, phrenological positivists argued in the early nineteenth century that behaviour was correlated with prenatally determined and varying sized regions of the brain, but they made little headway against the view that attitude and conduct were influenced by environment.

The Darwinian evolutionist intellectual revolution of the mid-Victorian era undermined this optimistic approach to prisoner reform. Evolutionist theorising had proceeded for several decades before Charles Darwin published *Origin Of the Species* in 1859 but had not been a mainstream preoccupation of British intellectual thought. By 1880, however, it was widely argued that the criminal, the pauper, the lunatic, the mental defective and others were examples of the workings of the laws of evolution whose deficiencies in the competition for survival and for life, if nature had her way, would ultimately lead their type to extinction. In Britain for example Herbert Spencer and Francis Galton argued that moral and intellectual qualities were not primarily the result of postnatal experience but were transmitted by heredity, according to evolutionist laws, and therefore differential behavioural propensities and moral predispositions were present at birth. In essence the notion was one of an eternal struggle for life and survival between types, the success of those most fitted through inherited capacities in that struggle and the gradual extinction of those who both inherited and bequeathed their unfit capacities through biological process.

The application of a Darwinian scientific framework to criminal man had the effect of weakening faith in the optimistic universality of Evangelicalism and the idea of reconditioning by associationism. This is not to suggest that in its extreme form it found acceptance in Britain. For example Cesare Lombroso claimed to have discovered in the 1870s that the majority of criminals were detectable by skull shape and more general physiological difference similar to lower orders on the evolutionary ladder. Therefore Lombroso believed that most criminals bore resemblance to primitive savage man and had physiological and psychological characteristics typical of less highly evolved man or higher orders of wild animal. His thesis was not accepted in Britain, although it was influential in Italy. However, the more general neo Darwinian view that there was constitutional deficiency amongst such people as habitual criminals or persistent vagrants or mental defectives and that this deficiency was transmitted by inheritance was moved to the centre of debate about such groups. By the 1880s, therefore, the idea of inheritance of predisposition was no longer a peripheral preoccupation of eccentrics but a question of great importance to contemporaries. So, both greatly influenced by Darwinian theory, Herbert Spencer and Francis Galton insisted that a qualitative characteristic difference existed from birth between the habitual offender or persistent pauper and the sturdy competitive average or indeed the highly talented stock of the race.

Such an approach cast into doubt the idea that by earnest Christian discourse, educational instruction or behaviour conditioning large numbers of criminals could be reformed. Furthermore, as belief in hereditarily transmitted characteristics was more strongly urged, two other major worries were created. Firstly by 1900 there was the racial anxiety that British national fitness was being undermined and that nations such as Germany, Japan or America would gain over Britain in economic and other forms of competition. Secondly it was increasingly feared by the end of the nineteenth century that the lower orders of human stock in Britain were not in fact dying out but, because protected from the harsh selective laws of nature by mechanisms of social policy such as lunatic asylums or the Poor Law, were in fact breeding at a faster rate than the higher. Indeed, one view was that there was an overall population decline in which the proportion of lower order fast breeders to the rest was increasing so rapidly as ultimately to overwhelm the rest. These concerns were forcefully argued by the Eugenics movement after 1900 and eugenicists maintained that 'in born potentiality' was 'largely derived from a similar capacity inherent in the parents or ancestry'.[8] Ideas therefore proliferated about the measures necessary to strengthen and protect nation and race whether sterilization, education or the segregation of criminal defectives 'with a view to non reproduction of the type'.[9] Furthermore, the debates among eugenicists became exceedingly technical for the more detailed scientific work of the nineteenth century such as the statistical studies of Francis Galton or the work of the Austrian monk and theorist Gregor Mendel on plant hybridisation made clear the profound nature of the matter and the necessity for most detailed inquiry. Thus eugenicists did not all subscribe to the same remedial measures but argued with one another continuously. Nevertheless, they were agreed that 'thanks to differential fertility the British race was not only losing its stock of great men but was becoming increasingly burdened with a social problem group or residuum at the bottom who bred recklessly and made up the bulk of paupers, criminals, lunatics, deaf mutes, alcoholics and feeble minded'.[10]

Concern about the physical and moral deterioration of the race was also an important element in the success of the British youth movements between 1890 and 1910. Baden-Powell, for example, frequently used the analogy of Roman imperial decline and believed that national efficiency required that the youth of the nation be organised so as to be fit for the government of empire, loyal, energetic, efficient, dutiful and clean. As he remarked: 'Don't be disgraced like the young Romans who lost the Empire . . . by being wishy washy slackers without any go or patriotism in them. Play up! Each man in his place and play the game.'[11] Baden-Powell clearly saw the boy scouts as a most important part of the building of a re-energised and strong imperial Britain. He emphasised the success of the fittest, the self-controlled and disciplined cultivation of endurance, self-reliance and service to the group and the contrast between the camps and jamborees of his troops of scouts and the loafers, criminals and hooligans of the street corner and prison was unmistakable.[12]

During the late nineteenth and early twentieth centuries there was a burgeoning international scientific criminological concern about the measures necessary to protect society from the criminal. In Britain much of this was in the context of anxiety about national decline and was heightened by the demands of eugenicists such as Francis Galton and his disciple Karl Pearson that there be dedicated study of 'all influences that improve the unborn qualities of a race'[13] together with laboratories and anthropometric devices to measure the physical differences between groups and types. In America enthusiasts urged that 'criminals, mattoids, paupers and other defectives are social bacilli which require as thorough scientific investigation as the bacilli of physical diseases'.[14] In Italy positivist criminologists, although frequently in dispute about particulars, condemned the traditional classical emphasis of sentencers and legislators on the free will of criminals and the probability of widespread deterrence by legal definition and enforcement of penalty. They urged the idea of the criminal act as a psychological entity, the criminal as deterministically created either by heredity or environment or both and the need for scientific differential treatment of criminals according to type and tendency of personality.[15] The influence of Darwinian and more general evolutionist theory upon these theorists was great although the weight assigned to hereditary transmission varied amongst them. However, they agreed that extreme measures of incapacitation were essential for those habitual offenders who were defective in the capacity to reform. So Raffaele Garofalo urged death, life imprisonment or transportation for those habituals found by scientific experts to possess a hereditarily transmitted moral anomaly.[16] For less recidivistic personality types a battery of measures was urged by Italian criminologists into which the scientifically diagnosed offender might be inserted, what Garland called 'an extended grid of . . . diverse dispositions into which the offender is inscribed according to the diagnosis of his or her condition and the treatment appropriate to it'.[17]

By 1895 the earlier pessimism of Lombroso and Garofalo about the likelihood of successful reformatory intervention was modified as increasing numbers of types of criminal were discovered and many kinds of hereditary and environmental causative factors in their criminality disclosed. For those who were not irreclaimable by severe hereditary defect a great number of strategies might therefore be tried, to be individually assigned according 'to which type of criminal he belongs, and, as a consequence, what degree of anti-social depravity and readaptability is indicated by his physical and mental qualities . . . whether he is a born criminal, or mad, or an habitual or occasional criminal or a criminal of passion'.[18] Treatment and cure were thus to be a matter for medical and other experts and the notion of indeterminate periods of treatment came to the fore, release being dependent upon diagnosed cure and pronouncement of safety of release. In such a scheme classical notions of the moral responsibility of the offender gave way to the positivistic analytical disposals of science.

Certainly there is evidence of these kinds of views being strongly urged in Britain. In 1892 Dr S. Strahan suggested that two-thirds of British criminals were born with criminal instincts and that their appearance was that of the idiot with 'ill shapen heads, paralyses, squints, asymmetrical faces, deformed shrunken and ill developed bodies, abnormal conditions of the genital organs, heavy large jaws, outstanding ears and a restless animal like or brutal expression'; for these prolonged and indefinite periods of incarceration were needed.[19] Bevan Lewis medical superintendent of Wakefield Asylum spoke of 'epileptoid' and 'convulsive' constitutions inherited from parents and prone to motiveless irresistible frenzy in 1893 and the medical officer of Portsmouth prison was convinced that in over half of a sample of prisoners 'the orbits were large and in the majority the frontal sinuses and zygoma were prominent'.[20] In 1894 the Home Office appointed an official to supervise the introduction of the French Bertillon method of measuring skull and bone structure of criminals and prison warders were instructed in this anthropometrical method.[21] At the turn of the century a good deal of attention was being paid by prison medical staff to scientific measurement of criminals in order to differentiate their types from one another and from the norm.[22]

However, in medical circles there was always caution about extreme forms of foreign psychology and criminology. Charles Mercier, President of the Psychological section of the British Medical Association, was a persistent and sarcastic critic of ideas such as that some murderers had a characteristic and constitutionally based craving for murder much as an inebriate craved drink and therefore, being incurable, should be destroyed. He was scathing about the treatment methods which he believed had resulted at Elmira in America based on such approaches. 'You are a degenerate and since your crimes are no fault of yours you shall not be punished for them. On the contrary you shall be entertained, amused and instructed. You shall be treated with Turkish baths and massage ... you shall exercise in a gymnasium to the strains of a band of music played by your fellow criminals. You are of weak mind and therefore you shall be aesthetically cultured by a course of lectures on Chaucer and Shakespeare ... you are a semi imbecile and therefore you shall be put through a course of Jowett's Plato ... your forehead recedes or worse it projects. Your chin projects or worse it recedes. You have no wisdom teeth. Your ears are too large, they are too small, they are misshapen.'[23]

Among most British lawyers and sentencers the distrust of these extreme criminological views was also marked. Admittedly in the mid nineteenth century juvenile offenders had begun to be differentially subjected to treatment in reformatory schools as an alternative to prison discipline and there had even been the experiment of a prison for young convicts set up at Parkhurst in 1838. Also there had been an attempt to divert first offenders from prison by means of a court order of release conditional upon good behaviour instead of a prison sentence in 1887 (50 and 51 Vict. cap. 25). However, in the mid Victorian era sentencing was essentially to one of a hierarchy of penalties imposed on the basis of perceived moral culpability, previous record and seriousness of the legally defined crime. The prevailing belief in Britain was that this classical dependence on statutorily limited punishment, measured by law so as to prevent political or judicial tyranny or administrative abuse and yet severe enough to deter others, was an entirely adequate basis for punishment. Nonetheless, although the great majority of sentencers shared this devotion to the classical approach to sentencing, there was by the end of the nineteenth century a growing concern in legal circles about habitual criminals as well as a fear that these were innately predisposed to crime. In 1895 the widely read professional journal, *The Law Times*, fiercely attacked lawyers and judges for adhering to outdated principles and unstintingly praised the Italian school for teaching the world to concentrate scientific endeavours on the criminal and his treatment rather than depend on futile classical assumptions.[24] The eminent barrister and sentencer, Montague Crackanthorpe, as early as 1872 was warning of the ill consequences of high birth rates among the poorest classes and was later president of the Eugenics Education Society.[25]

It seems clear that by 1900 there was widespread concern about the possibility of hereditary transmission of inferiority or tendency in Britain and that eugenists, in particular, attracted a good deal of attention even though British sentencers and penal officials adhered to classical ideas of responsibility and culpability. However there was another approach to social pathology which was more reminiscent of the original spiritual mission of the evangelicals than of the Darwinian age. The New Liberalism grew out of the teachings of Thomas Hill Green at Oxford in the late 1870s. He argued that the liberal political theoretical conception of individual freedom had to be grounded upon a theological conception of human nature. Urging that earlier liberal theorists had not understood that spiritual striving was at the heart of man's true destiny, Green insisted that spiritual growth occurred when the rich set aside luxury and self-indulgence, which vitiated their own spiritual progress, to engage in dedicated voluntary action amongst the poor. Essentially he demanded a voluntarist, self-denying, atoning service on the part of the well to do so that spiritual and moral potential would be realised among all sections of society. Consequently, dedicated service and social action would create conditions among the poor which would enable them also to reach their true spiritual destiny at present obscured by the vice and squalor to which they were abandoned.

Green and the new liberal theorists, such as L.T. Hobhouse, who succeeded him, placed moral improvement, social responsibility and collective progress at the heart of their ideas. The connection between such a theoretical trumpet blast and the Darwinian era was not immediately obvious and indeed Green himself was disdainful of the new scientific positivism whilst Hobhouse distrusted the extremes of 'eugenicists . . . efficiency advocates and all forms of bureaucratic authoritarianism'.[26] However, new liberal theory incorporated evolutionism and positivism in two major ways. Firstly new liberals universally argued that there was evolving a new kind of society, interconnected in its parts, highly ethical, dutiful, harmonious, a higher type of society in which would be naturally mitigated the struggle for survival. Members would become much more deeply secured in cooperation and reason. Secondly, however, the society would evolve systems of voluntary endeavour designed to protect the poor from the effects of unrestrained economic competition and state institutions to train those who fell into vice, crime and pauperism to a higher personal morality. Such systems would make use of scientific knowledge to a great degree for 'social arrangements, to be just and efficacious had to reflect what science had discovered about the structure and working of society'.[27] Such a society would place a strong conception of social welfare and moral improvement alongside the older Gladstonian liberal emphasis on individual liberty and economic freedom and it would be pervaded by 'the awareness of the need for constant action of an optimistic and rational spirituality upon a world which at best was only dimly conscious of ultimate ethical values'.[28]

All these currents of thought were in varying ways to influence the theory and practice of social policy and voluntary action. So, T.H. Green's teaching was directly influential in the creation of the settlement movement whereby graduates of universities went to reside and give service in centres of education and charitable work in the midst of urban slums and it is beyond doubt that large numbers of future administrators and educators were influenced by him: indeed Evelyn Ruggles-Brise who was at Oxford at this period and was later the Chairman of the Prison Commission for over twenty-five years believed that Green was 'one of the clearest and profoundest thinkers of the end of the last century'.[29] Sydney and Beatrice Webb the Fabian social theorists were greatly influenced by the eugenic and national efficiency debate, Beatrice Webb advocating measures in the well known 1909 Minority Report of the Poor Law Commission aimed to contain the irreclaimably unfit and to train other able bodied unemployed in camps 'to the highest state of physical and mental efficiency of which they were capable'.[30] Other Fabians such as H.G. Wells and George Bernard Shaw were similarly influenced by the anxiety about national physical efficiency and indeed Seebohm Rowntree emphasised this aspect in his survey of the condition of the people of York.[31] As David Garland drily remarked 'the prominence of the eugenic programme in establishment circles may be gathered from simply listing the names of Sydney and Beatrice Webb, G.B. Shaw, J.B.S. Haldane, J.M. Keynes, Cyril Burt, Dr Barnardo and William Beveridge all of whom were members or active supporters of the eugenic cause';[32] a letter to *The Times* in 1911 calling for eugenic intervention and control of the sub-normal was signed by eight peers, an archbishop, six bishops, three M.P.s, two heads of Cambridge colleges, a number of professors, the editors of *Lancet* and *Mind*, the heads of the Free Church of Scotland, other religious leaders, General William Booth of the Salvation Army and Ramsay MacDonald.[33] In 1906 a departmental committee recommended that medical knowledge, voluntary effort and long-term detention colonies for unreformable recalcitrants be utilised to combat the spread of vagrancy.[34]

At the turn of the century therefore attitudes to the reform of prisoners were effected by a mixture of differing bodies of discourse. On the one hand there was a renewed environmental crusade to kindle the spiritual and moral energies of the poor and to construct more interventionist institutions of social policy together with an insistence on the importance of stewardship, personal relationship, charity and education. On the other was the scientific positivist approach, drawing often from the evolutionist framework of analysis, which emphasised the careful analysis of personality and defectiveness so as to assign the individual to the correct category or type and to treat him or her by the most effective of the increasing number of methods differentiated by science. Alongside both approaches ran the hope that by measures of social policy national decline would be arrested as well as the eugenic fear that many of the least fit would be constitutionally inferior as a result of biological transmission, unlikely to be reclaimed and liable to procreate their own kind. For them measures of social protection by long-term institutional containment would be necessary and indeed, as Garland has recently pointed out, plans for such long-term incarceration of irreclaimable able bodied unemployed, mental defectives and habitual criminals multiplied between 1890 and 1910.[35]

As far as British prison administrators and officials were concerned there was an overall deep respect for the classical notions of punishment and culpability to which they added elements of the new human scientific ideas which seemed to them to be compatible with this traditional classicism. In point of fact most British criminological writing between 1895 and 1935 was the work of officials working within the penal system who wished theory to serve the objective of concrete solutions to practical problems.[36] They tended to be suspicious of abstract or extreme ideas and indeed Radzinowicz and Hood made clear that new initiatives, which in part drew from positivistic, criminological or psychological theory occurred within a predominant general faith in punishment, deterrence and culpability as the foundations of penal policy.[37] As will emerge the application of practice in the new borstals or the preventive detention system strongly suggests that environment, heredity, personality and selective differential treatment of varying types of offender were all seen as important by administrators and policy makers. However these notions were grafted onto a prison system which unambiguously emphasised defined and measured punishment for the culpable act of criminality unless insanity could be proved. Prisoners were therefore morally responsible and not the result of deterministic forces even though their physical, moral and mental qualities might be inferior because of heredity and / or environment. Whatever measures were devised to alter their attitude and conduct should therefore take full account of the new sciences but would none the less exist within a traditional framework of punishment, deterrence and moral reformation. Indeed, increasingly after 1895 prison administrators argued that those groups who were generally viewed as unable to make moral choices, such as the feeble minded or the inebriate, should not be in prison at all.

## NOTES

1. G. Kitson-Clark, *Churchmen and the Condition of England 1832-85* (Methuen 1973): 9.
2. W.Wilberforce, *A Practical View of the Prevailing Religious System*. 13th edn. (T. Cadell and W. Davies 1818): 22.
3. Ibid: 112.
4. Ibid: 364-5.
5. O. Chadwick, *The Victorian Church*, vol. 1 (Adam &Charles Black 1966): 5.
6. R.A. Soloway, *Prelates and People 1783-1852* (Routledge &Kegan Paul 1969): 258.
7. W.J. Forsythe, 'The Power of the Dog: Moral Reformation in Victorian Prisons' (PhD thesis, University of Exeter, 1985): 34-51.
8. E. Schuster, *Eugenics* (Collins 1912): 10 and 11.
9. A.R. Whiteway, *Recent Object-Lessons in Penal Science* (1st edn 1898, 3rd edn 1902): 24. Also Resolution of the Malthusian League to Sir Matthew White Ridley, HO 144/522/X73874/11. Cited in L. Radzinowicz and R. Hood, *A History of the English Criminal Law and its Administration from 1750*, vol. 5, *The Emergence of Penal Policy* (Stevens and Sons 1986): 33.
10. J. MacNicol, *The Movement For Family Allowances. A Study in Social Policy Development* (Heinemann 1980): 80.
11. R.S. Baden-Powell, *Scouting for Boys* (1909): 267. Cited in J. Springall, *Youth, Empire and Society. British Youth Movements 1883-1940* (Croom Helm 1977): 58.

12. J. Springall, *Youth, Empire and Society*: 124.

13. D.A. Forrest, *Francis Galton: The Life and Work of a Victorian Genius* (Elek 1974): 256-7.

14. PRO HO-45-10563-172511 Arthur MacDonald to Home Office 21 July 1906. Arthur MacDonald to Home Office with copy of article entitled 'The Study of Man' 28 Nov. 1912.

15. C.R. Jeffrey, 'The Historical Development of Criminology' in H. Mannheim (ed.) *Pioneers in Criminology* (Stevens & Sons 1960): 366.

16. F.A. Allen, 'Raffaele Garofalo' in *Pioneers in Criminology*: 262.

17. D. Garland, *Punishment and Welfare* (Gower 1985): 28.

18. E.Ferri, *Criminal Sociology* (Fisher Unwin 1895): 163-4.

19. *Lancet*, 13 Feb. 1892: 369-70.

20. W. Bevan Lewis, 'The Origins of Crime' *Fortnightly Review*, Sept. 1893, CCCXXI: 344,342,340. J. Baker, 'Some Points Connected with Criminals' *Journal of Mental Science*, July 1892, XXXVIII: 368.

21. *Lancet*, 28 July 1894: 208.

22. W. Norwood East, 'Physical and Moral Insensibility in The Criminal' *Journal of Mental Science*, Oct. 1901, XLVII: 737-58. East at the time was deputy medical officer of Portland. He measured 100 convicts to compare their deficiencies of physical senses such as awareness of colour, susceptibility to pain, 'moral sensibility'. He found professional recidivists had weak moral and physical sensibility compared with non criminal and accidental or occasional criminals.

23. *British Medical Journal*, 1 Oct.1904: 861. Charles Mercier to *BMJ*, 15 Oct. 1904: 957.

24. *Law Times*, 6 April 1895 98: 535. *Law Times*, 16 March 1895: 463-4.

25. Obituary on Montague Crackanthorpe, *Eugenics Review*, Jan. 1914, 5 (4): 352-3.

26. S. Collini, *Liberalism and Sociology: L.T. Hobhouse and Political Argument in England 1880-1914* (Cambridge University Press, 1979): 141.

27. M. Freeden, *The New Liberalism: An Ideology of Social Reform* (Clarendon Press 1978): 201.

28. Ibid: 259.

29. E. Ruggles-Brise, *Prison Reform at Home and Abroad* (MacMillan 1924): 193.

30. G.R. Searle, *The Quest for National Efficiency* (Blackwell 1971): 242. See also S. Webb, 'Eugenics and the Poor Law' *Eugenics Review*, Nov. 1910, 2 (3): 233-41. See also the Minority Report of the Royal Commission into the Administration of the Poor Law, PP 1909, XXXVII.

31. G.R. Searle, *National Efficiency*: 64-5.

32. D. Garland, *Punishment and Welfare* (Gower 1985): 150.

33. Ibid: 150-1 cited from S. Hynes, *The Edwardian Turn of Mind* (Oxford University Press 1968): 287.

34. Report of the Departmental Committee on Vagrancy, PP 1906, CIII.

35. Garland, *Punishment and Welfare*: 265-76.

36. D. Garland, 'British Criminology Before 1935' *British Journal of Criminology*, 1988, 28 (2): 1-17.

37. Radzinowicz and Hood, *Penal Policy*: 1-33.

# Chapter Two

# The End of An Era

In the early 1890s there began to be voiced widespread criticism of the government of the local and convict prisons of England and Wales. These prisons were administered by two official bodies, a Prison Commission set up in 1877 by statute (40 and 41 Vict. cap. 21) to take over running of local prisons from the county and borough magistrates and a Directorate established in 1850 to administer the convict prisons (13 and 14 Vict. cap. 39). In these latter institutions were served the long sentences of penal servitude, which came into being as a result of the decline of transportation in the mid nineteenth century, whilst in the local prisons remand and short sentence prisoners were held. Despite a legal distinction between the Prison Commission and the Convict Directorate the membership of these two bodies was the same by the early 1890s and they were both chaired by Sir Edmund Du Cane, a Royal Engineer, who had been involved in the management of convicts transported to Western Australia in the 1850s and who had been appointed Chairman of the Directors of Convict Prisons in 1869. He was made Chairman of the Prison Commission at its inception. The Commission as a whole consisted of up to five members at any one time.

During the time of Du Cane there occurred a reduction both in the number of prisons and the daily average number of prisoners held. For example between 1880 and 1895 the daily average of those held in local prisons fell from around eighteen thousand to around thirteen and a half thousand;[1] in penal servitude the numbers fell from around ten to around four thousand between 1878 and 1894.[2] Furthermore, the number of local prisons declined from 113 in 1877 to 56 in 1895, of convict prisons from 13 to 5 during the same period.[3]

Du Cane maintained that these figures were evidence of the success of the methods which he employed. He had been appointed to ensure uniformity of administration throughout the prison system and economy in its management and he applied both principles rigorously. He was scornful

of the idiosyncratic and reformatory approaches which had once characterised the local prisons when run by the county and borough magistrates
and was also critical of one of his predecessor chairmen of the Directorate
of Convict Prisons, Sir Joshua Jebb, who had in the mid nineteenth century
insisted upon the importance of reformation as a part of convict prison
discipline. Du Cane operated a very severe and deterrent regime in both
convict and local prisons with prisoners proceeding through a series of staged
improvements of their conditions, earned by their industry and docile
behaviour. He relegated such personnel as chaplains to the periphery of
prison administration and clearly paid much less attention to education,
moral improvement and Christian ministry than had been the case in English
prisons earlier in the nineteenth century.

Du Cane's theoretical position reflected the pessimism of the early
evolutionist era and he viewed the majority of prisoners as unamenable to
reformatory influence. In 1886 for example, reviewing Adolphe Prins' work
*Criminalité et Repression* he pointed out that education and other influences
had little effect on them for, in the main, 'a large proportion of the criminal
classes were more or less mentally deficient' having 'low brain power . . .
want of balance between the impulses and the power of resisting them . . .
a condition which is held to differ from madness only by reason that in the
latter the power of resistance to impulses is totally absent . . . heredity . . .
is probably included among mental and physical causes as it is generally the
origin of them'. Around the same time he quoted from the work of
contemporary mental scientists to the effect that many prisoners 'form a
class of fools whom even experience fails to teach'.[4] He mocked the
'burlesque absurdity' of the evangelical approaches in the 1840s at Reading
gaol and was determined that reformatory endeavours should not undermine
the deterrent severity of prisons.[5]

It is important to point out that Du Cane did have a place in prison
discipline for education and the learning of improved behaviour by rewards
and punishments. However, in his view such approaches were of minor
importance. Consequently, Du Cane transformed the purpose of the
structures which he inherited. The separate cell was no longer to be the
vehicle of spiritual growth but an instrument of penality. The staged
promotion system was to be used to inflict very severe conditions of privation
to be ameliorated by docility and obedience. So, in the local prisons the
emphasis was on hard labour on treadmill and crank and cellular isolation.
In the convict sector, after a nine-month period of separate confinement,
the prisoner proceeded to the public works prisons such as Portland or
Dartmoor to be subjected to the most stringent regime of unremitting penal
labour, nocturnal cellular isolation, most basic diet and prohibition of
conversation until eventual release under police supervision. Of the value

of this system in achieving reduction in crime by deterrence Du Cane had no doubts: 'the remarkably steady and sustained decrease in our prison population of late years must be considered to show that recent legislation ... has in principle and in execution not only completely succeeded in its object of promoting uniformity, economy and improved administration but also in that which is the main purpose of all, the repression of crime'.[6]

Between 1890 and 1895 Du Cane was subjected to mounting criticism. In the first place it is clear that within the Home Office there was a concern about the independent and autocratic style of his management. For example, in November 1889 a prisoner named William Gatcliffe was found dead in Manchester prison with broken ribs, fractured breastbone and covered in bruises. Although the court acquitted a warder charged with Gatcliffe's manslaughter, the Home Secretary was gravely disturbed that Du Cane had failed to inform the Home Office about the matter. Du Cane characteristically repudiated the implied censure and informed the Home Office that 'the enquiries made in your letter will be replied to when the Commissioners are able to give categorical answers to all of them. The Commissioners conceive that it should not be necessary for them to point out that they invariably make enquiries into abuses and defects in the prisons ... without waiting for special instructions from the Home Office ... they believe that they have fully justified their appointment by Her Majesty ... which they would certainly not have done if such letters as that under reply were necessary to stir them up to their duty.'[7] Enraged permanent Under Secretary Godfrey Lushington pressed the conservative Home Secretary, Henry Matthews, to demand that Du Cane be ordered to withdraw this 'disgraceful and even insolent' letter or be censured:[8] in the event Du Cane grudgingly amended the offending remarks.

Within the Prison Commission and Convict Directorate also there was unease. One of the commissioners, Robert Mitford, commented that Du Cane seldom called the members together for policy discussions rather preferring to govern alone and notify Home Office and other commissioners of decisions made.[9] Another, Evelyn Ruggles-Brise, remarked that Du Cane never spoke to him again after he had criticised one of Du Cane's proteges.[10] Furthermore, a number of prison chaplains were critical. As early as 1878 there had been allegations that convicts were subjected to cruelty, violence and neglect but the Royal Commission[11] which had heard these reports had not considered them proved although a number of prison chaplains had argued this to be the case.[12] In addition in the 1890s one of the chaplains at Wandsworth, William Morrison, argued that the Du Cane system was based upon false philosophical principles and that the pessimism which it engendered led to a failure of reformatory endeavour. Morrison fused constitutional and environmentalist approaches to cause and cure of crime to argue that the inherited weak constitution of the offender interacted with environment to produce a fixed habit of criminality in early adult life. This fixed habit was however preventible by a special reformatory regime along the lines of American experiments and applied to prisoners when relatively young. He therefore suggested that the Du Cane system in fact confirmed young offenders in a criminality which was rapidly becoming fixed. 'Take a child now who comes into Wandsworth. He has got . . . no home . . . he has got no occupation . . . he has nowhere to go when he gets out. What happens to him? He goes back into exactly the same conditions of life that produced the offence . . . he goes on repeating the offence; he becomes an habitual criminal and goes away to penal servitude.' Between 1890 and 1895 Morrison published numerous attacks upon Du Cane's system alleging in addition that it drove some offenders mad and atrophied and debilitated mental processes which were already constitutionally weak by hereditary process.[13]

There was also a great deal of criticism from those who had experienced imprisonment during the Du Cane era. Those who recorded their experiences complained of harsh unforgiving attitudes to prisoners, bare and at times inedible diets, long periods of cellular isolation and silence, brutality which was said to be institutionalised at some prisons, immediate and very severe punishment for even the suggestion of breach of prison rules, ignorance of real conditions on the part of the commissioners.[14] Michael Davitt, the Irish nationalist member of parliament who had served a sentence of penal servitude wholly condemned 'the abominable and inhuman punishment of treadmills, cranks and all that sort of thing' and maintained that brutal beatings occurred in a system which was characterised by inhumanity, monotonousness and heartlessness.[15] Another in a petition to the Home Office after Du Cane's retirement remarked: 'our overall system is one of degradation. Du Cane, the coryphoeus if not the oracle of a little coterie, has expounded this system in his book . . . Du Cane is gone . . . I hope to a place where perhaps his earthly errors are being expiated by a penance which Sisyphus himself might not envy—a perpetual perusal of books like his own' the departed overlord of 'a little oligarchy of official fiends'.[16]

Attacks on the Du Cane system also became intense outside the Home Office and the prison system. For example, a number of well known voluntary organisations were, on varying grounds, very critical of Du Cane. The Howard Association and its secretary William Tallack had long duelled with Du Cane. Tallack desired prisons to return to the earnest spiritual evangelicalism which, he believed, had once characterised their management and had indeed given evidence to the 1878 Royal Commission on Penal Servitude in which he alleged moral and physical neglect of prisoners and brutality to them. In 1891 Tallack complained further to the Home Office that many 'unsuitable and objectionable persons' were employed as warders to which Du Cane replied that 'this little piddling assoc'n is like the frog which tried to persuade itself and its neighbours that it was a bull—but it has considerable powers for mischief'.[17] Another group, the Humanitarian League, with which W.D. Morrison was associated, publicly stated that the prison system was 'pitiless, indiscriminating and needlessly and culpably severe'.[18]

By mid 1894 Du Cane's position was substantially weakened. William Morrison was spearheading a widespread campaign against him in the popular and professional press, arguing that under the Du Cane system serious crime was actually on the increase[19] and that the decrease in prison population was not the result of Du Cane's system but of changed sentencing practice.[20] In January 1894 the *Daily Chronicle* ran a series of long articles entitled 'Our Dark Places'. In this series, very probably written by Morrison, Du Cane was depicted as an autocrat governing 'a thoroughly pernicious bureaucracy' which ran a 'cumbrous, pitiless, obsolete, unchanged' system with prisons 'as clean as the deck of an ironclad' but characterised by 'the gloom, the monotony, the nervous strain of a prisoner's life'.[21] In the prisons it was alleged that the prisoners were subjected to silence, morbid introspective hopelessness and even the chapel services were a sacrilege for there 'oaths and jests mingle with the words of the creed and the hymns; prisoners substitute for the responses or the Magnificat the message to wife or comrade which finds its way outside quite as surely as the official letter'. Appealing to the liberal Home Secretary Herbert Asquith for a major enquiry into the system the writer, 'our special commissioner', added that he would never have bothered to appeal to the government had the conservative Matthews still been Home Secretary for the latter would not have been willing publicly to challenge Du Cane.[22]

To be sure some of the news media rallied to Du Cane, the *Pall Mall Gazette* accusing the *Chronicle* of 'journalistic neurosis',[23] but, following the *Chronicle* articles, letters from prison staff, prisoners and penal reformers added strength to the case advanced by that newspaper.[24] Du Cane was now clearly on the defensive and fulminated to the Home Office about misrepresentation, distortion, 'the inaccuracy and the animus of the writer' charging that 'awkward facts are suppressed' and accusing Morrison of 'mere loose reasoning supported by partial and perverted statistics'.[25]

By the early 1890s a small number of members of Parliament such as liberals Edward Pickersgill and Henry Labouchere and conservative Sir Robert Fowler were plainly concerned about neglect and brutality in English prisons. Over such matters as William Gatcliffe's death they questioned the Home Office's policy in Parliament and were clearly distrustful of government reassurances. However, in mid 1893 the liberal M.P. for Peterborough,

Alphaeus Morton, asked an apparently innocuous backbench parliamentary question about over crowding in the London prisons. Du Cane mishandled this request for a detailed breakdown of figures and concluded—rightly —that an opponent of the centralising 1877 Act had put Morton up to the parliamentary question in the hope that further attacks might be launched on the prison authorities. He argued to the Home Office that the necessary information would be difficult to find but three months later produced a report which suggested no overcrowding.[26] Clearly Alphaeus Morton disbelieved this when it was laid before Parliament and widened his criticisms to allege cruel treatment of prisoners and constitutional impropriety on the part of the Prison Commission whose 'officialism' led to delay and inaccuracy in submitting information desired by Parliament. By January 1894 Morton was demanding that Du Cane resign.[27]

One aspect of all this was the lingering resentment of the 1877 Act. Du Cane suspected that the desire to return to local government of prisons by magistrates was one of Morrison's motives but certainly among many local justices there was deep dislike of the Prison Commission which had replaced them. It is true that the magistrates continued to be associated with prisons by virtue of the visiting committees which were appointed to punish more serious offences against prison discipline and to provide a local watch dog in prisons. However, it was generally believed that the Prison Commission paid little attention to these committees. One magistrate referred to the 1877 Act as 'one of the most centralizing, confiscating and despotic of acts passed during the present century' adding that 'as long as Sir Edmund Du Cane continue Chairman' the Association of Visiting Justices would not even bother to meet, deeming such meetings a waste of their time.[28] The mood was well summed up fifteen years earlier when the Prison Commission had inquired into an alleged over familiar and lewd relationship between the governor of Dorchester and male sex offenders without reference to the Visiting Justices. 'The Committee can only gather . . . that the government set no value on their services . . . treated with such scant courtesy as not even to be informed of occurrences that most vitally effect the discipline of the prison.'[29]

Sir Edmund Du Cane had ruled the prisons certain of the correctness of his own views and methods. Most criminals were not amenable to reformatory influence—as he illustrated in his lectures their photographs often revealed them to be 'the type of what Professor Darwin calls our arboreal ancestors',[30] He had been intolerant and hostile to outside influences, refusing for example to have any part in the International Penitentiary Congresses which met quinquennially in various parts of Europe to debate resolutions on a wide variety of aspects of criminal disposal and prison discipline. He had been resentful and suspicious towards all questioning and criticism and he ruled the Commission and Convict Directorate with a fierce energy doing battle with Home Office and other government departments whenever they overstepped the boundaries which he had erected around his authority. Now however the tide was running against him and the criticisms too intense and public to suppress by dictatorial memorandum to the Home Office. On June 5th, 1894 Herbert Asquith signed the warrants of appointment of a committee to investigate the workings of the English and Welsh prison system and in April 1895 Du Cane retired claiming to the last 'to have assiduously endeavoured to carry out the objects of the (1877) Act and to have spared no effort to make the English prison system effective for its purpose of diminishing crime'.[31]

The report of the Departmental Committee on Prisons was the work of a group which was chaired by the liberal Herbert Gladstone parliamentary Under Secretary at the Home Office from 1892-94 also the son of William Ewart Gladstone the liberal Prime Minister and included three other members of parliament, the Liberal Richard Haldane, a lawyer and later theorist on the philosophy of education and public administration, Conservative Sir John Dorington with experience as lunacy commissioner and Chairman of Quarter Sessions and Arthur O'Connor an Irish Nationalist member and Chairman of the Public Accounts Committee. Also included were a Metropolitan Magistrate Albert De Rutzen, a doctor J.H. Bridges and an expert on women's labour questions, who was highly critical of the treatment of women in the British economy, Miss Eliza Orme. The Committee heard evidence from a wide range of opinion both within and without the prison system and themselves visited six convict prisons and seventeen local prisons together with various associated institutions.[32]

The evidence before the Gladstone Committee was of five main types. In the first place a number of protesters such as William Morrison and William Tallack from different starting points argued that the prison system no longer pursued the reformation of offenders and because of this deficiency prisons were not effective instruments for the reduction of crime. They also argued that foreign experiments and theories had been disregarded in England and added that there was a need, not merely to pursue energetically a reformatory policy, but also to ensure lengthy periods of incapacitation for those who were beyond reform. Plainly, the Committee treated the evidence of Morrison in particular with caution feeling that in his allegations against Du Cane he was straying into wild statements unfounded in his own experience.[33]

Secondly, a large body of evidence was given by others who worked in the prison system—commissioners, inspectors, medical officers, governors and so forth. The two commissioners, Evelyn Ruggles-Brise and Robert Mitford, were in fact critical of Du Cane although Ruggles-Brise was careful to support his Chairman whenever he agreed with his policy. Nevertheless the evidence of these two put together suggested that Du Cane was isolated from his commissioners whom he dominated by diktat rather than discussion. Thus he did not invite the participation of the commissioners in the preparation of the annual report, decided alone upon the appointment of warders, chaplains and medical officers, called the commissioners together infrequently for discussions and Ruggles-Brise added that there was urgent need for promotion of more effective schemes for aiding discharged prisoners.[34] The evidence of the majority of official witnesses was however less critical and Du Cane himself made a sturdy defence of his system. Prisons, he said, had to be severe places of privation adding that cellular isolation was essential to the prevention of contamination and that 'a great number of prisoners . . . are below par mentally . . . the thing to do with them . . . is to put them under control permanently'.[35]

Thirdly, a number of ex prisoners spoke of their experiences and these remarked upon a poor quality of staff incapable of exercising personal influence over prisoners and upon the severity of the system as a whole. One of these who had served twenty-four years in penal servitude and local prisons declared that 'I then became fairly reckless. I thought to myself I have done wrong and I deserve punishment but I did not deserve to be punished so severely. I felt that there was no God. I felt that there was no religion.'[36] Most referred to the collective very deprived and regimented existence of prisoners and the absence of reformatory approaches to the individual.[37]

Fourthly, the evidence of the Home Office was given by Sir Godfrey Lushington, very recently retired Under Secretary of State. Lushington had already been involved in frequent conflict with Du Cane who believed that the former deliberately blocked his access to the Home Secretary and encouraged mere Home Office clerks to question the authority of the Prison Commission.[38] Lushington clearly disliked Du Cane's behaviour towards the Home Office yet he himself was no advocate of a sustained reformatory base to prison administration. He, nevertheless, described the system in terms which left his hearers in no doubt as to his view of the overall effect of the Du Cane system 'I regard as unfavourable to reformation the status of a prisoner throughout his whole career; the crushing of self-respect, the starving of all moral instinct he may possess, the absence of all opportunity to do or receive a kindness, the continual association with none but criminals'.[39] It was these remarks which the Gladstone Committee quoted in their report as one of the bases of their conclusions—the fact that Lushington actually doubted the possibility of reforming prisoners at all was mentioned and cast aside. Lastly, there was a considerable body of evidence from specialist workers outside the prison system whether voluntary workers with charitable aftercare organisations or medical experts in the theory and treatment of inebriates or the psychological traits of criminals.[40]

The Gladstone Committee recommended substantial change. The members were careful to avoid any direct attack on Du Cane whose implementation of the 1877 Act was praised as 'strong and masterful action', the creation of an 'absolute system of uniformity . . . discipline and economy'.[41] Nevertheless, the Committee at once stated that although such a system paid great attention to 'organisation, finance, order, health of the prisoners and prison statistics the prisoners have been treated too much as a hopeless or worthless element of the community and the moral as well as the legal responsibility of the prison authorities has been held to cease when they pass outside the prison gates'.[42] Taking a stance on the potential of most prisoners to reform if subjected to correct influences the Committee insisted on the need to change prison administration radically, for the present system 'while admirable for coercion and repression is excessively deficient on the reformatory side'. Prisoners were to be subjected to a 'more elastic' system,[43] 'adapted to the special cases of individual prisoners' and designed to 'maintain, stimulate or awaken the higher susceptibilities of prisoners . . . develop their moral instincts . . . train them in orderly and industrial habits . . . turn them out of prison better men and women, both physically and mentally than when they came in'.[44]

The Committee therefore recommended new measures of education, classification, special reformatory approaches to young prisoners, training in productive labour, regular consultation between Commissioners and prison staff, staff training, radically improved discharged prisoners' aid systems, and above all the exercise of personal influence of staff over the prisoner so that the latter would 'humanize the prisoners . . . prevent them from feeling that the state merely chains them for a certain period and cares nothing about them beyond keeping them in safe custody and under iron discipline'.[45] For those who proved unreformable the recommendation was for segregation of habitual criminals for long periods of detention under a new preventive incapacitatory sentence to be made available to the higher courts. Lastly the Committee suggested a relaxation of some of the more extreme severities of the Du Cane system, urging a reconsideration of the period of separate confinement inflicted on convicts, association for work and education, increased visits, reduction of severe punishments for breach of prison rules and abolition of the hard labour machines, the treadmill and crank.

Such a vision of prison discipline contrasted with the ideas of Sir Edmund Du Cane with its emphasis on the hatching of reformed attitudes and conduct among prisoners. Plainly the Gladstone Committee was responding to the greater optimism and the rescuing emphasis of the New Liberal ethos and its insistence on the need for personal influence of prison staff, 'auxiliary effort'[46] of aftercare agencies, education and training reflected this. Also there was evidence of the influence of the newer criminological theories in the emphasis on increased classification of types of offender and the suggestion of specialist medical regimes for inebriates.[47] Thirdly the demand for gymnastic and physical exercises reflected the concern with physical efficiency and improvement and lastly the emphasis on preventive in-capacitation of unreformable prisoners in more comfortable and less penal detention than penal servitude[48] reflected the fear that habitual criminals had inferior character traits as a result of inheritance or environment which required that they be prevented from committing the depredations towards which their character tended to push them. The Gladstone Committee clearly retained the overall traditional classical approach to the punishment of offenders but it wished to graft onto that approach measures derived from new ideas which had already rendered obsolete many of the assump-tions upon which Du Cane had worked. In so doing Gladstone left to Du Cane's successors an immense and onerous task of reconstruction which almost at once fell upon his replacement, Evelyn Ruggles-Brise.

The wider significance of the Gladstone report has been disputed by writers about the history of English prisons and criminal justice. Tradi-tionally the report has been viewed as a major event in the evolution of the prison system towards more humane and enlightened treatment of prisoners. However recent authorities such as Christopher Harding have emphasised that the discrediting of Du Cane was less because of outrage at the severity of his system than because a welfare / reformative emphasis made much more possible substantial increase of state control through the differential disposition of numerous deviant groups and types.[49] In a concrete way therefore the discourses of liberal paternal stewardship, youth improvement, criminological analysis of habitual criminality and so forth required the replacement of the limited field of deterrence and collective symmetrical punishment by a more discriminating, penetrative and apparently beneficent penal order, the prison as merely one element of a more wide-ranging reformatory system of individualistic analysis and control. As Harding pointed out, Du Cane's prisons appeared to have become anachronistic, out of kilter with the emphasis upon improvement and philanthropy and an 'increasing measure of social regulation and control; in the workplace, in relation to children, as regards problems such as venereal disease, inebriety and mental deficiency, to mention some of the more obvious areas'.[50]

It is important to avoid mere repetition of the harsh stereotype of Du Cane reproduced by so many writers about the history of English and Welsh prisons and to reiterate that Du Cane was a determined fighter for healthier conditions in prisons as well as an advocate of more efficient prisoner aid societies. Yet all the evidence of prisoners to state committees between 1877 and 1895 and all the writings of prisoners about their experience of Du Cane's prisons attest to an extreme severity which crushed and demeaned prisoners.[51] The Gladstone Committee accurately picked up and reflected that experience. At the same time the Committee emphasised an approach which incorporated a traditional early Victorian emphasis on moral improvement, elements of differential selective treatment, stewardship and training within the overall framework of punishment and deterrence. The Committee did not therefore propose any abolition of the traditional view of imprisonment rather that its excessive severity should be ameliorated and its reformatory base strengthened.

## NOTES

1. RCP PP 1881 LI: 1; RCP & DCP PP 1902, XLVI: 20.
2. Report from the Departmental Committee on Prisons, PP 1895, LVI: 3.
3. RCP PP 1878, XLII, App. 8: 36; RDCP PP 1878, XLIII, Frontispiece. RCP & DCP PP 1896, XLIV App. 8: 121-2.
4. E. Du Cane, *Law Quarterly Review*, April 1886, VI: review of A. Prins *Criminalité et Repression*, 229. E. Du Cane, *The Punishment and Prevention of Crime* (MacMillan 1885): 3.
5. Du Cane, *Punishment and Prevention*: 57.
6. Ibid: 109.
7. PRO HO 144-230-A51041/9, E. Du Cane to HO, 18 Jan. 1890.
8. Ibid: HO Minute 26 Jan. 1890.
9. Departmental Committee on Prisons, PP 1895, LVI: 356-7.
10. S. Leslie, *Sir Evelyn Ruggles-Brise* (Murray 1938): 87.
11. Report of the Royal Commission Appointed to Inquire into the Working of the Penal Servitude Acts, PP 1878-9, XXXVII.
12. W.J. Forsythe, *The Reform of Prisoners 1830-1900* (Croom Helm 1987): 202-3.
13. Departmental Committee on Prisons, PP 1895, LVI: 110. See also W.D. Morrison, 'Are Our Prisons A Failure?' *Fortnightly Review*, April 1894, CCCXXVIII: 459-69.
14. Forsythe, *Reform of Prisoners*: 206-15.
15. Departmental Committee on Prisons, PP 1895, LVI: 386-7, 391. See also M. Davitt, 'Criminal and Prison Reform' *The Nineteenth Century*, Dec. 1894, 214: 875-89.
16. PRO HO 144-203-A47874/16, petition William Bundy to HO, 13 Feb. 1896.
17. PRO HO 45-9707-A50752/3 Howard Association Memorial to Home Secretary 7 Feb. 1891. E. Du Cane to HO 20 Feb. 1891.
18. PRO P.Com. 7/38-1 Cut. from *Daily Chronicle* 1 Feb. 1894.
19. W.D. Morrison to *Lancet*, 7 April 1894: 904.
20. W.D. Morrison to *Lancet*, 10 March 1894: 640-1.
21. *Daily Chronicle*, 23 and 25 Jan. 1894.

22. *Daily Chronicle*, 25 Jan. 1894.

23. Cut. *Pall Mall Gazette*, 1 Feb. 1894, in PRO P.Com. 7/38-1.

24. *Daily Chronicle*, 1, 5 and 7 Feb. 1894.

25. PRO P Com 7/38-1, printed memorandum E. Du Cane to HO, no date; obs by Sir E. Du Cane on Mr Morrison's article in *Fortnightly Review*, April 1894, no date.

26. PRO HO 45-9958-V20544/1 E. Du Cane to HO, 21 June 1893. -/6 Du Cane to HO 4 Sept. 1893.

27. Alphaeus Morton to *Daily Chronicle*, 29 Jan. 1894.

28. PRO HO 45-9958-V20544/20 Henry Manton to H. Asquith, 11 June 1894.

29. PRO HO 144-53/89940 Chairman Visiting Committee Dorchester Prison to Home Secretary 19 Jan. 1880.

30. L. Radzinowicz and R. Hood, *A History of the English Criminal Law and its Administration from 1750*, vol. 5, *The Emergence of Penal Policy* (Stevens & Sons 1986): 9.

31. RCP PP 1894, XLIV: 44.

32. Report from the Departmental Committee On Prisons PP 1895, LVI: 7.

33. Ibid. Minutes of Evidence: 117-26.

34. Ibid: 337-49; 353-6.

35. Ibid: 362-75.

36. Ibid. Evidence Mr E—: 322.

37. Ibid. See for example Evidence M. Davitt: 386-91.

38. J. Pellew, *The Home Office 1848-1914: From Clerks to Bureaucrats* (Heinemann 1982): 45-6.

39. Report, PP 1895: 8.

40. Ibid. See for example  Evidence of William Wheatley: 242; Colonel Buchanan: 248-51; Dr Bevan Lewis: 302-6; Dr T. Clay Shaw: 194-6.

41. Ibid: 7.

42. Ibid: 7.

43. Ibid: 14.

44. Ibid: 8.

45. Ibid: 13.

46. Ibid: 13.

47. Ibid: 32.

48. Ibid: 31.

49. C. Harding, 'The Inevitable End of a Discredited System? The Origins of the Gladstone Committee Report On Prisons 1895' *Historical Journal*, 1988, 31 (3): 591-608.

50. Ibid: 601.

51. Forsythe, *Reform of Prisoners*: 206-15.

# Chapter Three

# Sir Evelyn Ruggles-Brise and the Prison Commission

The new Chairman of the Prison Commission and Convict Prison Directorate was born in 1858 the second son of an established, influential family of Essex landowners. After Eton, for whose first team he played cricket and a first-class degree in Literae Humaniores at Balliol College, Oxford, Ruggles-Brise entered the Home Office in 1881 and served three Home Secretaries as principal private secretary. In 1891 Home Secretary Henry Matthews recommended him for royal appointment as a Prison Commissioner and the Gladstone Committee resulted in his final promotion to Chairman by Home Secretary Herbert Asquith who had been impressed by the evidence which Ruggles-Brise gave to Gladstone and considered that he would energetically implement the reforms recommended. He was to occupy this post until 1921; in 1902 he was knighted.[1]

These details are of more than antiquarian interest. Ruggles-Brise was one of a new cadre of young elite civil servants who were selected by open competition and rapidly promoted between 1880 and 1900 in order to improve radically the efficiency and professionalism of the civil service. Indeed, Home Secretary Sir William Harcourt who first appointed Ruggles-Brise to be his assistant private secretary was bitter in his condemnation of drunkenness, inefficiency and ineptitude within the Home Office[2] and appointed a number of young men of similar character to Ruggles-Brise to posts in his department.

From the outset Ruggles-Brise had realised that he must make his own way in the world for Spains Hall, the family country seat, would pass to his elder brother. His father continually urged him to success throughout his schooldays warning him repeatedly that failure to work exceedingly hard would mean that he would never 'rise above the rank and file', and when his progress faltered his father withdrew affection from him for 'so much now depends on the next few years of your life as to whether you are a man or a mouse in the future'.[3] Eton brought to bear an intense moral, athletic and intellectual influence, an emphasis on Christian and Romano-Greek notions of physical and moral courage, sincerity and integrity. As Ruggles-Brise's tutor wrote to him during one vacation: 'Let Eton boys be types of manly character. They cannot aim higher . . . Christianity has done little for the world if it has not exalted moral courage above physical. If a boy, from high motives of duty, tries to stem evils which he sees existing around him, has the courage not to laugh at vice, shows his disgust plainly and unmistakably, is this boy honoured and respected?'[4]

From Eton Ruggles-Brise went immediately to Balliol College, Oxford. Here he tended to mix almost entirely with students from Eton and Harrow backgrounds[5] and, whilst at Oxford, he was influenced greatly by T.H. Green who was at the height of his reputation at Oxford at this time. To his already formidable Greek and Latin expertise[6] was added an understanding of T.H. Green's philosophical teachings as well as a familiarity with modern and classical philosophers. The impact of Eton and Balliol on Ruggles-Brise was immense and it was not difficult for one accustomed to Aristotle, Bentham, Kant and Fichte later to master the essentials of the new criminology.[7]

As Jill Pellew recently pointed out, there was at this time a great faith in the capacity of the intellectual training at Oxford and Cambridge to prepare young students for later government of a reformed professional civil service. In tutorial the work of the student was subjected 'to a ferreting, worrying, persistent examination, accompanied by suggestion to the student, recommendation of further or alternative reading, the indication of alternative solutions or points of view'.[8] However the mixture of Eton and Oxford was also believed to promote a manly virtuous integrity and it was felt by Ruggles-Brise's superiors that his evidence to Gladstone showed that he would do his duty to the state with energy and frankness, yet he expressed no personal animus against Du Cane.[9] Furthermore, although his own views were in part along the lines of Gladstone, he made clear that in certain respects he adhered to Du Cane's views and he spoke warmly of Du Cane's contribution to English prisons shortly after the retirement of the latter.[10] Ruggles-Brise's integrity, sincerity and fairness were indeed greatly valued by Home Secretaries such as Herbert Asquith and Herbert Gladstone and Gladstone later commented on Ruggles-Brise's capacity to accept criticism without resentment.[11]

Ruggles-Brise was never apparently at ease with the aristocratic influence in British society during the late nineteenth century. He detested ceremonial and court etiquette—'swarms of officials crawling slavishly to court'—and was later disappointed when he saw Labour politicians adopting the same postures. He questioned religious assumptions and disliked ecclesiastical conventions—'in the chapel at Eton they used to sing that beautiful anthem

"I know that my Redeemer liveth" and I would say to myself "why should I have a Redeemer? Why should I be redeemed? What are we but crawling lizards? We are born into this world . . . just like any other animals and why should I be held responsible for anything?" '[12] Furthermore, although Ruggles-Brise appeared self-assured, even on occasion arrogant, to the outside world with his emphasis on individual achievement rather than inherited grandeur and on the superior ability of the inner circle of civil servants of which he was a member, in fact he often felt an outsider for his own family had lavished affection on his elder brother who inherited the Finchingfield estate. 'Archie was their darling, the eldest son and everything centred around him. Don't think I'm jealous . . . but it would have just made the difference to have had a home to go to.'[13]

Whilst Ruggles-Brise may have fulminated in private against Royal Family, House of Lords, Bishops, and state religion he was yet the able and efficient servant of these. Notwithstanding, during his career he was at times attacked by senior judges and administrative personnel who feared that under his influence the ground of crime and punishment was decisively shifting. The Lord Chancellor of England Halsbury accused him of following 'maudlin and sentimental' policies whilst Lord Justice Darling was later accustomed to dwell upon an imaginary country which he called 'Ruggles-Brisia'[14] whose psychologists and sociologists governed the treatment of criminals and whose judges had to take into account the possible bad influence of the nursery rhymes learned by the offender as an infant when passing sentence.

That Ruggles-Brise's penal theory was influenced by the new approaches of the late nineteenth century is evident in his writings and many of his policies. He therefore frequently referred to the importance of the 'personal factor' in prisoner management so that 'the upright and manly attributes of our warder class' would operate to reform the prisoner by a mixture of kindliness and discipline.[15] He also advocated the application of a new regime based on athletic and physical development and moral, industrial and spiritual training to young prisoners. This institutional model of training, which will be discussed in greater detail later, was ultimately known as the Borstal system and may be seen in the context of the widespread contemporary popularity of new preventive and curative specialist institutions designed to remedy the defects and improve the physical and mental functioning of diagnosed problem groups. In this regime for young prisoners there would be an 'appeal to the honour' . . . 'keen activity, admirable order and precision of the parade ground, the swing and go of the gymnasium, the busy hive of industry . . . the glow and keenness of the youngsters in the foot ball or cricket field', the accomplishment of 'a wonderful metamorphosis' from 'slow stubborn impenetrable . . . material' to alert, dutiful, energetic and loyal citizens.[16]

Furthermore, Ruggles-Brise was influenced by the emphasis of much foreign penological literature and opinion on the need for a strong state coordination of the numerous agencies—official and voluntary—which worked in the field of prisoner reformation. He was an ardent enthusiast for the critical study of foreign penal systems both in America and Europe and from 1895 onwards he represented his country at the quinquennial International Penitentiary Congresses held in various capital cities being president of the executive body overseeing these congresses from 1910 to 1926. Along with the majority opinion at these congresses Ruggles-Brise often urged an interlinked state coordinated system of preventive, reformatory, educative, supportive and penal provisions in which the individual at risk of crime would be trained or preventively treated. So there would be educational and rescue measures aimed at children and those at risk of developing criminality, a streamlined and regulated system of aid to discharged prisoners, differentiated penal classes in prisons, systems of probation, admonition or sentence suspension, preventive detention and so forth. All at risk from the tiny waif and stray to the aged sick convict about to be released would be provided for by extended preventive services.[17]

Ruggles-Brise was knowledgeable about both foreign and British criminological trends. Like most theorists in Britain he rejected Lombroso's extreme views believing that 'nothing . . . has so much retarded progress . . . as the old idea of a criminal type . . . persons predestined to crime by certain inherited or atavistic stigmata, mental or physical'[18] and scorned the idea of the 'bogeyman . . . the stealthy enemy of peaceful persons, ever ready to leap in the dark . . . without pity and without shame and with the predatory instincts of a wild beast'.[19] He was, however, keen to encourage research by prison medical and other staff and played a notable part in promoting British criminological studies. Thus he greatly encouraged the work of one of his deputy medical officers, Charles Buckman Goring, who led a prison medical research project which in the event pointed to a tendency to inherited defective intelligence and physique among criminals.[20] Ruggles-Brise was quick to deny that this implied any inevitability of criminal behaviour, rather insisting that Goring's findings made clear the need for improved diagnostic and curative facilities as well as emphasising the poor physical and intellectual condition of most prisoners.[21]

Despite all this, however, Ruggles-Brise retained a traditional classical approach to crime and punishment as the basis of his thinking and he consistently argued that crime should be viewed primarily as a matter of culpability and choice. He was therefore critical of systems which seemed to him over dependent on deterministic psychological or hereditarian theories and indeed he followed T.H. Green surmising that a punishment system based entirely on reformatory theory was unjust in that it violated the reversionary rights of humanity, treating man as patient not agent, liable to sap or vitiate the will rather than activate it.[22] Notwithstanding, he wished to incorporate elements of reformatory theory into the traditional concepts of retribution and deterrence but he saw the purposes of prisons as being 'coercive as restraining liberty, deterrent as an example and retributory in the sense of enforcing a penalty for an offence'.[23] What was so different from Du Cane however was the greater theoretical emphasis which Ruggles-Brise placed on reformation and the need for a range of facilities and institutions operating on the basis of theoretical knowledge and through the sort of personal influence and developmental programmes which existed in the best English public school.[24]

From the outset of his chairmanship there was a substantial change in the relationship of the Prison Commission with the Home Office. The founding act of 1877 had made it clear that the Commission, which consisted of up to five members, was to operate 'subject to the control of the Secretary of State' and it had originally been envisaged as an executive body to assist the Home Secretary in the discharge of his duty of superintending prisons.[25] As has been described, Du Cane showed an energetic independence in the running of the Commission which had caused much concern in the Home Office and there can be no doubt that Ruggles-Brise's promotion was intended to bring the Commission into greater subordination to the Home Secretary after the earlier conflicts and disputes. In June 1895 Home Secretary Asquith was 'glad to note the sympathetic spirit' of the response of the Commission to the Gladstone proposals[26] and thereafter Ruggles-Brise submitted to the Home Office an immensely detailed series of proposals for the implementation of Gladstone's recommendations. Clearly, throughout his period of office, Ruggles-Brise wished to work closely with the Home Office and largely succeeded in this. However there were times when Ruggles-Brise found the Home Office slow to move and lacking in enthusiasm and other times when he was put under great pressure by Home Secretaries.

There was in general a tendency to scepticism and cautiousness among Home Office officials about new theories emanating from Prison Commission staff. The long and detailed investigation of Charles Goring serves to illustrate this. In general, attempts to interest the Home Office in scientific studies of criminals had not been well received. Home Office officials sarcastically noted of one American project that it sounded like 'a much to be desired extension of the Vivisection Act but unfortunately public opinion lags behind scientific yearnings'.[27] Notwithstanding, the Home Office gave cautious support to the idea of testing theories about the 'physical progress of the race'[28] by the study of convicts and in 1912 Ruggles-Brise submitted to the Home Office the gigantic report based on complex biometric statistical analysis drawn up by Charles Goring. This research was grounded on data about three thousand English convicts and a control group of university students, schoolboys and military personnel. It was critical of Lombroso and, as earlier described, found a tendency in the convicts to what Goring called a 'criminal diathesis' the chief symptoms of which were inherited physical and intellectual defect.[29]

Ruggles-Brise was initially enthusiastic about this study, not least because he interpreted it as a justification for his approach to young offenders but the Home Office was highly critical. One of the new breed of rapidly promoted public school/Oxford-educated civil servants, H.B. Simpson, a senior official in the criminal department, complained that Goring's study was unnecessary for Lombroso had long been refuted, not least in Britain, and that Simpson himself had played a part in that refutation. Furthermore, officials were irritated by the style of the report. 'His arguments are so elaborate and so much disfigured by an excessive use of algebraical symbols . . . that it is exceedingly difficult for anyone not an advanced mathematician to follow them'; H.B. Simpson in particular felt that Goring had made a number of elementary errors of fact and that the idea of an inherited criminal diathesis was, in a different way, as deterministic as Lombrosian criminology, likely to 'appeal to the popular imagination . . . a superstition as difficult to eradicate as was Lombroso's'.[30] He argued later, somewhat inconsistently, that publication of the report was a waste of public money and would be read by few except 'admirers of Dr. Carl Pearson' the biometric eugenicist who had advised Goring on the execution of the project.[31] Plainly the Home Office was not only suspicious of policies based on mere intellectual theory but were worried more generally about the effect of publication by employees of the Prison Commission on public opinion. Ruggles-Brise was sharply chided by Home Secretary, Sir Matthew White Ridley, when he allowed one of his inspectors to publish an article on penal discipline in America which contained thinly veiled references to Oscar Wilde who had recently been imprisoned and whose case was the subject of great public controversy.[32]

Tension also arose between Home Office and Prison Commission as a result of what was viewed as more serious misbehaviour of employees of the Prison Commission. An example of this was the outrage expressed to Ruggles-Brise by the Home Office over the conduct of the first female inspector of prisons, Dr Mary Gordon. At the height of the suffragette protests Gordon was in secret correspondence with one of the leaders of the movement who had herself been imprisoned in this connection, Emmeline Pethick-Lawrence. In 1914 Gordon's letters to Pethick-Lawrence were discovered during a Scotland Yard raid and sent by the police to the Home

Secretary.[33] A further example was the sharp exchange between Home Secretary Winston Churchill and Ruggles-Brise in 1910 which related to the dismissal by the Commission of two warders at Warwick prison who had taken a prisoner under escort for a drink in a public house. Churchill characteristically felt that the punishment was over severe and argued that the Home Secretary should exercise the right of dismissal rather than the Chairman of the Commission. Ruggles-Brise strenuously denied this saying that 'by long custom and for administrative convenience' the Prison Commission decided such matters and acted as 'the interpreters of (the Home Secretary's) pleasure'.[34]

Another source of tension was the differing weight given to plans of penal reform by Prison Commission and Home Office. Ruggles-Brise was often placed in the role of catalyst in the face of Home Office delays and reluctance. Thus, in keeping with the European emphasis on new penal codes to suit a new era of criminal justice, Ruggles-Brise pressed early on for consolidation and amendment of the law regarding local and convict prisons. A Prisons Act of 1898 (61 and 62 Vict. cap 41) fell short of his aspirations and in November of that year he complained that 'so far as convict prisons are concerned no steps . . . have been taken to consolidate the very ancient and confused enactments at present regulating the administration of Convict Prisons'.[35] Despite the fact that he sent voluminous memoranda on the urgency of this to Sir Kenelm Digby, permanent under secretary at the Home Office, such legal reform was not achieved in his time.

The Home Office was influenced by the likely public response to new measures of prison discipline and nobody reading the mountainous Home Office archive material at the Public Record Office can fail to note the immense attention paid to public opinion by officials there. Cuttings from the local and national press were collected with meticulous care and individuals, penal reform groups, professional organisations and protest groups maintained pressure on the Home Office to adopt a great variety of measures. The Home Office was exceedingly sensitive to criticism that penal discipline was either over severe or had become soft and treated outsiders with the greatest caution. Answers to parliamentary private members' questions were prepared with very careful thought about the motivation which had prompted them and the likely use to which the answer would be put. Some of Ruggles-Brise's proposals, such as Borstal or Preventive Detention, posed substantial constitutional issues about the liberty of the subject and Home Office officials constantly wished to test public and parliamentary opinion before committing the government to a new policy.

Yet even this cautious and restraining tendency of the Home Office was not a consistent feature of Home Office interaction with Prison Commission.

The most remarkable exception to this rule was undoubtedly the approach to prison discipline of Winston Churchill, who was appointed Home Secretary in 1910, and was the sixth Home Secretary with whom Ruggles-Brise had to deal as Chairman. Churchill at once began to act with an energy and independence which was entirely different from his predecessors who had relied heavily on their senior advisors and on Ruggles-Brise himself. Churchill was at this time close to David Lloyd George and the radical reforming wing of the Liberal Party but he added his own characteristic suspicion of the executive branches of government to his programme. He was convinced that the civil service was slow to move and that Home Office and Prison Commission were paying insufficient attention to the demands of new scientific knowledge and the human suffering of the poor caught up in the institutional systems of social and penal policy. He was averse on constitutional grounds to prolonged detention of individuals who did not by virtue of their diagnosed mental condition require such detention and he wanted a radical extension of non custodial sentences available, in particular for young offenders. He also demanded far reaching differentiation in the treatment of prisoners according to new classifications and methods. Furthermore, he insisted on general ameliorations of severity such as special relaxed conditions for aged convicts or the abolition of some of the more harsh physical restraints like the figure of eight handcuffs.[36]

Against the advice of his officials Churchill therefore began to interfere in individual cases almost always with a view to mitigation of punishment. He insisted on the release of certain aged or in other ways vulnerable prisoners and indeed on occasion was subjected to much public ridicule, as when he released an aged recidivist who apparently enjoyed his life tending the sheep at Dartmoor and who subsequently reoffended in order to be sent back there.[37] He ordered a warrant to be withdrawn so that an 'anaemic and delicate' woman should not be rearrested at the prison gate for offences not dealt with at her original trial[38] and was enraged when the police complained about this.[39] He tried in vain to ameliorate the conditions of imprisonment of a convict who had in all been sentenced to a total of over fifty years of penal servitude during the previous half century.[40]

As far as Ruggles-Brise and the Prison Commission were concerned it was over matters of grand policy that the relationship between Home Office and Commission was altered dramatically. Suddenly Ruggles-Brise's role of advocate of new measures to the Home Office was reversed for he was now the recipient of a bombardment of memoranda demanding the immediate abolition of separate cellular confinement, labour colonies for weakminded prisoners, the abolition of sentences of one month or less, a new system of twenty classifications of prisoners, reduced use of borstal for young offenders, suspended sentences, 'defaulters' drill' instead of prison as well as many relaxations of the severity of prison discipline.[41] Ultimately, as will be seen, Ruggles-Brise and Churchill formed a formidable alliance for promotion of various penal schemes but initially Ruggles-Brise enlisted the aid of Sir Edward Troup, permanent under secretary at the Home Office since 1908, in a successful attempt to persuade Churchill to pause for thought. Ruggles-Brise was indeed at first astonished by the onslaught of this extraordinarily energetic and demanding Home Secretary and, when Churchill had informed him that it would be easy to reclassify prisoners into twenty new categories, he had apparently 'burst into Homeric laughter'.[42]

Andrew Rutherford has recently made clear that Churchill was deeply committed to the reduction of use of imprisonment in the penal system partly because he had painful memories of his time as a Boer prisoner of war and because he was in close contact with a number of critics and ex-inmates of the system whose views influenced him. He therefore persuaded King George V at his accession to grant remission to a very large number of prisoners, thus striking 'five hundred years of imprisonment and penal servitude from the prison population'. Churchill aimed overall to reduce the daily average population of prisoners by 10 to 15 per cent by extending use of the existing non custodial options and adding to them. Indeed Rutherford believed that Churchill left an enduring commitment at the Home Office to reduction of the prison population. This, he argued, later bore fruit in such measures as the 1914 Criminal Justice Administration Act which obliged the courts to consider allowing time to pay fines rather than order immediate imprisonment if the offender could not produce the money.[43]

Other Home Secretaries with whom the Commission had to deal did not possess Churchill's unremitting attention to individual cases or his indefatigable somewhat ferocious energy in promoting far-reaching programmes of reform. On these Ruggles-Brise had to bring to bear detailed and lengthy arguments and the new sentences of Preventive Detention and Borstal Training were not indeed passed into law until fourteen years after the original Gladstone proposals. Then Herbert Gladstone was himself Home Secretary and was able to steer the Prevention of Crime Bill through Parliament in 1908.

The Prison Commission was intended to be relatively insulated from political pressure, for attacks on the prisons by Members of Parliament and protesters were, in the first instance, dealt with by the Home Office which at once requested information about the issue in question from the Chairman. Between 1895 and 1914 there were a number of liberal backbenchers such as Edward Pickersgill, Sir William Byles, Hilaire Belloc and Llewellyn Atherley-Jones who were deeply critical of the prison system and persistently questioned it in the Commons. There was also strong feeling amongst many Irish nationalist members such as Arthur O'Connor, John Dillon, Michael Davitt and John Redmond, for many of their number had experienced imprisonment and condemned outright all aspects of the system. Later Labour members such as Keir Hardy, William Thorne and Philip Snowden paid much critical attention to the prison officers' strike of 1919 and the general issue of the right of prison officers to form a federation.

The persistence of backbench criticism ensured a good deal of interchange of information between Home Office and Prison Commission between 1895 and 1906. After this, however, the operation of the system was placed at the centre of public controversy by four events—the imprisonment of suffragettes between 1906 and 1914, the imprisonment of conscientious objectors during the Great War, the 1919 prison officers' strike and the publication of a swingeing condemnation of the entire Ruggles-Brise system by the research department of the Labour Party in 1922.[44] The effect of these events was to ensure a close working relationship between the Home Office and Prison Commission and thus by the end of Ruggles-Brise's tenure of office all vestiges of the old independent autonomy of Du Cane's time had wholly disappeared, for the two bodies depended upon one another for defence against determined and well organised critics.

In a different sense, however, under Ruggles-Brise the status of the Prison Commission as a self-contained highly professional organ of government increased in relation to the Home Office. The number of commissioners was limited to five by law and during Ruggles-Brise's time it became customary for one of these to be medically qualified in keeping with the mental scientific direction of much criminological theory and as a result of persistent pressure from medical organisations. Shortly after Gladstone Horatio Donkin was appointed the first medical commissioner and remained in office until 1910 and, after a hiatus which drew immediate condemnation from contemporary medical opinion,[45] the medical inspector Herbert Smalley was promoted to commissioner status. Thereafter one of the commissioners was always a doctor with previous experience as medical inspector. Furthermore, other specialist posts, unknown in Du Cane's time, resulted from Gladstone's recommendations. Thus a new post of visiting chaplain, subsequently converted to chaplain inspector, was created shortly after Gladstone and first occupied by Reverend G.P. Merrick chaplain of Holloway and an authority on aid for discharged prisoners whose duty was to supervise and report on spiritual and educational work in prisons. Around the same time a Controller of Industries was appointed to facilitate the movement from the traditional hard labour machines or severe labour of oakum picking to a more diversified system of prison labour.

Although individual commissioners were responsible for the oversight of a regional group of convict and local prisons and spent a great deal of time focussing on and if necessary visiting these,[46] the Commission itself also maintained a team of inspectors who were responsible for liaising with the prisons and ensuring that the policies of the Commission were in fact being implemented. Their office predated the foundation of the Commission itself, for the inspectorate had been set up in 1835 to act as a body of advisers and watchdogs in respect of the local prisons administered by the county and borough magistrates. Between 1895 and 1921 there was a tendency towards professional specialisation amongst the inspectors so that, alongside general duties relative to a regional group of prisons, there were strengthened medical, spiritual and female prisoner specialisms within the inspectorate.

In this latter connection, until the early twentieth century, the headquarters staff of the Prison Commission was entirely male. Considerable pressure was brought to bear on the Home Office about this by militant women's organisations which argued that a body responsible for the safety and care of large numbers of women should most certainly have a woman at headquarters, preferably at commissioner level. The Gladstone Committee had favoured the appointment of a woman inspector of prisons, but Ruggles-Brise was clearly unwilling to make the appointment. He argued that he had met the spirit of the Gladstone report by greatly increasing the number of female philanthropic visitors to female prisons and by using the voluntary services of Adeline, Duchess of Bedford, whenever female help was needed at top level. The issue of the suffragettes, however, brought this to a head and Home Secretary Herbert Gladstone insisted. In early 1908 Dr Mary Gordon, a Harley Street physician, was appointed, although she was not at first allocated office space working from her rooms in Harley Street which had the facility of 'telephonic communication with the Home Office'.[47]

The appointment was not a happy one either for Dr Gordon or the Commission. She later described that she was constantly referred to as 'a new departure' and felt that her work was more closely scrutinised than that of other personnel: 'I am closely watched and have to do my duty with all the tact I can get together'.[48] Certainly there was no doubt in the Home Office that she had been appointed as a 'sop to feminism' and, when she applied for leave to serve in a first world war military hospital abroad, it was noted that 'she will not be missed';[49] her suffragist sympathies and secret letters to Pethick-Lawrence had not, it appeared, been forgotten or forgiven although she returned to the Commission after the war.

At the centre of this body of experts Evelyn Ruggles-Brise was assisted by secretaries such as Edward Clayton (1895-1908) and Basil Thomson (1908-1913) who were themselves ex governors and recognised as experts on the prison system in their own right. The Prison Commission had throughout been strengthened and adapted in order to implement the Gladstonian programme and, soon after Ruggles-Brise took office as Chairman, regular decision-making meetings came to characterise its work with an increasing flow of information between inspectors, Commissioners, secretary and Home Office. Ruggles-Brise himself maintained an extra-ordinary volume of correspondence and his memoranda to his officials and the Home Office were often exhaustive and detailed analyses covering ten or twenty closely typed pages. There can be little doubt that Ruggles-Brise brought great energy and attention to detail to his work. Initially he found some opposition from those who had served the Commission under Du Cane. For example, M. Clare Garsia, who had been Commission secretary and an intimate of Du Cane before being appointed commissioner in 1895, clashed with Ruggles-Brise. 'I felt very hurt on Wednesday when you threw the papers on the ground', Garsia wrote to him on one occasion; 'you seemed to ignore me for the rest of the meeting . . . I assure you that you are in error in thinking that I have elevated into the dignity of a personal quarrel . . . a slight difference of opinion on the subject of penal reform.'[50]

The emphasis on specialist knowledge and professional experience among Prison Commissioners and headquarters staff continued throughout the inter-war years. Ruggles-Brise's three successor chairmen during that period had experience as civil servants at the Home Office and the tendency to recruit other commissioners with specialist expertise persisted. Thus Alexander Paterson was appointed Commissioner in 1922 having had experience as a youth worker with the poor of Bermondsey and organiser of aftercare of borstal boys as well as experience of administering Ruggles-Brise's new scheme for assistance to discharged convicts. William Norwood East, the Medical Commissioner during the 1930s, had been prison medical officer and medical inspector of prisons and was a leading writer and researcher on medical and psychological aspects of crime and punishment. Lionel Fox, the secretary, had been a Home Office civil servant before transfer to the Commission and published books on the prison system. Close engagement with the Home Office and a general restraining Home Office influence in that relationship continued and two Home Secretaries, Sir William Joynson Hicks between 1924 and 1929 and Sir Samuel Hoare between May 1937 and September 1939, took a very close personal interest in the work of the Commission.

The Prison Commission had been reformed in the late 1890s specifically to set up the approach to prison management recommended by Gladstone. Thereafter the Commission advertised itself as a scientifically informed professional body which under Ruggles-Brise retained an emphasis on punishment and deterrence yet also claimed that it was committed to the creation of various projects to reform the attitude and conduct of prisoners along the lines of the original committee. It is now necessary to look closely at the four major sectors of the prison system—borstals, convict prisons, the preventive detention system and the local prisons—to discover the extent to which these were effected by the new emphasis on reformation and amelioration of disciplinary severity. Furthermore, it is necessary to consider the extent to which the elements of segregation, quarantine, categorisation, classification and positivist differentiation and management emphasised in David Garland's account of penality generally between 1895 and 1914 actually obtained in the English prison system.

## NOTES

1. For the life of Sir Evelyn Ruggles-Brise see S. Leslie, *Sir Evelyn Ruggles-Brise* (Murray 1938).

2. W.V. Harcourt to A. Liddell, 31 Jan. 1885, ECRO ACC 5909 Personalia of Sir Evelyn Ruggles-Brise, no. 3 of 3.

3. Sir Samuel Ruggles-Brise to Evelyn Ruggles-Brise 21 Oct. 1876, 6 Dec. 1874, ECRO ACC 5909, Personalia, no. 1 of 3, no. 3 of 3.

4. E. Stone to E. Ruggles-Brise, no date, ECRO ACC 5909 Personalia no. 1 of 3.

5. E. Ruggles-Brise to his father, 13 Nov. 1878, ECRO ACC 5909, Personalia, no. 1 of 3.

6. E. Ruggles-Brise, Translations and Miscellanies, Oct. 1873. In private collection of Sir John Ruggles-Brise.

7. E. S. Ruggles-Brise, a note book. No title. No date. Jottings made about various philosophers and his view of their work, no date. In private collection of Sir John Ruggles-Brise.

8. J. Pellew, *The Home Office 1848-1914* (Heinemann 1982): 200.

9. Leslie, *Sir Evelyn*: 87.

10. Report from the Departmental Committee on Prisons. Minutes of Evidence: 340, 341, 348. RCP PP 1895, LVI: 12.

11. H. Gladstone to E. Ruggles-Brise, April 1910, ECRO ACC 5909, Personalia, no. 2 of 3.

12. Leslie, *Sir Evelyn*: 187-8, 179, 194.

13. Ibid: 184.

14. Ibid: 168.

15. E. Ruggles-Brise, *The English Prison System* (MacMillan 1921) 10.

16. Ibid: 11, 99.

17. See E. Ruggles-Brise, *Prison Reform at Home and Abroad* (MacMillan 1924).

18. Ibid: 195.

19. Ruggles-Brise, *Prison System*: 200.

20. Ibid: 198-212.

21. Ibid: 215.

22. Ruggles-Brise, A note book.

23. Ruggles-Brise, *Prison System*: 1.

24. Ibid: 10.

25. An Act to Amend the Law Relating to Prisons, 40 &41 Vict. c. 21, ss. 9, 6.

26. PRO HO 45-10025-A 56902/2, HO Minute, H. Asquith, 27 June 1895.

27. PRO HO 45-10563-172511, HO Minute, 19 Jan. 1907.

28. Ibid. HO Minute, 15 Oct. 1906.

29. E. Driver, 'Charles Buckman Goring' in H. Mannheim (ed.) *Pioneers in Criminology* (Stevens and Sons 1960): 335-48.

30. PRO HO 45-10563-172511, H.B. Simpson, HO memo 5 Nov. 1913.

31. Ibid. HO Minute, H.B. Simpson, 27 July 1915.

32. PRO HO 45-9754-A60246/1.

33. PRO HO 45-10552-163497.

34. PRO HO 45-10609-193551. HO Minutes, W.S. Churchill, 9 June 1910, 24 June 1910, E. Ruggles-Brise to HO, 29 June 1910.

35. PRO HO 45-9752-A59678/2 E. Ruggles-Brise to HO, 9 Nov. 1898.

36. PRO HO 45-18366-122929/10, W.S. Churchill to PC, 13 July 1910.

37. Sir Alfred Wills to *The Times*, 16 Jan. 1911: 9 col. f.

38. PRO HO 144-1144-209195/4, Description of Beatrice Carter, 1 June 1911.

39. PRO HO 144-1144-209195/9, W.S. Churchill, HO Minute, 15 June 1911.

40. PRO HO 144-1067-189934/5 W.S. Churchill, HO Minute, 23 March 1910.

41. PRO HO 144-1085-193548/1,2,3. HO 144-18869-196919/1 W.S. Churchill to E. Ruggles-Brise *et al.* 13 Aug. 1910./2 W.S. Churchill to E. Ruggles-Brise 30 June 1910.

42. R.S. Churchill, *Winston S. Churchill*, vol. 2, *Young Statesman 1901–14* (Heinemann 1967): 392.

43. A. Rutherford, 'Lessons from a Reductionist Era', paper delivered to the 10th International Congress on Criminology, Hamburg, 6 Sept. 1988: 6.

44. S. Hobhouse and A. F. Brockway (eds.), *English Prisons Today* (Longman, Green & Co. 1922).

45. *Lancet,* 30 April 1910: 1213-14.

46. B. Thomson, *The Scene Changes* (Collins 1939): 224-5.

47. PRO HO 45-10052-A63072/5 HO to Treasury, 13 Dec. 1907. /6, Sir Edward Troup, HO Minute, 12 March 1908.

48. M Gordon, *Penal Discipline* (Routledge 1922): 4. PRO HO 45-10552-163497, M. Gordon to E. Pethick Lawrence, 26 Oct. 1908.

49. PRO HO 45-10552-163497, HO Minutes, 9 July 1916, 21 Dec. 1919.

50. M. Clare Garsia to E. Ruggles-Brise, ECRO ACC 5909, Personalia, no. 3 of 3. 17 Dec. 1897.

# Chapter Four

# Juvenile Adults and the Borstal System
# 1895–1921

During the mid-nineteenth century there had begun to be instituted Reformatory Schools for the training and reformation of children and young people previously sent to prison and by 1895 there existed a cross-country system of these schools to which under sixteens were committed following conviction. They had come into being as a result of assumptions that young offenders were contaminated by prolonged contact with older prisoners, that they lost their dread of prison if sent there at an early age for lengthy periods and that, because of youthful plasticity of personality and susceptibility to environmental influence, they would respond to a regime of training and education. By 1895 there were around 24,000 in these schools which were run, for the most part, by voluntary committees, and offenders could be committed to them up to the age of sixteen and held for between three and five years with the proviso that they could not be held beyond the age of nineteen. Lastly up to 1893 the court was obliged to order a very short period of preliminary imprisonment prior to removal to a Reformatory School but this requirement was removed by an Act of that year (56 and 57 Vict. cap.48 sec. 1).[1]

The history of Reformatory Schools and Ships (designed to train for a life at sea) falls outside the scope of this study because these were never viewed as prisons or administered by the Prison Commission. However, the intention to screen young offenders below the age of sixteen out of the prison system was not entirely successful before 1900. Indeed in 1896 sixty under twelves and just over fourteen hundred between twelve and sixteen were in fact committed to prison.[2] Of the age group sixteen to twenty-one around thirteen and a half thousand young men and three thousand young women were committed to prison in the same year.[3]

The new liberalism and the criminological thrust towards selective and differential treatment on the basis of assessed physical, mental and moral deficiency unanimously emphasised special treatment for the young prisoner.

Thus William Morrison had argued strongly for this on the basis that inborn deficiency and predisposition did not result in a fixed recidivistic habit until the mid twenties and that large numbers of young prisoners could be successfully influenced to lead law abiding lives if subjected to education and training.[4] Almost all New Liberal philosophers insisted upon the value of programmes of moral and spiritual improvement of the young by educational and personal influence, whilst those concerned with physical deterioration of the race supported measures which promoted the conversion of down-at-heel, cigarette-addicted, street corner, youthful lounger to alert, muscular athlete.

Ruggles-Brise's policy towards the younger prisoner was two dimensional. In the first place, like Du Cane, he gave unstinting support to the idea that all under sixteens should be removed from the prison system and during his period in office a good deal of success was achieved in this. So between 1st April, 1906 and 31st March, 1907 only four under twelves were sent to prison and 704 boys and 20 girls aged between twelve and sixteen[5]—a plain contrast to the figure of nearly ten thousand under sixteens sent to local prisons during 1870, four and a half thousand in 1890.[6] Clearly the reduction in numbers of the under sixteen prisoner was partly effected by the general decrease in the daily average of prisoners between 1870 and 1921. But it was also brought about by the unremitting condemnation of such sentences by Prison Commission and Home Office who argued that prisons were entirely harmful to these young people and that a selective programme of reclamatory facilities was necessary to include reformatory schools at one end, the supervision in the community by earnest philanthropic and morally uplifting Police Court Missionaries and Probation Officers at the other.

With regard to the prisoner aged between sixteen and twenty-one Ruggles-Brise's policy was an amendment of the original Gladstone view that the committal age to Reformatory Schools should be raised to eighteen and that a new kind of regime should be erected for prisoners aged between eighteen and twenty-three, designed to operate 'half way . . . between the prison and the reformatory'.[7] In making this recommendation Gladstone had been influenced by the spread of reformatories for prisoners aged between sixteen and thirty in America. The first of these had been opened at Elmira, New York in 1876 and they were aimed at offenders who were in danger of drifting into habitual crime: at them it was intended that the regime would emphasise release on parole at the discretion of the institution with a minimum and maximum set by the Judge, supervision after release, physical and military training, educational and occupational programmes and the use of marks as an indication of progress made.[8]

The American Reformatories of the late 1890s were the subject of controversy in Britain where many saw them as dependent upon the positivist idea that personality not criminal act should become the focus of attention and condemned Elmira with its baths, gymnasia, class rooms, lecture halls and libraries.[9] However in 1897 Ruggles-Brise was sent by Conservative Home Secretary, Sir Matthew White Ridley, to America to study the Elmira system. As a result of his observations in New York and Massachusetts particularly he became convinced that the American Reformatory with its 'elaborate system of moral, physical and industrial training ... the enthusiasm which dominated the work, the elaborate machinery for supervision of parole ... if stripped of their extravagances' was an excellent model for Britain.[10] However, he believed that the Americans were wrong to depart from 16—21 as the dangerous age and intended to operate the new training for those sixteen to twenty-one year olds who were plainly drifting into habitual crime and those he defined as 'the young hooligan advanced in crime, perhaps with many previous convictions, and who appeared to be inevitably doomed to a life of habitual crime ... the young ruffian ... of the London streets, the callous and precocious young criminal' who could up to twenty-one be saved from a life of crime 'by the exercise of civil and firm restraint ... twisted and turned and converted up to the age of his civil majority'.[11] From the beginning, therefore, Ruggles-Brise had in mind the young offender well advanced towards recidivism.

Ruggles-Brise took personal charge of devising this new scheme for 'juvenile adults' who were to be reformed by a 'stern and exact discipline, tempered only by such rewards and privileges as good conduct with industry might earn: and resting on its physical side on the basis of hard manual labour and skilled trades and on its moral and intellectual side on the combined efforts of the chaplain and schoolmaster'.[12] Initially this system was carried out with young male prisoners from the London prisons serving the twelve months or more required to allow the approach to be applied and these were collected together at Bedford prison. Soon the enthusiastic governor at Bedford reported that 'they are more susceptible to good advice and teaching, are beginning to gain self-respect and the value of being respected for their efforts ... they show a decided spirit of candour ... speak of the past with regret ... understand that everything is being done for their ultimate good'.[13] Thereafter the scheme was also begun for exactly the same group at Borstal Convict Prison near Rochester and the London Prison Visitors Association (later the Borstal Association) coordinated and planned arrangements for the young men after release also visiting them at Borstal before release. By 1905 Bedford was specialising in under sixteens from London who were sentenced to lengthy periods despite state condemnation of the practice and Borstal was dealing with the older 'Juvenile Adult' group. By the spring of 1904 the regime at Borstal was available to all juvenile adults serving twelve months or over throughout England and Wales.

In 1905, because of pressure on Borstal, parts of Lincoln prison were utilised for 'juvenile adults' serving over twelve months from the North and a part of Dartmoor converted to the regime in respect of young male convicts serving penal servitude. In addition the three elements of physical improvement by exercise and drill, 'mental improvement by training, scholastic and industrial' and post release 'shepherding' began to be applied to the under twenty-ones who were serving shorter sentences than twelve months.[14] These were placed in special 'collecting prisons' for this purpose or, if the sentences were very short, dealt with according to a rudimentary version of the regime at their local prison.

The plan was to create a regime of physical drill and exercise, classroom education, technical, moral and spiritual instruction and trade training in such occupations as printing, book binding, masonry, carpentry, tin smelting and boot making. At Bedford to begin with there were two hours instruction in numeracy and literacy per week, gymnastics for nearly an hour a day, lectures, weekly choir practices and twice weekly cellular visits by the governor and chaplain 'for straight talk and sound moral advice'.[15] At Borstal prison itself in 1902 a set of grades and sub grades was created with an ascending scale of privileges such as lights allowed on in the evenings in cells or cubicles, association in a reading room, carpet, mirror and photographs allowed in cells, good conduct badges each carrying a set money allowance. Each grade was dressed in a distinctively coloured uniform— drab for the initial penal grade, brown for the ordinary and blue for the special.[16]

In 1908, following very detailed planning and negotiation between Ruggles-Brise and Herbert Gladstone the Home Secretary, the Prevention of Crime Act was passed (8 Edward VII cap. 59). In Part One of this an entirely new sentence was created of 'detention under penal discipline in a borstal institution for a term of not less than one year nor more than three years'.[17] The sentence could only be passed by the higher courts and was to apply to sixteen to twenty-ones whose 'criminal habits or tendencies' or 'association with persons of bad character' were heading them into persistent crime and the Home Secretary was given permission to raise the maximum age to twenty-three if he later wished. Lastly, at any point after six months had been served (three for girls) the trainee might be released on revocable licence at the order of the Prison Commission.[18] Shortly after this act a part of Aylesbury convict prison was converted into a borstal institution for girls and when Ruggles-Brise retired in August 1921 there were these institutions at Borstal, Feltham and Aylesbury and Portland Convict Prison was converted for use as a fourth. By 1921 at Borstal and Feltham there were over nine hundred young men undergoing borstal training, at Aylesbury nearly two hundred girls.[19]

Between 1903 and 1921 the borstal system therefore consisted of the actual institutions where the new sentence was served at Borstal, Feltham, Aylesbury and at the very end of 1921 Portland. But it also referred to the way of handling sixteen to twenty-one year olds who were serving ordinary lengthy sentences of prison and who were collected in special prisons where the regime was known as 'modified borstal' and elements of 'borstal' such as local 'borstal' aftercare societies were also applied at local prisons where the same age group were serving very short terms.

The outside world was thus assured that a self-contained individually oriented and systematic programme of intellectual, physical and moral development was under way in each of the full borstals. Through the annual reports of the Prison Commission and of the Borstal Association the public were told that rigorous gymnastics, sports, class instruction, personal influence and lectures were in operation. Ruggles-Brise and his associates emphasised that as the trainee worked up to the higher grades more trust and responsibility would be given in order to stimulate a 'sense of honour and self respect'[20] and that promotion to the higher grades would teach the advantage of industry and effort with privileges such as team games, meals in association, newspapers, organized debates, club rooms and monetary rewards being allowed. Furthermore those who won through to the top grade would be appointed 'monitors' so as to exercise the self-discipline and responsibility which they had learned to the benefit of all. All would learn occupational skills and the habit of hard work in the workshops and farms attached to the borstals and each day there would be 'silent hours' for study, religious ministry at chapel services and drill to promote physical coordination, mental alertness and obedience. The girls would learn the skills and duties of wife and mother through 'laundry work, housework, needlework and cooking'[21] and particular attention was to be paid to individual progress and difficulty and personal influence of the staff on the trainees was to be emphasised. The borstals were later divided into 'Houses', so that 'the spirit of friendly rivalry and competition might be developed' and 'something like the public school spirit ... generated'.[22] Then, at the end, in accordance with Gladstone's emphasis on post release 'patronage' and concern, the inmate would emerge to the regulating supervision of the Borstal Association which set up systems of pre release planning meetings with trainees, arranged accommodation, occupation and maintenance and supervised adherence to the conditions of the licence. This supervision was carried out by the officers of the Association led by its Honorary Director Wemyss Grant Wilson in the London area and in the provinces delegated to voluntary associates such as clergy, philanthropists or police court missionaries recruited on a case by case basis.

Both the full and modified borstal systems were hailed throughout England as a radical and most promising reform. Imperial governments and foreign countries eagerly asked for details of the scheme.[23] Large numbers of magistrates, judges and journalists extolled it.[24] Claims were made that around 70 per cent of the trainees were successfully reclaimed.[25] Eulogists vividly depicted the change in demeanour: 'the shifty eyes have grown steady, the sullen brows and lips are clear. Heads are held erect; they walk without a slouch'.[26] Governors regaled the public with tales of string quartettes and brass bands of borstal boys giving concerts at local work houses and from chaplains came assurances that the public school spirit was flourishing down at Feltham although their readers must bear in mind that such transformation required much time and effort before the disappearance of that 'street corner, hand in pocket slouch that he had on reception . . . that deceitful and bobby-coming expression which is so often marked on the face of the guilty conscience-smitten young thief'.[27]

The reality was somewhat different. In the first place the staff operating the system were almost all accustomed to the routine of prisons and were placed in the position of having to carry out a demanding and testing system with a host of young men and women sent to them with only the briefest of preliminary enquiries. Ruggles-Brise himself frequently emphasised the importance of the personal factor in the conduct of public school and penal regime the default of which 'no perfecting of machinery or method will ever be able to replace'.[28] It was in fact the lack of the rare qualities of combined firmness and personal magnetism and sensitivity which tended to frustrate the borstal system. Thus some of the staff concealed their disciplinary problems believing they would be blamed if the Commissioners got to know of these. As one governor of Borstal itself put it, 'if I was to send a sheet up to the Home Office with all these reports against juvenile adults they'd think I didn't know how to 'andle the lads. As things are now we've got a good name 'ere'.[29] Beneath the surface there was a tendency to monotonous deadening reliance on the institutional routine, the faith that, if all is done exactly according to the book of rules, the needs of the system would be served, an approach described thus in respect of a reformatory school: 'we gets up when we hears the bugle and we makes our beds. We goes to breakfast when we hears the bugle and then when the bugle goes we goes to school. We comes home to dinner when we hears the bugle and in the evening we sits and mends our clothes and when the bugle goes we goes to bed'.[30]

There is no doubt, however, that some of the governors were successful in the work as was Charles Rich at Borstal itself just after the Great War and whose work will be shortly described. Another was Basil Thomson governor of Dartmoor when first a juvenile adult class of convicts was set up. In 1905 he described the gradual change in motivation and commitment that occurred for, at first, the young convicts felt insulted by their new juvenile adult status. However, before long even the most defiant and contemptuous begged to be allowed to rejoin the class and he concentrated juvenile adults on care of the animals at the prison farm. Soon all 'vie with one another in turning out the horses clean and well groomed'[31] and many participated frankly and thoughtfully in the debates organised by the assistant chaplain.

Yet more often the complaints were that the staff did not know how to operate the system effectively. So in 1910 at Holloway, where a modified borstal for girls operated, the Lady Inspector emphasised that there was 'a want of harmony and understanding on the part of the superior officers' which resulted in an institutional, monotonous and mechanical implementation of the system.[32] On another occasion at Liverpool modified borstal wing the chaplain inspector was astonished to find utter confusion in a small room where a number of different classes were being conducted simultaneously.[33] Indeed the introduction of tutors such as Paterson Owens at Feltham towards the end of Ruggles-Brise's chairmanship was intended to bring into the system personnel who were familiar with problems of education and not conditioned by prison experience.

Staff often seemed unable to cope flexibly with the trainees, whose experience of life bore little relationship to what was happening to them in these institutions. Through Aylesbury there trooped a succession of girls who failed to remain at the refuges and homes in which they were placed as a condition of release licence[34] and whose deepest concerns and loyalties seemed to puzzle their custodians, who frequently turned to the Prison Commission for advice. So, bundles of love letters from distressed boy friends to Aylesbury girls found their way to the Prison Commission with a recommendation that they should be withheld from the girls as unsettling to them or because they invited immorality.''My darling Vera . . . how happy I was when you were here, how I used to look forward to the time of seeing you to be with you again and kiss you passionately.' 'Dear Maggie, I have not been the same since you went away. I have been good for nothing. Dear, I don't care what anyone says I am going to wait for you . . . true loving sweet heart, goodnight John XXXXXXX'.[35]

There was often an abruptness of manner and a watchful suspiciousness on the part of staff. As one visitor to Borstal itself remarked in early 1921, 'wherever one goes, in class room, shop, recreation ground or refectory, (the warders') ubiquity is apparent. One wonders whether it is really essential to impress upon the youths the fact that . . . they have to be as carefully shadowed as any hardened criminal . . . the uniform does not assist the man but it must be detested by the youths who regard the wearers as their natural enemies'.[36] On occasion Ruggles-Brise had to insist on greater tolerance and compassion towards the trainees. So, in 1911 he remonstrated with the Director of the Borstal Association who did not want to receive at his office, or find work for, boys who had been sent to a special unit at Canterbury prison following revocation of licence and recall to borstal or rejection in the first instance as untrainable by the borstals themselves. Ruggles-Brise insisted that these were not to be treated as 'unworthy of assistance' or refused help on release.[37]

Staff undoubtedly were judgemental towards the very group for whom Ruggles-Brise had devised the system, the energetic and heavily convicted youth headed for a life of crime. They preferred the docile, apprehensive and obedient. So, Wilfred Law was 'a thorough waster, badly disposed and without intention of improving himself. A slave to vicious impurity'. John McLaughlin was 'quite the worst boy here. He is my idea of a real brute.' Frank Skinner was 'one of the most deceitful and wrong headed boys who have been to Borstal. He is clever enough to keep out of report but is doing harm here . . . a dangerous character . . . one of our worst—crafty and deceitful.'[38]

Further difficulties arose because many of those sent to borstal were suffering from disabilities and deficiencies, often brought on by the extreme poverty or destitution in which they had lived. Courts were supposed to consider reports about young men and women before making a borstal order and these reports were drawn up by the local prison governor. However these were usually perfunctorily done and frequently young people were committed suffering physical illness. 'James Nesling. Health poor. Suffers from abscesses in neck and under arms. Has not been able to work . . . but waits on the others.' 'Alfred Smith—poor physique and not intelligent enough for the workshop', 'Robert Wallace. Physically and mentally defective. Does his work carefully but in my opinion is a hopeless case.' The Home Office complained in 1910 that 'Parsons (deaf) and Hill (almost weak minded) are unsuitable for borstal. It is doubtful whether they could get any benefit from the training . . . which requires at any rate some mental and physical capacity for development.'[39] However, courts persisted in the practice of sending 'a large body of infirm, weakly lads' to borstal and indeed Feltham was opened partly because Ruggles-Brise found it impossible to stop this practice and therefore had to create a more relaxed less physically demanding regime for them.[40]

Yet on the other hand many courts continued to send the heavily convicted young men and women for whom the system was designed to short sentences of prison. In 1910 Ruggles-Brise complained to the Home Office that a young woman 'who had been five times before convicted of larceny' was yet again sentenced to a short prison term.[41] In the same year philanthropic bodies from Manchester protested about the failure to use borstal for young girls whom they saw as immoral and in need of reclamation and tutelage, who passed 'to and fro between the common lodging house, the prison and the work house maternity ward'.[42] Indeed, the reluctance of courts to impose the long borstal terms on girls was general and the Home Office complained about it to sentencers in late 1910.[43]

By no means all sent to borstal accepted the lengthened and indeterminate training. At Feltham and elsewhere there were 'smashings up' of cubicles and 'insolence to officers and foul language, coupled with refusal to work or destruction of Institution property' . . . 'exceptionally obscene, blasphemous and abusive' language.[44] To break such rebellious spirit a severe penal grade of hard labour and cellular isolation had been designed but towards the end of Ruggles-Brise's tenure there were very widespread complaints that a spirit of mutiny and defiance prevailed and that the standards of discipline and training had fallen drastically. Furious visiting committees of magistrates expostulated to Ruggles-Brise that the boys could be heard 'yelping, whistling, barking and shouting to one another'[45] and the Borstal Association made swingeing criticisms of what they saw as a departure from the original vision.[46]

The full borstal system was, indeed, profoundly effected by the Great War. From 1914 onwards a policy of early release for military service was pursued and three hundred and forty were so treated by March 1915. In 1916 conscription was introduced nationally and, thereafter, training for the older inmates was reduced to six months drill, trench digging and road building before compulsory enlistment.[47] At Borstal itself the entire programme was thus overthrown on account of the national crisis and it remained in a poor state after the war with the trainees resentful, grudging and ill disciplined.

Ruggles-Brise at first tried to reform the system by encouraging and urging the staff,[48] but in January 1920 he appointed an experienced prison governor, Colonel Charles Rich, recently returned from war service to restore order at Borstal where discipline had all but collapsed. Rich at once introduced strict military discipline and confronted his startled charges with dire warnings about the consequences of defiance and slackness. He particularly emphasised military parades and sports such as cricket, football, swimming and boxing.[49] Thus he got them 'drilled disciplined and taught that they had a country to serve',[50] and he organised the borstal into 'wings' and 'companies', with staff as wing commanders and trainees in the top grades as 'company leaders' 'platoon leaders' and 'orderlies'.[51]

Rich also, at the request of some of the trainees, created a group called 'the circle' which was an association of trainees with some staff to which a member could gain admission by election. This 'circle' of trusted trainees bound all its members explicitly to obedience, cleanliness, self-control and diligence. Members were bound to 'always play the game', 'think twice', 'take your punishments in the right spirit', 'show the difference between a member and non-member' and the circle emphasised such ideas as duty, honour, loyalty and concern for each other and called on members to propagate these qualities throughout the borstal by example and influence.[52] Furthermore, Rich introduced fortnightly camps annually on the sea coast and set up an institution newspaper called 'The Borstalian' (subsequently significantly renamed 'The Phoenix') which was written by staff and trainees. In September 1920 there was a public display of this new spirit when a sports day was held with sack races, tug of war, 'grenade throwing', 'bayonet display', gymnastic pyramids and a mock infantry battle whilst the borstal band played 'Rule Britannia' with one of the warders' daughters acting the role of Britannia.[53]

Colonel Rich, like Basil Thomson, had a powerful, sympathetic, authoritative and self-assured personality. He wanted trainees bound together in mess committees and associations to promote honour and loyalty and set great store by addresses to trainees individually or collectively. 'You are sent here in order that you may have a chance of learning the rules of the game and of acquiring the habit of playing fair . . . the reason why you are here is that you have been playing the game with no rules, not as a sportsman nor in the true British way and now the referee has blown his whistle and ordered you off the ground to go and learn the rules before you attempt to play again . . . think always for five seconds before answering back. Many a man has saved himself by acquiring this habit . . . Don't loll about and talk with your mouth full and don't eat as if you had not seen food for a week. Your food is not going to run away'.[54]

At the end of his tenure Ruggles-Brise introduced new rules to strengthen the educational, occupational and physical developmental programmes[55] at all the borstals. In April 1920 tutors were appointed at Feltham to devise an entirely new curriculum and to relate more closely and personally to each inmate[56] and to plan educational programmes upon a more individual basis. Furthermore the Prison Commission strengthened the application of morally uplifting and educational approaches. In 1920 and 1921 appropriate films were used at Feltham, although on one occasion later the governor was gently reprimanded for showing a film for mere entertainment rather than education[57] and outside organizations allowed access. So International Correspondence Schools encouraged trainees in the study of mechanical engineering and draughtsmanship and examined those who took the courses[58] and at Aylesbury girl guides were introduced in 1919. This endeavour began well with a visit by Lady Baden Powell but the chaplain and staff distrusted the enthusiastic young guide leader and resentments developed between the girls over the award of badges. The governor felt that the guide leader lacked experience 'in the ways and villainies of the type with whom she is dealing' and, despite complaints about this attitude by the Prison Commission, the experiment eventually had to be discontinued.[59]

There were times when Ruggles-Brise had to fight hard to sustain faith in his most cherished project. In mid 1910, for example, Churchill expressed considerable reservations about it because he was convinced that borstal was a very severe sentence inflicted for 'very slight offences arising from the rowdy moods of youth'. He believed that the new system represented a shift towards the view that 'no punishment other than the longest and the most severe can be inflicted upon youths of the working classes with any hope of beneficial result'[60] and demanded more use of probation and a new sentence of 'defaulters' drill' to be served in the community in evenings or at weekends. Ruggles-Brise was himself concerned that courts were committing too many young trivial offenders to borstal, as was Churchill, and himself believed very strongly in the extension of probation yet was obliged to defend the borstal idea against Churchill's swingeing condemnation of the use to which it was being put.

The most damning attack on the system was made by the Labour Research Department enquiry set up in 1919[61] which concluded that borstals were severe and institutional in character, failed to equip trainees with occupational or educational skills and depended too heavily on prison staff who lacked the skill and enthusiasm of outside educators or trained teachers. Those who submitted evidence to this enquiry suggested that the trainees worked long hours at the various trades such as laundry work, building, painting, farming, blacksmithing, cooking, gardening, shoemaking and carpentry and that the tendency was to undiscriminating collective management rather than individual training and development. The enquiry forcefully questioned Ruggles-Brise's view that moral, physical and intellectual improvement was being achieved and called for radical reform of the system.

There is thus much evidence that the regimes in borstals were often largely penal in character, quite apart from the issue of lengthened sentences for reformatory purposes which would preoccupy academics examining twentieth century criminal disposal overall. Plainly Ruggles-Brise's original vision was only in part fulfilled and he himself, aware that there were deficiencies, felt that the Great War had thrown all parts of the penal system into 'an inextricable confusion': indeed he blamed that war for the ruin of many of his deepest hopes.[62]

Yet it is necessary to reflect on what was done in the years of Du Cane and compare that with the borstals as they were by 1921. Admittedly some would have received shorter sentences under Du Cane although others would have gone to long years of penal servitude. However, the monotonous cellular separation of the local prison and the inflexible and most severe regime of Du Cane's convict system were a different and much harsher approach to juvenile adults. So, even in the most sustained attack on the borstals produced by the Labour Enquiry the regimes described were more relaxed and gentle. Thus at Aylesbury by 1921 the gates of the borstal and the internal doors stood open all day, girls in the higher grades had 'small but cheerful and well warmed' rooms of their own with flowers and photographs and selected girls were allowed to go in twos into the town unaccompanied to spend their earnings. For the middle and higher grades at male borstals outdoor games were organised, meals taken in association, conversation allowed at certain times of the day and in the evenings 'after the education hour games are allowed including parlour games ... cards, chess, dominoes, draughts ... football is taught and encouraged and sometimes the borstal team plays away. Boxing is also permitted ... a stage has been erected the boys having painted scenery and constructed a drop curtain, footlights etc. Lantern lectures are given on Saturday nights and outside concert parties give performances. Certain of the boys are allowed to go without a warder for country walks, visiting etc.'[63] Furthermore, there were not lacking letters to governors and staff expressing gratitude for what had been done: 'it is your kindness and ... interest in us boys that has enabled me to obtain a real good start again in life' ... 'Dear Sir, us lads here (at the front) will always try our best ... to keep up the name of the old place'.[64]

The Liberal and Ruggles-Brisian vision of digging up the roots from which recidivism sprang, reformation of the young by example, influence and individualisation, the dream of legions of grateful, glowing, bright and fit young men and women streaming, cured, out of the borstals was not fulfilled. Clearly borstals were often stern, institutional and collective and at other times paradoxically seemed to contemporaries to be in a state of near chaos with boys slouching around, defiant and refusing to call warders 'Sir'[65] or with girls wrecking the monitor (prefect) system by persistently electing 'the very worst characters' to these posts.[66] Yet between 1895 and 1921 very great change had occurred and Sir Edmund Du Cane would have been aghast at any idea of elected monitors, football matches or theatrical performances.

Their most recent historian, Victor Bailey, was critical of Ruggles-Brise's borstals which he saw as 'primarily penal' establishments 'based on strict discipline, obedience and uniform treatment'.[67] However it is important to recognise that considerable relaxation of severity of treatment of young offenders in Prison Commission institutions had occurred between the retirement of Du Cane and 1921. It is true that radical reform of borstals occurred subsequent to Ruggles-Brise's chairmanship and it is also true that, as Bailey pointed out and as one would expect, Ruggles-Brise, true to his classical notions of criminal treatment, resisted any idea that the penal element should be altogether removed from the borstals.[68]

Nonetheless, putting to one side the marked relaxation of penal discipline compared to Du Cane, it is also clear that Ruggles-Brise's objectives were seriously upset by the Great War and conscription. It is also clear that in his last years as chairman Ruggles-Brise wished to improve the system by the introduction of tutors, better education, 'wing' groups and so forth. Clearly, as Bailey pointed out, these later projects were often explicitly based on a post war enthusiasm for military discipline among officials, yet this does not alter the fact that they had as their object the stimulation of energy and enthusiasm and certainly under Colonel Rich at Borstal itself they met with a good deal of success. The public criticisms of the Labour Research Group, the Howard Association and the Borstal Association should not therefore be taken as the last word on the borstals of Ruggles-Brise.

It is however clear that the borstal system illustrated problems which were inherent in the optimistic liberal ideal of reclamation by example, close engagement and energetic stewardship. In particular selection of staff, their attitudes, preference among them for the safety of monotonous institutional regimes, resistance among trainees who resented the long periods of training all posed difficulties. However the system also showed up flaws in the criminological enterprise of pre planned purposeful total institutions designed to identify mental, physical and moral defects and rectify these on the basis of individualised training programmes. In the event the actual practice in the borstals fell far short of the aspirations of the Commission which in any case found it difficult to secure improvement of practice after shortfalls between practice and policy had been brought to light. Indeed Ruggles-Brise seems to have been somewhat naive in his expectation that staff attitudes and practices would change when required to do so or when staff were placed in new situations. Thus in 1917 he himself confronted staff at Borstal because of allegations that the regime was 'too much like a prison'[69] and ultimately had to draft Colonel Rich there. Yet, only four years later, he founded a new borstal at Portland Convict Prison and—scarcely surprisingly—there was swift outrage in the press and among reformers at the severity and unsuitability of Portland borstal, which was of course entirely staffed by officers whose only experience was that of running a convict prison.[70] Lastly sentencers frequently ignored Home Office circulars advising them that the borstals were intended for a particular type of offender, tough, healthy, recidivistic in inclination and often sent sick or infirm young people there or sent suitable candidates to short sentences of prison. So, although penal severity of treatment of young offenders by the Prison Commission was much relaxed in comparison to Du Cane's time, in terms of the reformatory assumptions of those who formulated the scheme in the first place, it left much to be desired.

Despite these short comings of practice the borstal system provides a good example of the new type of reformative/welfare based institutional system which both Foucault and later Garland believed was coming to dominate penality and to take a major part in the normalising mechanisms and discourses which Foucault so strongly emphasised. Indeed the actual relaxation of disciplinary severity and indeterminacy and lengthening of period of custody fit well with Garland's notion of the state taking to itself functions of rescue, assistance, welfare, assessment and differential intervention and a strengthening of the power and influence of the state at the expense of classical sentencing principles of uniformity of punishment and judicial fixing of penalty independent of the executive. Indeed, Foucault would have expected the actual reformatory programmes to have been out of kilter with the propaganda of the state about their effectiveness, for to him all such penal institutions were essentially bricks in an encircling, crushing, intruding carceral wall.

## NOTES

1. For an account of these institutions see Report to the Secretary of State for the Home Department of The Departmental Committee on the Reformatory and Industrial Schools, vol.1, PP 1896, XLV.
2. RCP and DCP yr end 31 March 1898, PP 1898, XLVII: 14.
3. Ibid.
4. W.D. Morrison, *Juvenile Offenders* (Fisher Unwin 1896): 103-18, 268-317.
5. RCP and DCP yr end 31 March 1907, PP 1908, LII: 13.
6. RCP PP 1890-91, XLIII: 4-5.
7. Report from the Departmental Committee On Prisons, PP 1895, LVI: 30..
8. J.L. Gillin, *Criminology and Penology* (Century 1935, rev. ed.): 452-3, 472
9. *The Times*, 8 June 1897: 7 cols c-d. Lancet, 7 May 1892: 1042.
10. E. Ruggles-Brise, *The English Prison System*, (MacMillan 1921): 91.
11. Ibid: 91-2. Borstal Prison 1900-1907, PRO HO 45-10046-A62024/1, E. Ruggles-Brise to Sir Kenelm Digby, 30 June 1900.
12. Ruggles-Brise, *Prison System*: 93.
13. RCP & DCP yr end 31 March 1900, PP, 1900, XLI: 20..
14. RCP & DCP yr end 31 March 1907, PP 1908 LII: 15-18.
15. PRO HO 45-10046-A62024/1, E. Ruggles-Brise to Sir Kenelm Digby, 30 June 1900. Instructions to Governor Bedford Prison, no date.

16. PRO HO 45-10046-A62024/8, Standing Order Borstal Juvenile Adults. RCP & DCP yr end 31 March 1907, PP 1908 LII: 24.
17. Prevention of Crime Act 1908, 8 Edward VII, c. 59, part 1, s. 1. Later the one year minimum was raised to two by the Criminal Justice Administration Act 1914. 4 & 5 George V, c. 58, s. 11, ss. 1.
18. Prevention of Crime Act 1908, s.1 ss.B, s. 5.
19. RCP & DCP yr end 31 March 1921 PP 1921 XVI: 4.
20. Ruggles-Brise, *Prison System*: 244.
21. Ibid: 262.
22. RCP and DCP yr end 31 March 1920, PP 1920 XXIII: 11.
23. E.g. Ceylon Colony, RCP and DCP yr end 31 March 1919., PP 1919, XXVII: 8. *Re.* Greece see PRO HO 45-10570-175865. The Borstal System. Foreign Office to HO on request Greek Ambassador for details, 22 Nov. 1922.
24. *Justice of the Peace*, 26 Aug. 1905, LXIX: 399. Ruggles-Brise, *Prison System*: 5-6. *The Times*, 1 Dec. 1904: 4 cols. c-d, 18 March 1921: 7 col. d.
25. Ruggles-Brise, *Prison System*: 95, 119.
26. Arthur Paterson, *Our Prisons* (Rees 1911): 33.
27. RCP & DCP yr end 31 March 1912 Pt 2,. PP 1912-13, XLIII: 166, 171, 173.
28. E. Ruggles-Brise, note book, no date, private collection of Sir John Ruggles-Brise.
29. W. Blake, *Quod* (Hodder and Stoughton 1927): 87.
30. M.A. Payne, *Oliver Untwisted* (Arnold 1929): 15..
31. PRO. P.Com. 7/281, The Church and Prisoners, address by B. Thomson to Church Congress, Oct. 1905.
32. PRO P.Com. 7/586. P.Com. 7/587
33. PRO P.Com. 7/594
34. PRO P.Com. 7/561
35. PRO P.Com. 7/574 Albert Chadwick to Vera Burville 22 June 1917, John Atkinson to Margaret Bristow, no date.
36. S. Hobhouse and A.F. Brockway (eds.), *English Prisons Today* (Longmans, Green & Co. 1922): 420.
37. PRO P.Com. 7/516, W. Grant Wilson to PC 3 Jan. 1911, PC to Basil Thomson, 5 Jan. 1911.
38. The Borstal System: Reports on Borstal Boys, no date, PRO HO 45-10570-175865.
39. Establishment of a Juvenile Adult Section of Borstal Prison 1900-1907. PRO HO 45-10046-A62024/1. Reports of the Governor of Bedford Prison 29 June 1900 and 3 April 1900. The Borstal System, HO 45-10570-175865, HO Minute, 1 June 1910
40. PRO HO 45-10570-175865, E. Ruggles-Brise to HO, 23 June 1910
41. Ibid. E. Ruggles-Brise to HO, 5 July 1910.
42. Ibid. Lady Visitors of Strangeways to W.S. Churchill 1 Nov. 1910.
43. Ibid. A. De Rutzen to HO, 6 Oct. 1910..
44. Borstals 1914-23, PRO HO 45-11160-271162, R. Vansittart Chairman Visitors Feltham to HO, 29 Jan. 1914, E. Ruggles-Brise to HO 5 March 1914, HO Minute, 28 Jan. 1922.

45. PRO P.Com. 7/521, E.Ruggles-Brise to Governor Borstal, 22 Jan. 1920., see attached Visiting Justices' report.
46. PRO P.Com. 7/521, W. Grant Wilson to E. Ruggles-Brise 14 Nov. 1919, P.Com. 7/541, Resolution of Borstal Association 1 Aug. 1917.
47. PRO P.Com. 7/536, PC to W. Grant Wilson, 9 Oct. 1917.
48. PRO P.Com 7/552
49. C.E.F. Rich, *Recollections of a Prison Governor* (Hurst Blackett 1932): 83, 96.
50. Ibid: 96.
51. PRO P.Com 7/521 C. Rich to PC, 14 June 1920.
52. PRO P.Com 7/521 C. Rich to PC, 14 June 1920.
53. PRO P.Com 7/572, Account of Sports Day at Borstal, 15 Sept. 1920.
54. PRO P.Com 7/521, June 1920 Address to Inmates Borstal.
55. PRO P.Com 7/522, New Borstal Rules 1921.
56. PRO P.Com 7/521, April 1920 New Education Scheme, Feltham.
57. PRO P.Com 7/556.
58. *Law Times*, 9 March 1912, 132: 446-7.
59. PRO P.Com 7/575.
60. PRO HO 144-18869-196919/2 W.S. Churchill to PC, 30 June 1910.
61. Published as Hobhouse and Brockway, *English Prisons*.
62. S. Leslie, *Sir Evelyn Ruggles-Brise* (Murray 1938): 127, 178
63. Hobhouse and Brockway, *English Prisons*: 436, 437, 423, 425, 426..
64. PRO P,Com 7/593 Herbert Brandon to Basil Thomson, 3 Oct. 1908, RCP & DCP yr end 31 March 1915, PP 1914-16, XXXIII: 9.
65. Rich, *Recollection*: 83.
66. Hobhouse and Brockway, *English Prisons*: 437.
67. V. Bailey, *Delinquency and Citizenship: Reclaiming the Young Offender* (Clarendon Press 1987): 189.
68. Indeed, Ruggles-Brise used the expression 'hypercritical sentimentalists' to describe those who failed to realise that borstals were primarily penal establishments. Bailey, *Delinquency:* 191.
69. PRO P.Com. 7/552 Note of a visit of Sir E. Ruggles-Brise to Borstal, 8 Aug. 1917.
70. Portland Conversion to a Borstal, PRO HO 45-16953-415065/18, W. Clarke Hall to HO 5 March 1922.. /6, Cut. *Manchester Guardian*, 3 Nov. 1921. Cut. *Daily Express*, 2 Nov. 1921.

# Chapter Five

## Penal Servitude 1895–1921

In 1895 offenders deemed to have committed serious crimes or to be habitual criminals were usually sentenced to penal servitude. This disposal was created in the 1850s as a result of the decline of transportation and indeed the last convict ship sailed for Western Australia in 1867. Furthermore, the centrality of penal servitude for major offenders was also emphasised by the increasing tendency to commute the death sentence to one of penal servitude for life and between 1880 and 1929 the actual rate of executions ran at 14.26 per year,[1] a notable decrease on the rate of fifty nine between 1805 and 1810.[2]

At the turn of the century all sentenced to penal servitude, known as convicts, served the initial nine months of their sentence in cellular separation at local prisons and were thereafter transferred to the convict prisons of Borstal, Dartmoor, Parkhurst, Portland and (for women) Aylesbury. Since 1869 there had been a remarkable fall in the number of convicts from around eleven and a half thousand to just over four thousand in 1896.[3] Furthermore there had already begun a trend towards shorter sentences of penal servitude and by 1900 four out of ten passed were for the minimum of three years permitted by law, a proportion which steadily rose until in 1936 seven out of ten were for the minimum period.[4] At the other extreme those sentenced to life terms were usually held for around fifteen years before release between 1895 and 1939 and the average length of a penal servitude sentence in 1901 was around five years for men (rather less for women).[5] Between 1900 and 1910 the daily average number of convicts in England and Wales ran at around three thousand but by 1919 this figure had fallen to around fifteen hundred.[6] Lastly it was predominantly a male sentence—on March 31st, 1908 there were only 130 women in penal servitude, the daily average of women for 1920-21 was seventy six.[7]

Sir Edmund Du Cane intended that penal servitude should be dreaded by all, served in impermeable and remote institutions, the convicts only visible to the outside world as they laboured at physically very severe labour in gangs, clad in a coarse drab uniform covered with broad arrows the original purpose of which had been to mark property which belonged to the government in the seventeenth and eighteenth centuries.[8] He also intended it to be a precisely administered regime the exact pains and severities of which would be known to judges so that sentence length could be precisely adapted to punishment deserved. So, after the nine month initial cellular isolation, there followed a second stage of eating and sleeping in the cell with labour in association on public works at the convict prisons. The third and last stage was conditional release on a licence which contained such requirements as obedience to law, regular reports to the police and notification of change of address to the police: for breach of the licence recall to serve the unexpired portion of sentence could be ordered. For women there was a stage between the period at Aylesbury and the licence in that they were often sent to 'refuges' which were 'establishments managed by private persons who interest themselves in preparing the women for discharge'[9] some months before licence.

The system of penal servitude in Du Cane's time was complex. Firstly, as a result of the conclusions of a Royal Commission in 1877-8, there was established a 'star' class of convicts 'not versed in crime' in order to prevent 'contamination by old offenders'.[10] Secondly, during the first and second stages (separation and public works), the convict had to work his or her way through a ladder of promotion (with demotion used as a punishment). So, there were four classes each with its own privileges and distinctive uniform and these privileges consisted of such things as money earnings paid after discharge, number of visits and letters allowed, amount of exercise permitted, a mattress instead of a plank bed, tea and bread instead of gruel: in the fourth or 'special' class a convict might be placed in a privileged position of trust.[11] Promotion from class to class was earned by the award of marks for industry over lengthy periods[12] and in addition by overall good conduct a convict might earn remission of time spent in prison (with earlier licence release) of up to one quarter of the period spent on the public work stage. The majority of longer sentenced penal servitude prisoners did in fact earn this remission[13] which was proportioned to the marks earned during sentence.[14] In the separation stage the work was tailoring, shoe-making, mat-making, weaving, oakum-picking and other tasks which could be performed in cells; in the public works stage it was 'severe labour'[15] such as sea defence, dock construction, quarrying and moor reclamation. Indeed the mid-Victorian convict hewed the stone out of which the two mile long Portland breakwater is built, constructed most of Chatham docks at St Mary's isle, greatly extended Portsmouth docks and reclaimed large portions of Dartmoor land.[16]

The Gladstone committee members suggested that the severity of penal servitude needed to be relaxed and throughout Du Cane's time there had been numerous complaints about its harshness and tendency to brutality. Gladstone urged that the nine month separation period should be shortened and that other ameliorations such as talking between prisoners under controlled conditions should be allowed. Secondly, however, the committee suggested that the system itself lacked an individualised reformatory basis and that the reformatory methods of education, instruction and training recommended for prisoners generally should be applied to convicts: indeed at one point the committee even called for a return to the serious and detailed programmes of improvement which had been used in convict prisons such as Pentonville in the 1840s.[17] Consequently, although Gladstone was much concerned with local prisons, the recommendations of the committee had plain implications for the convict sector.

Between 1895 and 1921 the Prison Commissioners claimed that they were vigorously pursuing these objectives. It was maintained that education of convicts was greatly improved by daily basic instruction during the initial separation phase[18] and that a regime similar to Borstal was in place for juvenile adult convicts at Dartmoor. Generally it was urged that lecturers, missioners and visitors were given much greater access to convict prisons, that numerous baptisms, confirmations and weekly bible classes were held, that labour was more diverse, religious services brightened and improved and convicts with special disabilities such as blindness given special training in such skills as braille reading so that one remarked 'I thought I should have gone mad but being able to read like this has saved me and given new life'.[19]

There had always been a tendency for specialisation in the convict prisons, but under Ruggles-Brise Aylesbury held female convicts (later replaced by Liverpool when borstal girls took over the whole institution rather than merely one wing), Parkhurst specialised in physically and mentally weak adult males, Maidstone in stars and Dartmoor and Portland in the more heavily convicted men. In addition Dartmoor specialised in juvenile adult males.[20] Furthermore Ruggles-Brise substantially altered the stages and classes which he had inherited from Du Cane establishing a new tripartite division of Star, Intermediate and Recidivist classes to replace the binary 'star' and 'other' classes of Du Cane.[21] He improved access to the less penal fourth 'special' stage by creating a new 'long sentence division' for those serving eight years or more in which meals were taken in association and conversation allowed at exercise and meals: to this stage more convicts would be admitted than was possible under the Du Cane arrangements.[22] Moreover an entirely new 'aged convicts' division', 'free so far as possible from all penal conditions', was set up.[23] Lastly the period of separation was reduced in 1899, set at three months for stars, six months for intermediates and nine months for recidivists in 1905, reduced to one month for stars and intermediates and three months for recidivists in 1911.[24]

Ruggles-Brise therefore claimed that he had markedly ameliorated the severity of the Du Cane system and he strenuously also argued that he had improved the reformatory base of penal servitude and the specialist care of physically or mentally weak convicts now collected at Parkhurst and concluded that by 1921 'the gloom and the mystery which was popularly supposed to envelope the convict system' has 'largely disappeared'.[25] The convict prison was now a place where magic lantern lectures might show 'the beauties of the Heavens' or 'the wonders of the Antipodes', where the chaplains might expatiate on 'Light Houses and Light Ships' and 'Travels in the Alps' and local male voice choirs visit to give 'a selection of sacred music'.[26] Ruggles-Brise emphasised particularly the value of an entirely new Central Association, announced in 1910, to supervise and help convicts after release: all were now to be interviewed before release and employment, accommodation and clothing to be provided either by the officers of the new state subsidised association or through its coordination of the services of the existing local societies.

Behind the optimistic claims of the annual reports and other publications of the Prison Commission there was an altogether more tortured and difficult process at which the official reports do not hint. The relaxation of separation dramatically illustrates this and also shows the immense pressure to which Ruggles-Brise was at times subjected as one who adhered to traditional classical notions of punishment and severity and was yet responsive to the need to reduce severity.

Ruggles-Brise, as made clear, without hesitation reduced the initial separation substantially between 1895 and 1906 and, as far as he was concerned, his new tripartite division each with its own 3, 6 or 9 month separation period met the requirements of classicism, the emphasis on scientific differentiation of positivism and the tendency towards relaxation of severity of the new liberalism. However in May 1909 the playwright and novelist John Galsworthy published two 'open letters' to Home Secretary, Herbert Gladstone, in which he condemned the initial separation of convicts and prisoners as 'prolonged starvation and agony of the mind' in which they must endure 'utter seclusion . . . from all sight and sound not only of human beings but of animals, trees, flowers and from the sight even of the sky'.[27] He argued that, far from causing reflection and sober self-examination, it led to 'mental vacuity', and 'unnatural indulgence in the one animal appetite of which he cannot be deprived'.[28]

Ruggles-Brise initially rejected Galsworthy's allegations as groundless invention by one who had no experience of prisons. He also maintained that many prisoners actually preferred their own company to that of other prisoners and that those who particularly longed for the fellowship of these were precisely the recidivists who were least suitable for association. However the Home Office was seriously concerned about such publicity and on May 20th, 1909 Ruggles-Brise undertook an enquiry of prison governors, chaplains and medical officers about the effects of separation.[29]

Those opinions varied but it emerged that some experimentation had been tried. So at Lewes a new system had been operated by which convicts in initial separation were taken out of their cells by day and placed in 'roofless pits', sunk in rows into the ground, in an immense shed so that they could have fresh air and see the staff patrolling the gangway above them but could not see or communicate with other convicts.[30] At other prisons the confinement was cellular and some staff emphasised that it was essential to sober down a newly convicted convict before he was placed in the public works prison, others that the prisoner did begin 'to realise what a fool he has made of himself'.[31] A number however had worries that separation had a tendency 'to brutalise, harden and stupefy' and one chaplain argued that it was morally degrading in that solitude was 'the happy hunting ground of foul thoughts and imaginations'.[32] A number of medical officers also argued that mental weakness tended to be exacerbated by separation.

Ruggles-Brise agreed to meet Galsworthy to discuss this matter and allowed him subsequently to interview convicts undergoing separation at Lewes and Chelmsford. Galsworthy sent Ruggles-Brise an account of these interviews and followed up with a very long letter condemning the system yet again.[33] He emphasised that he saw Ruggles-Brise himself as a reformer of prisons but warned him to beware of the attitude of his own prison staff who would always support the status quo. Galsworthy also insisted that prisoners were victims of heredity and environment whose lives had usually been of poverty, deprivation and misery, 'bred in slums and garrets where the only real God is drink'.[34] He added that, when he had interviewed the convicts, many had wept most piteously in their isolation and despair and again voiced his condemnation of separation.

By now Ruggles-Brise had realised that he was not dealing with an eccentric enthusiast whose attentions move rapidly from one thing to another, but rather with a man of conviction and determination. Nevertheless, he was convinced that separation was an essential element of penal servitude because he was sure that without it the convict would be precipitated straight into association after sentence. The convict would thus arrive at the public works prison flushed with the glory of his crime, full of news of outside associations and criminals, the centre of admiring attention 'with fresh news and incidents causing general unrest in convict prisons'.[35] Reluctantly, however, Ruggles-Brise suggested that separation be reduced to three months for all to Home Secretary Herbert Gladstone and permanent undersecretary Sir Edward Troup. In point of fact Gladstone himself had grave doubts about the necessity for separation at all, believing that it neither deterred nor reformed,[36] but the Home Office officials shared Ruggles-Brise's faith in it[37] and Gladstone and Ruggles-Brise agreed eventually that it should be reduced as proposed.

On February 19th, 1910 Gladstone was replaced as Home Secretary by Winston Churchill and two days later at the Duke of York theatre in London the premier of a tragedy called Justice was held. In this play, written by John Galsworthy, the central character committed suicide after serving three years penal servitude. The prison chaplain was depicted as a pious unfeeling man and the other staff as woodenly administering a system exactly according to regulations. In scene three of the third act there was no dialogue at all, merely the convict in his separate cell, the actor's rubric of instruction being to portray 'a man so lost in sadness'.[38]

On February 24th Churchill, who went to see the play, demanded that Ruggles-Brise lay before him 'in a compendious form the main arguments against the total and immediate abolition of solitary confinement'.[39] Ruggles-Brise at once enlisted the support of Home Office civil servants and these warned Churchill against precipitate action, Troup indeed suggesting that if Churchill did act it would appear that His Majesty's Secretary of State had been influenced by a playwright.[40] By then Galsworthy was in correspondence with Churchill, insisting that the play was an accurate and exact reflection of what he had seen among the convicts and that he was not driven by any animus towards the Prison Commission or Ruggles-Brise 'who have been kind and courteous to myself'.[41]

The dispute by now had ramified out into criminology for Churchill was raising the issue of the fairness of subjecting to separation convicts who could not help their conduct but whose recidivism showed them to be 'insane' or 'criminal by nature'[42] Ruggles-Brise was more confident in his capacity to convince Churchill on these theoretical grounds and at once urged on Churchill the view of one of his most respected criminologists, the French Professor Gabriel Tarde, that crime was the outcome of weakness of the will rather than disease or degeneracy and patiently explained to Churchill that recidivism existed because, whatever reformatory approaches were tried, there was, as Tarde argued, an 'irreducible minimum . . . a sort of hopeless residuum in all civilized communities'.[43] This did not, however, invalidate reformatory approaches to convicts, many of whom could respond to reformatory programmes and strengthened the case for separation which kept such a residuum isolated for longer periods (i.e. the recidivist class) and which was the main element of penal servitude which they feared. He appealed; 'can the instinct of acquisitiveness or cupidity—the most elementary and universal of all be regarded as a disease? and is the dream of the philanthropist, that the prison system, instituted primarily for the punishment of crime and the protection of the community, should exist only for the purpose of the moral reformation of a man, capable of practical realisation?'[44]

It was, as many would later find to their cost, not wise to attempt to baffle Churchill with science. On May 27th, 1910 a memorandum arrived on Ruggles-Brise's desk that all convicts except those who had served more than two previous sentences of penal servitude should serve one month only in separation.[45] Ruggles-Brise pleaded that on administrative grounds this was inoperable[46] but on March 25th, 1911 it was so ordered, save only that the recidivist class must serve three months separation.[47]

This episode revealed the influence which a literary figure could have on events, although it also makes clear that a single letter of protest or a literary broadside on its own might achieve little. On this occasion Galsworthy followed through with a process of pressure and operated at a high level of tactical skill. Certainly he was fortunate in his Home Secretaries, Herbert Gladstone and Winston Churchill, and clearly his reputation as a highly respected literary figure of probity and loyalty were indispensable to his gaining a hearing. Had he been of a lower class or in any way suspect on moral or political grounds he would have been dismissed as unworthy of serious attention. So, the far more devastating *Ballad of Reading Goal* and *De Profundis* of Oscar Wilde may have led to private reflections and journalistic comments but did not result in any concrete changes. Wilde was beyond the moral pale and neither he nor the Prison Commission ever imagined that they could do business with each other after his release in mid 1897.

The episode also illustrated Ruggles-Brise's desire that penal conditions should not be relaxed to a point at which, in his view, the essential punishment and deterrence ceased to operate. Yet here his freedom of decision was greatly restricted by figures outside the Prison Commission and, although he was able to stave off demands for abolition of separation, he had in the process to concede more than he wished. This indeed was a feature of his relationship with Churchill and there were lengthy inter-changes between Ruggles-Brise and Churchill over the desire of the latter to introduce more musical concerts, magic lantern lectures and military band performances in convict prisons.[48] Ruggles-Brise pointed out to Churchill that solo artistes and military bands regularly visited convict prisons and had 'a most admirable influence, the convicts being affected greatly both at the time and afterwards'[49] but Churchill insisted that more of these were needed and eventually Ruggles-Brise obtained tenders for such concerts from a Fleet Street agency. For a time he and Churchill haggled over numbers of such concerts before, on this occasion, Ruggles-Brise got his way on the grounds that supervision of convicts in darkened rooms was difficult and that 'the entertainments should be so rare and of so interesting a quality that the attention of convicts will be riveted . . . their appreciation of a great privilege and indulgence . . . will counteract the temptation to make mischief'.[50] Subsequently Churchill himself found the Treasury reluctant to agree to the purchase of magic lanterns[51] and angry letters appeared in the press about the new Home Secretary's sentimentality towards criminals and the insult to the King's Uniform implied by military bands forced to play to convicts.[52] The Home Office was able to assure anxious patriots that the military bands did not actually come into contact with the convicts but sat in the galleries above them to play.[53]

Churchill was very active in trying to mitigate the hard life of convicts. So he ensured remission of time to large numbers on the accession of George V[54] and battled with his reluctant civil servants to reduce such sentences as six years for theft of three billiard balls[55] and to release old convicts early who had served many sentences on occasion, as with the famous case of the Dartmoor shepherd, with unfortunate results; on that occasion the shepherd swiftly reoffended. He was also active in demanding better treatment for elderly convicts individually[56] and indeed it was his idea that a special class should be set up for aged convicts—'they will be our old guard'—[57]for whom 'the punitive element should be largely excluded'.[58] He ignored the sarcastic remark of his permanent under-secretary that 'it is hardly the proper function of a prison to provide a home of rest for these aged sinners'.[59] Another of his plans was for a strenuous regime of military and industrial discipline for one hundred convicts, selected for their promise of reform, who would be able to earn a much larger remission by participating in the programme.[60]

Ruggles-Brise greatly respected Churchill but was disturbed by the many proposals emanating from the Home Office whenever Churchill had an idea about reforms and ameliorations in penal servitude and prison discipline generally. In October 1910, after the arrival of a fresh wodge of proposals, he asked Home Office officials to tell the Home Secretary that 'the Commissioners see great difficulty in carrying out the changes . . . and are not in favour of many of the proposals . . . I should be glad if the Secretary of State could be made acquainted with the views of the Commissioners in regard to these very grave and important matters.'[61] Churchill tersely minuted 'had better come and see me'.[62]

Churchill's concerns were wider than just penal servitude but in 1910 and 1911 he was under a great deal of fire from both the press and his own officials because he seemed determined to act in defiance of all who sought to restrain him. Yet he worked closely and successfully with Ruggles-Brise at establishing the new Central Association for the aftercare of convicts which operated with the same premises and Director as the Borstal Association and utilised the same methods of pre release interview, provision of clothing, maintenance and accommodation, supervision through its own officers for some convicts but through coordination of existing aid societies for most. In part this stemmed from Churchill's dislike of the traditional police supervision of convicts which he believed marked a man as a convict in the eyes of the world and obstructed his rehabilitation.[63]

With regard to penal servitude the Prison Commission were under attack from various organisations which believed that the pace of relaxation was too slow. The Penal Reform League, which in 1921 merged with the Howard League, was exceedingly critical of penal servitude during Ruggles-Brise's time. This organisation had roots in radical liberalism, the Independent Labour Party and the Suffragette movement and prepared reports based upon the testimony of ex prisoners which indicted penal servitude. The Penal Reform League argued that the warders were often tyrannical bullies who gained promotion by cowing the prisoners and dismissed the view that a serious religious atmosphere and encouragement to moral improvement characterised Dartmoor and other convict prisons. So, at Dartmoor prisoners and officers were said to mock religion, the chaplains bawled at prisoners not singing hymns from the pulpit and books given out were unsuitable, one highly educated convict given Jack and The Beanstalk, an illiterate man given a dense theological treatise.[64] Against such groups Ruggles-Brise and the Home Office closed ranks and viewed them as potentially subversive and certainly disloyal, their secretary a 'mischievous person' proposing 'wild and eccentric devices' aiming to attack the prison authorities by 'subterraneous methods', such people in general tending to be adherents of 'the feminist section'.[65] The Labour Party Research Department was another group which condemned penal servitude: from the beginning this group was viewed with deep suspicion by the Home Office and Prison Commission and seen as 'probably hostile' and susceptible to the lies of suffragettes and conscientious objectors.[66]

Although Radzinowicz and Hood drew attention to the reduction of some of the brutalities of the Du Cane era, such as very severe and frequent floggings of convicts, they concluded that penal servitude under Ruggles-Brise tended towards the description by the Labour Research Group —'silence, separation and slave morality .... punitive slavery rather than . . . penal servitude',[67] and they characterised the system as 'Men . . . dressed in ill fitting and depressing clothes, plastered with broad arrows, their heads closely shaved . . . expected to turn their face to the wall whenever persons in authority or visitors passed by'.[68] Clearly convicts spent long hours alone during the entire evenings and nights in their cells and laboured in groups by day. Equally clearly the ameliorations introduced by Ruggles-Brise and the Home Office did not—nor were ever intended to—alter the basic purposes of penal servitude which were severe punishment, deterrence and the demonstration of the awesome power of the state over those who defied its laws. Indeed, as far as convicts were concerned, there was a strong tendency to pessimism about reformation. Basil Thomson, at one time governor of Dartmoor and later Secretary of the Prison Commission, asserted that 'no less than 87 per cent of the inmates of convict prisons belong to the professional class . . . proof against reformatory influences',[69] a view widely accepted at a time when the habitual criminal was the subject of very frequent and prolonged debate. Certainly there are indications that some convict prison chaplains felt overwhelmed by the difficulties of reforming their charges. So at Parkhurst the chaplain lamented that so many of them were 'senile and debilitated old men' who seemed to prefer life in the prison to the outside, while at Portland the chaplain complained that they were so accustomed to obedience to and dependence upon the regime that they lost their 'sense of responsibility'.[70]

Notwithstanding, there was a degree of relaxation of the severity of what Radzinowicz and Hood called 'the screw of repression'[71] although to later generations accustomed to different attitudes this may seem to have been slight in its scope. During Ruggles-Brise's tenure outside individuals and groups did gain a much greater access to convicts; concerts and lantern lectures did become regular features of the regime; aged convicts were given special relaxed conditions with their own day room, light work and freedom to talk; annual missions were held in all convict prisons; education was improved and some conversation permitted more generally.[72]

Some convicts considered that by the end of Ruggles-Brise's chairmanship there had been a remarkable relaxation since Du Cane's time. For example in 1922 Guy Dashwood praised the regime at Parkhurst and pointed especially to the changes made during Ruggles-Brise's last years. At Parkhurst the governor gave his consent to set up two clubs for convicts, the Unique Fellowship Club for stars and the Mutual Benefit Society for recidivists, at which both staff and convicts gave lectures on such subjects as wireless or a miner's life and held debates. A committee held regular meetings to plan activities and games and to these clubs staff gave a good deal of help lending gramophones and so forth. At each club there was a convict 'captain' and one of these wrote after release to urge the importance of the clubs as an experiment and exhorting his fellows to ensure the extension of the clubs by 'strictly playing the game'.[73] In addition the governor and chaplain at Parkhurst enthusiastically set about trying to establish a convict orchestra in the prison. Although the idea was accepted by the Prison Commission it fell through because there was no money for the numerous instruments needed.[74] Ruggles-Brise's keenness on 'debates and discussions', 'readings and recitations and lectures' continued throughout his years of office and indeed at the convict prisons there were patriotic showings of films about the Great War which, it was believed, were hugely enjoyed by the convicts.[75]

Convicts who served their sentences early in Ruggles-Brise's time made clear that the regime was at that time exceedingly strict and monotonous. Jabez Balfour, a liberal member of parliament who served nine years between 1895 and 1904, pointed out that convicts spent from 5.15 p.m. to 6.55 a.m. in their cells and that the regime at Portland was a 'heart breaking, soul enslaving, brain destroying hell' dominated by capricious and vindictive officers, with prisoners under employed so that they felt 'deadly dulness . . . a monstrous monotony . . . so palpable that it can almost be felt and handled'.[76] Yet Balfour also spoke of Colonel Plummer governor of Parkhurst as 'the most apostolic man I ever met in my life' whose chapel addresses were listened to with 'scarcely a movement or a sound . . . the kindly, sagacious, acute, sympathetic, engrossing talk of a single hearted earnest man who believed every word he spoke'. He also described the Church Army missioner in terms of great respect and gratitude and recalled one convict who would have preferred to remain at Parkhurst where he was 'very kindly treated' than to have returned to an unfeeling and uncaring world.[77] Balfour was nonetheless very sceptical of the claims of the Prison Commission that moral reform and training were occurring. He pointed out that during the seven hours a day labour the work parties were by no means hard pressed for the warders had an agreement with their men that as little would be done as possible. So, each warder and work party appointed a 'warder's crow' from among their number whose job was to 'flap his wings' at the approach of a principal or governor grade member of staff—one finger up for governor, two for deputy governor, three for chief warder.[78] Thus the convicts had an easy life, the warder escaped any disciplinary proceedings from superiors for allowing laziness, or mutiny or threat from his labour gang, and reports about work done could be happily fabricated at the end of the day. Another convict in 1905 argued that the prison authorities deliberately made the men work at their slowest pace because work was so difficult to find for them.[79]

Balfour believed that most chaplains were naively idealistic and were invariably thwarted by staff and convicts.[80] However, another convict of aristocratic family, who was sentenced in 1897 to five years for falsification of a security, spoke very highly of the ministry of the Roman Catholic priest at Parkhurst although he criticised the Church of England chaplain for his long theological discourses which the prisoners could not understand. He believed that the warders were usually strict but kindly, although subject to very severe discipline themselves. Of one principal warder he remarked: 'if either an officer or a prisoner did anything wrong he let him know it and did not mince his words. But though rough and ready he was absolutely fair and straightforward, and a rebuke from him could never be taken in ill part.'[81]

Later accounts of the system between 1918 and the early 1920s were a good deal less condemnatory than had been Balfour. A lawyer sentenced to penal servitude spoke warmly of the changes since 'the awful conditions of the old regime at the very mention of which old lags shudder today' when 'no-one cared whether we were mad or sane' and he greatly valued the 'lectures, concerts and debates' organised by prisoners and staff and the permission to converse for four hours a week after two and a half years had been served.[82] Another, an ex army captain who served seven years for robbery with violence after the Great War, spoke highly of missions and concerts and remembered the visits of London singers to Dartmoor and the simple sensitive concern of the Church Army missioners towards the convicts.[83]

By the end of Ruggles-Brise's period of office there had been an amelioration of the severity of the convict prison system since 1895 and it was plainly more humane and considerate than in Du Cane's time. So, the convict gangs kept at very severe penal labour in the 1870s and 1880s became a thing of the past and even the very critical Labour Research Group noted that convicts now worked in workshops at such occupations as tailoring, shoe making, carpentry, smithing and that in the later stages of sentence convicts worked on the prison farms and land reclamation schemes outside Dartmoor and Parkhurst prisons. Here, the Labour Research Group noted, convicts were often devoted to the farm animals and, apart from their clothes, could hardly be distinguished from cheerful, hard-working, ordinary farm labourers. At Maidstone convict prison, where after 1900 stars tended to be concentrated, especially light industrial work in workshops was practised.[84]

Clearly the reduction of penal severity was initially a slow process in penal servitude despite the fact that Ruggles-Brise acted swiftly to implement some of Gladstone's recommendations, such as the first lessening of the initial period of separation. It is however clear that the process of amelioration was speeded up by Winston Churchill. Indeed Andrew Rutherford[85] persuasively argued that Churchill left a legacy of greater humanity to all sections of the prison system which was plainly in evidence in the convict prisons despite the perturbed reactions which he caused in both Home Office and Prison Commission. So the last decade of Ruggles-Brise's chairmanship witnessed a plain tendency towards relaxation of severity.

Furthermore there was one remarkable new reformatory enterprise, the Central Association for the aftercare of convicts set up by Ruggles-Brise and Churchill, which is discussed in more detail in chapter 14.

The physical and extreme psychological abuse of convicts which was widely reported during Du Cane's time[86] had largely disappeared from the system by 1921. Certainly there is evidence that Ruggles-Brise was himself aware that members of parliament took a keen interest in reports of brutality to convicts and it is obvious that he paid very careful attention to outrages which came to his notice. For example, in 1897 he ordered that firearms were to be used in a much more careful way after William Carter was precipitately shot dead escaping from Dartmoor—warders were not to use revolvers unless actually attacked by an escaping convict and all shots from carbines must be fired in such a way 'that there shall be no danger of (their) taking effect fatally'.[87]

In criminological theory as well as in more traditional notions of prisoner reformation, such as evangelical mission, there was always a marked pessimism about convicts and a tendency to see them as difficult to reclaim. This was partly because they were often commonly believed to have behind them long histories of recidivism and partly because the sentence of penal servitude was widely seen as reserved for the most defiant and predatory of all criminal groups. It was therefore logical that the major thrust of policy during Ruggles-Brise's time was not towards reformatory programmes for convicts and indeed even Central Association aftercare supervision was not compulsory for those sentenced to penal servitude. It is therefore very difficult to detect any radically different reformatory principle in operation in convict prisons or, despite Ruggles-Brise's preoccupation with tripartite classifications, any strikingly different mode of managing, categorising or classifying them according to the requirements of eugenic or any other criminological theory.

What was radically different by 1921 was that the number of convicts had fallen by half and that the average length of their sentences had fallen substantially. In addition it is clear that the overall result of the policy of the Prison Commission was that a process of cautious amelioration of severity had occurred which was evident soon after Gladstone and gathered pace after 1910. By 1921, therefore, there was a more humane regime in convict prisons evidenced, for example, by the debating classes, permission to talk under controlled conditions, twice weekly evening recreation to convicts who had served over two years and much easier and improved labour conditions for all.

David Garland's view of such relaxations was that they were put into effect so that the welfarist controlling paternalist interventionist modes of the post Gladstone penal system could more plausibly and effectively be sustained. Yet this view does not take into account the singular reluctance of the state to accomplish some of the relaxations, as, for example Ruggles-Brise's and the Home Office's caution in the face of Galsworthy's pressure. Nor does it give room for the strong feeling amongst some ministers and officials that penal servitude in Du Cane's time had been intolerably severe. Certainly Churchill himself was convinced that the discipline of the convict prisons was overly harsh and was subjected to a good deal of public ridicule because he attempted to moderate it. Lastly, whilst relaxation occured to a limited extent, more extensive plans to segregate and manage convicts and prisoners generally according to their propensity and characteristics (such as other proposals made by Churchill) tended to be resisted successfully by the Prison Commission on the very ground that these would erode the constitutional powers of the sentencer as 'a grave infringement on the authority of courts of law which would be strongly resisted'.[88]

## NOTES

1. Special Report from the Select Committee on Capital Punishment PP 1929-30, V: XIV.
2. L. Radzinowicz, *A History of English Criminal Law and its Administration since 1750*, Vol. 1, *The Movement For Reform* (Stevens and Sons 1948): 153.
3. RCP and DCP yr end 31 March 1896, Pt 1, PP 1896, XLIV: 12-13.
4. L. Radzinowicz, 'The Present Trend of English Penal Policy' *Law Quarterly Review*, April 1939, CCXVIII: 276.
5. 5.03 years for men, 4.35 years for women. RCP & DCP yr end 31 March 1902, PP 1902, XLVI: 19.
6. RCP and DCP yr end 31 March 1902, PP 1902, XLVI: 20. Figure is 2695 for 1902, 2716 for 1900. RCP & DCP yr end 31 March 1921, PP 1921, XVI: 4. Daily average is 1553 for 1919-20, 1435 for 1920-21.
7. RCP and DCP yr end 31 March 1908, PP 1908, LII: 5. RCP & DCP yr end 31 March 1921, PP 1921, XVI: 4.
8. PRO HO 45-12566-209069, Broad Arrow Use and Origin HO to A.J. Carey, 29 March 1927.
9. E. Du Cane, *The Punishment and Prevention of Crime* (MacMillan 1885): 156-7
10. Ibid: 162.
11. PRO HO 45-9958-V20544, Standing Order No 494, Convict Prisons, 15 Nov. 1892.
12. Du Cane, *Punishment and Prevention*: 163.
13. Ibid: 166.
14. Ibid: 168.
15. Ibid: 177.

16. Ibid: 178-9.
17. Departmental Committee on Prisons, PP 1895, LVI: 28.
18. RCP & DCP yr end 31 March 1898, PP 1898, XLVII: App. 25: 155.
19. RCP & DCP yr end 31 March 1901, PP 1902, XIV: 537, 540, 549, 553, 571-2, 573, 574. RCP & DCP yr end 31 March 1909, Pt 2, PP 1909, XLV: 214-5.
20. Maidstone first became a convict prison in Jan. 1906 and began to specialise in star convicts in 1910. Thereafter it became the major Star Convict Prison. Borstal ceased to be a convict prison as Juvenile Adults took over more and more of it.
21. RCP & DCP yr end 31 March 1906, PP 1906, L: 24.
22. E. Ruggles-Brise, *The English Prison System* (MacMillan 1921): 41.
23. Ibid: 41.
24. Ibid: 45-6.
25. Ibid: 47.
26. RCP & DCP yr end 31 March 1911, PP 1911, XXXIX: 224. RCP & DCP yr end 31 March 1909, PP 1909, XLV: 227.
27. Separate Confinement 1909-1930, PRO HO 45-13658-185668, *The Nation*, 8 May 1909.
28. PRO HO 45-13658-185668, *The Nation*, 1 May 1909.
29. PRO P.Com. 7/308, Enquiries Into Separate Confinement.
30. PRO P.Com. 7/308, H. Donkin to E. Ruggles-Brise, 22 May 1909.
31. PRO P.Com 7/308, Chaplain Portland to PC, 22 May 1909.
32. PRO P.Com 7/308, Chaplain Chelmsford to PC, No day May 1909.
33. Separate Confinement 1909-1930 PRO HO 45-13658-185668, J. Galsworthy to E. Ruggles-Brise, Oct. 1909.
34. Ibid. Letter J. Galsworthy to E. Ruggles-Brise: 30.
35. Ibid. E. Ruggles-Brise to HO 10 Nov. 1909: 18.
36. Ibid. H. Gladstone to E. Troup, 23 Nov. 1909.
37. Ibid. HO Minute, 17 Nov. 1909.
38. J. Galsworthy, *Justice A Tragedy In Four Acts* (Duckworth 1927): 83.
39. PRO HO 45-13658-185668, W. Churchill to E. Ruggles-Brise, 24 Feb. 1910.
40. Ibid. HO Memo, 26 Feb. 1910.
41. Ibid. J. Galsworthy to W. Churchill, 9 March 1910.
42. Ibid. W. Churchill to Sir E. Troup and Sir E. Ruggles-Brise, 7 March 1910.
43. Ibid. E. Ruggles-Brise to Sir E. Troup, 18 April 1910.
44. Ibid. E. Ruggles-Brise to Sir E. Troup, 18 April 1910.
45. Ibid. Memo W.S. Churchill, 27 May 1910.
46. Ibid. E. Ruggles-Brise to Sir E. Troup, 9 June 1910.
47. Ibid. Statutory Rules and Orders, 24 March 1911.
48. Entertainments in Prisons, PRO HO 45-16483-192637. E. Ruggles-Brise to W.S. Churchill, 18 April 1910; W.S. Churchill to E. Ruggles-Brise, 23 April 1910; E. Ruggles-Brise to W.S. Churchill, 5 May 1910.
49. Ibid. E. Ruggles-Brise to W.S. Churchill, 18 April 1910.
50. Ibid. E. Ruggles-Brise to HO, 11 May 1910.
51. Ibid. Treasury to HO, 7 July 1910.
52. Letter to *The Times*, 6 Sept. 1910: 13 col. f.

53. PRO HO 45-16483-192637 HO Minute, 22 Sept. 1910.
54. PRO P Com 7/430.
55. PRO HO 144-1009-143484/11.
56. PRO HO 144-1067-189934/5, W.S. Churchill HO Minute, 23 March 1910.
57. PRO HO 144-926-A49225/6, W.S. Churchill to Sir E. Troup 19 June 1910.
58. Ibid. /6, W.S. Churchill HO Minute, 8 June 1910.
59. Ibid. /6, Sir E. Troup HO Minute, 1 June 1910.
60. PRO P. Com. 7/413 W.S. Churchill to E. Ruggles-Brise, 28 March 1910.
61. PRO HO 144-18869-196919/5, E. Ruggles-Brise to E. Troup, 29 Oct. 1910.
62. Ibid. W.S. Churchill HO Minute, 2 Nov. 1910.
63. PRO P.Com 7/413 Meeting of W.S. Churchill, E. Troup and E. Ruggles-Brise *et al.* with deputation of Prison Aid Societies at HO July 1910.
64. General Report and Recommendations of the Penal Reform League, received HO 15 July 1910: 42-4, PRO HO 45-10617-195485.
65. Prison System in the United Kingdom, PRO HO 45-11543-357055, HO Minute, 22 Oct. 1918, PC Memo to HO, no date.
66. Ibid. HO Minute, 23 Dec. 1919, Sir E. Troup to Sir Sydney Olivier, 21 April 1919.
67. Quoted in Radzinowicz and Hood, vol. 5, *Penal Policy*: 587.
68. Ibid: 587.
69. B. Thomson, *The Criminal* (Hodder & Stoughteon 1925): V of preface.
70. RCP & DCP yr end 31 March 1910, XLV: 237, 245.
71. Radzinowicz and Hood, *Penal Policy*: 526.
72. RCP & DCP yr end 31 March 1911, PP 1911, XXXIX: 221, 215, 223, 211.
73. PRO P.Com. 7/283, Humanitarian Ideals in Modern Penology by Guy Dashwood a Parkhurst Prisoner. Memo Governor of Parkhurst Prison 26 April 1921.
74. PRO P.Com. 7/322, Concerts in Prisons 1919-1920.
75. PRO P.Com. 7/321, Film of the Battle of the Somme 1916-1917.
76. J.S. Balfour, *My Prison Life* (Chapman & Hall 1907): 67, 122.
77. Ibid: 147, 131, 159.
78. Ibid: 277.
79. H.J.B. Montgomery, Ex prisoner of Parkhurst. Views described in *Law Times* 20 May 1905, 119: 65.
80. Balfour, *Prison Life*: 375, 334-7.
81. W.B.N. *Penal Servitude* (Heinemann 1903): 49, 79, 94.
82. S. Scott, *The Human Side Of Crook and Convict Life* (Hurst & Blackett 1924): 91, 93, 111.
83. Jock of Dartmoor, *Dartmoor from Within* (Readers Library Publishing Co. 1933): 139-41.
84. S. Hobhouse and A.F. Brockway (eds.) *English Prisons Today* (Longman, Green & Co. 1922): 320-1. For original removal of Stars to Maidstone see RCP & DCP yr end 31 March 1910, Pt 2, PP 1910, XLV: 229.
85. A. Rutherford, 'Lessons from a Reductionist Era', paper delivered to the 10th International Congress on Criminology, Hamburg, September 1988: 9-10.
86. W.J. Forysthe, *The Reform of Prisoners 1830-1900* (Croom Helm 1987): 199-215.

87. Firing at Escaped Convicts 1896-7, PRO HO 45-9743-A55944/20, Prison Commission and Directors of Convict Prisons Circular to Convict Prisons, 23 Feb. 1897.

88. Memo on Prison Reform HO 144-18869-196919/4, E. Ruggles-Brise to E. Troup, 9 Sept. 1910.

# Chapter Six

## Preventive Detention – A Tale of Disappointment 1895–1921

In their report on the prisons the Gladstone Committee recommended that a special sentence be created to incapacitate habitual criminals. This new disposal, members envisaged, would not be as severely penal as was penal servitude but would hold persistent offenders under a relaxed regime for prolonged periods in order to incapacitate them from further crimes.[1] In recommending this the Gladstone Committee inaugurated a process of conflict, dispute and disappointment which ran for thirty years and which culminated in the failure of an entirely impracticable scheme. Indeed the committee members must have realised that they were stirring up a hornets' nest in making such a suggestion, for the proposal at once attracted the attention of theorists who had since Lombroso's day controversially urged that those adults, whom positivist science declared to be temperamentally recidivistic, tended also to be unreformable and should be dealt with exclusively with social protection in mind: whatever reformatory techniques were tried, they would continue to live by crime and indeed could not help being what they were and doing what they did.

Preventive detention was not the only scheme resonant to science and positivist criminology to be proposed by Gladstone. Members had also reminded the public that there were close links between habitual drunkenness and crime and that inebriates ought to be dealt with as a medical problem. This suggestion led to a notable debacle, for the Prison Commission set up two institutions called State Inebriate Reformatories, one for men adjoining Warwick prison and another for women at Aylesbury convict prison. These were intended to deal with the most recalcitrant inebriates with whom the ordinary local inebriate reformatories (not run by the Commission) were unable to cope and a long and sorry failure ensued at these two places. Very swiftly it was borne in on the Commission that they had become involved with a highly problematic situation and as early as 1902 they were referring to 'refractory and violent' inebriates and could scarcely conceive of 'humanity fallen to a lower state' than the women.[2] At Aylesbury an entire new block was built with all modern facilities but the inebriates at both institutions remained explosive, violent, sullen and intractable showing 'jealousy, dislike and passion' believed to be intensified by the disinhibiting influence of alcohol.[3] In vain were lady visitors, lectures on abstinence, ministers of religion, concerts, aftercare associations and missions launched at them; they remained 'noisy and refractory . . . they disturb everyone by shouting and swearing, sometimes with little or no cessation for days altogether'.[4] Ruggles-Brise rapidly concluded that the state reformatory inebriates were more closely akin to the criminal or the insane than the 'inebriate type' and thereafter the system became much less relaxed and more severe.[5] By 1921 there were no inebriates left in the two institutions and during the three years prior to the Great War their numbers never rose above nineteen men and fifty seven women.[6] Nobody in the Home Office or Prison Commission doubted that this experiment had been a failure and both Ruggles-Brise and permanent undersecretary Troup were greatly concerned about soaring costs and the 'tremendous strain on staff' resulting from the fact that the ordinary inebriate reformatories were transferring their 'worst and incorrigible cases' to Warwick and Aylesbury.[7] Nonetheless, at first, Ruggles-Brise had with enthusiasm applied his favourite tripartite classification to them and allowed very relaxed conditions with day rooms, exercise facilities, chess, draughts dominoes, newspapers and smoking before, in 1904, replacing the original with a more severe regime. However, with enthusiasm for special treatment of special groups unabated, he devoted very great thought and time to the matter of the habitual criminal unaware that he was headed for a debacle of rather greater proportions.

By 1900 there was a most vociferous demand for action to be taken to incapacitate the habitual criminal. Yet from the early days of this movement there was also a failure to define precisely the terms used in the debate. For one thing the term Habitual Criminal was ambiguous in that it could be applied, say, to an offender who persistently stole an empty milk bottle on the first day of release from prison imposed for the previous milk bottle or it could connote a character such as Professor Moriarty of Sherlock Holmes fame, the ruler of a huge and voracious criminal empire, governing by terror and extortion and ever planning new and more daring crimes. If the term habitual criminal was not intended to cover the former type of criminal but to fall somewhere between him and Professor Moriarty where should the line be drawn? Yet if there were two or indeed more types of habitual criminal what were these?

The arguments and disputes about this were protracted. Sir Robert Anderson, Head of Scotland Yard between 1888 and 1901, argued that there were indeed two kinds of habitual and made a distinction between the weak, incompetent, 'hopelessly wicked' criminal who could not desist from crime by virtue of his personality and for these suggested 'asylum prisons'.[8] However, for professionals, by which he meant serious and major criminals who deliberately and repetitively calculated their life of crime, he suggested that a prison be set aside for very long or permanent preventive detention after the offender had been convicted by a jury of being a habitual criminal.[9] Anderson insisted that there would only be a small number of the latter group and that sentencers and juries in such cases must concentrate not on the most recent crime for which the criminal had happened to have been caught but on the actual historically authenticated criminal record of the offender.[10] Anderson strongly repudiated the suggestion that his solution was harsh and pointed out that there was pressure for elimination by execution of this group.

However, although he had drawn his line between the two groups, he had not cleared up the ambiguity. Still it was not clear whether he included in his professional group the persistent petty rather inefficient larcenist or had in mind more the skilled safe cracker or cat burglar as well as the Fagins and Moriartys of the criminal world. He had emphasised the smallness of the numbers of professionals but precisely where the line should be drawn remained a mystery.

The argument about the type of offender to be subjected to the new disposal was also joined by eugenists such as Montague Crackanthorpe,[11] Recorder in Westmoreland, and the President of the Eugenics Education Society Major Leonard Darwin.[12] Darwin argued that the habitual criminal possessed 'innate defects which (they) are certain to pass on . . . to their descendants for an indefinite number of generations',[13] but again it was very unclear who was to be the subject of this incapacitation. Eugenists tended to suggest certification of many habitual criminals as mental defectives and preventive custody for the rest but if the class as a whole were to include the petty repetitive offender then thousands of institutional places would be needed. Certainly Captain St.John, the secretary of the Penal Reform League, urged the application of eugenic protective measures to large numbers of loafers and delinquents who would breed paupers and criminals.[14]

Between 1895 and 1908 there was most prolific discussion about who were the habituals but no general consensus, although there was a tendency towards the idea of labour colonies for petty delinquents and special prolonged prison for more dangerous ones. However, ex-prisoners, judges, doctors and prison administrators exchanged arguments and at times insults.[15] Some attempted laborious distinctions between 'aggressive, noxious and anti-social' criminals and 'passive, idle, debauched and un-productive' offenders[16] or between criminals of 'low morals, very poor, not very intelligent or well equipped, either physically or mentally, who under pressure of poverty, loss of employment, severe weather, sickness at home, or other unfavourable circumstances cannot, or do not, resist the temptation to pilfer and get convicted many times, who yet do not belong to the criminal class' and those who made a career of crime, teaching it, recruiting for it and living well off it.[17] At the same time disputes arose between those who wished to extend the realm of mental science far into criminal jurisprudence and criminal disposal and those who insisted that all talk, such as Goring's, about diathesis or neurosis, was nonsense and must be resisted in favour of the traditional emphasis on punishment and culpability.[18]

If there was dispute about the precise nature and categorisation of habitual, professional or persistent criminals, there was also long argument about what to do with them. On the one hand were those who advocated 'lethal chambers'[19] and others were sure that eugenic and cost considerations required sterilisation of them by X ray.[20] However, the solution most commonly proposed was institutional containment, an approach which meshed with the contemporary enthusiasm for labour colonies for vagrants and idle paupers and the use of science and purpose designed specialist institutions more generally as mechanisms of social policy.

This was not as simple as it sounded. One problem, which was to haunt Preventive Detention, was whether a sentence aimed entirely at in-capacitation of a habitual criminal who, it might be argued, could not help his or her condition, should exist in its own right or be combined with other penal measures. Certainly foreign positivist criminologists emphasised incapacitation and type of personality and rejected entirely any idea that habituals or recidivists should be punished for being what they were. So, there were, in Britain as elsewhere, those who argued that prisons of incapacitation for habituals should merely aim to detain preventively and that therefore they should be, relative to say penal servitude, relaxed places with much easier 'more elastic discipline'.[21] Some suggested that, once the court had found the offender to be a habitual, he or she should be sent straight off to a preventive detention prison, others that a sentence of preventive detention should be passed to begin at the instant that the punitive sentence of penal servitude imposed for the current crime expired. So the judge, after the jury had found the defendant guilty of a current crime and of being an habitual criminal, would sentence him to so many years penal servitude for the crime to be followed by so many years preventive detention for habitual criminality.

Furthermore it was not entirely clear what was to be done with these persistent criminals once they were safely in custody. Some suggested that the intelligent, predatory, calculative, professional and the inefficient petty recidivist were victims of their own heredity and environment and had since early childhood become fixed in their attitude and conduct. So, were these merely to be held in relaxed conditions or was any reformatory strategy to be operated regarding them? Again there was no consensus on this although some suggested that there was a place for reformatory approaches, a view which drew much bitter sarcasm from one ex-prisoner who rebuked Judge Alfred Wills for implying that reformation might exist anywhere in the English prison system apart from 'the jejeune attempts recently made in regard to young offenders'.[22]

It was, however, agreed that, if petty habitual and grave professional criminals were taken together, whoever they were, there were a lot of them. So, Dr R.F. Quinton, who had been a staunch defender of Du Cane against his attackers and had been both governor and medical officer of Holloway, was sure that four fifths of convicts were habitual criminals.[23] Horrified reporters, hot foot from Dartmoor, regaled their readers with accounts of hordes of convicts there, 'a study in human degeneracy . . . cunning, hard, shifty eyes . . . suppressed murder and devilment . . . animal ferocity lurks in every line of the enormous jowls of these men'.[24]

Solutions to the problem were also seen to be complicated by the diversity in sentencing practice before the Great War which suggested that, even if preventive detention were made available, it would be a matter of chance whether the right offenders received it. The Recorder of Liverpool, Charles Hopwood, made it policy to pass much lighter sentences than his colleagues and demanded an overall reduction of sentence length by two thirds, whilst other judges apparently were very much more severe.[25] In general however it was well known to contemporaries that the overall tendency was to shorter sentences and this judicial tendency might well have made advocates of lengthened preventive detention pause for thought.[26]

Shortly after Gladstone, pressure on the Home Office began to mount as many different schemes were proposed and officials were irritated by some 'so vague as to elude' criticism.[27] However, enquiries were made about foreign systems of indeterminate sentencing and letters and articles by well known contributors to the debate, like the retired Sir Edmund Du Cane and Mr Justice Wills, assiduously collected and studied whilst outside the Home Office the demand for action grew stronger.[28] In 1901 the Lord Chief Justice wrote to the Home Secretary that, as a matter or urgency, the Home Office should consider 'the best way of dealing with habitual and professional criminals' and make proposals about this.[29]

Radzinowicz and Hood have described in great detail the intense, detailed and lengthy discussions which occurred in the Home Office[30] and, indeed, the archive material at Kew Public Records Office on the subject is extensive and need not be recapitulated here. However, as early as 1899 Ruggles-Brise warned the Home Office that it was most important to distinguish between the habitual petty offender and 'recidivists guilty of repeated serious crime'. His proposal was that a penal colony be set up in a remote spot, such as Dartmoor, and a new form of sentence invented especially suitable for incapacitation of serious recidivists such as those committing repeated 'crimes of acquisitiveness i.e. all forms of burglary, larceny etc. when the record shows that there have been more than four previous convictions'.[31] He argued for a system, for these serious recidivists, of penal servitude for the current conviction followed by preventive detention in the penal colony for an indeterminate period up to the maximum allowed by law for the offence, with provision for earlier release on licence at the discretion of the executive. In 1900 Ruggles-Brise advocated to the Brussels International Penitentiary Congress that this hybrid disposal be created consisting in the one part of penal servitude and the other preventive incapacitation. He argued that it would be an integration of the classical and positivist schools including 'immediate adaptation of suffering to sin' or 'penalty to offence' but also sentence on the basis of the nature of the criminal.[32]

The Home Office referred the Lord Chief Justice's letter to him and in late 1901 he replied and advocated his scheme. He also suggested that the penal servitude system should itself be substantially amended so as to classify convicts more accurately according to their criminality and reformability and to allow the creation of a new fifth stage with relaxed conditions in which less serious petty recidivists not requiring preventive detention could be held having been given very long sentences of penal servitude.[33] His intention in part was that there should not be greater comfort for the serious offenders serving preventive detention compared to the long penal servitude served by petty recidivists.

The Lord Chief Justice called the King's Bench Judges together and they resolved that there was indeed a class of professional criminals for whom crime was a career but they were also worried about the petty recidivist —'weak and immoral beings'—and believed that society required protection from these also. However, they were very unwilling for juries to have any say in the decision as to who was habitual and were therefore deeply opposed to the idea that a new sentence of preventive detention should be created, only to be passed after conviction on a charge of being a habitual criminal: this emphasis on juries and method of conviction was urged particularly by the Home Office. The judges also disliked the indeterminacy aspect of preventive detention. They therefore proposed an alternative idea, that Ruggles-Brise's penal colony should indeed be created to serve as a fifth stage of penal servitude: whenever a judge wished to sentence an offender to a prolonged sentence of penal servitude because he was a habitual, whether serious or petty, he would also have power to order that up to three quarters of the sentence would be served in the more relaxed penal colony.[34] A bill to this effect was drawn up, unanimously supported by the judges,[35] but failed to surmount protracted parliamentary opposition.[36]

In May 1908 Home Secretary Herbert Gladstone proposed a bill which was much closer to Ruggles-Brise's hybrid notion in that it contained provision for a sentence of penal servitude to be followed, after appropriate jury conviction for habitual criminality, by a sentence of preventive detention during royal pleasure. Gladstone had been Home Secretary since December 1905 and clearly wished to do something to put into effect the wishes of the original 1895 Gladstone Committee with regard to habituals. However the precise shape of the proposal resulted because Edward Troup also believed strongly in the need for a special indeterminate sentence up to life, jury conviction and Director of Public Prosecution's authorisation before police could charge a habitual under the act and all these elements appeared in the bill.[37]

Gladstone distinguished between two types of habitual in his defence of the bill, those who were a nuisance 'because of physical or mental deficiency rather than by reason of a settled intention to pursue a life of crime', and those deliberate calculating professionals who 'laugh at the present system of imprisonment'.[38] For this latter class the new sentence of preventive detention was proposed to be served in relaxed conditions at a special prison subsequent to the initial penal servitude. An additional advantage would be the removal of these from the convict prisons where 'progressive improvement' could continue unabated, relieved of the presence of these unreformables.[39]

The Conservatives supported the Liberal bill with minor reservations but it ran into a storm of opposition from backbench liberals such as Edward Pickersgill, Sir George Radford, Hilaire Belloc and from Irish nationalists such as John Dillon, who had himself served a period of imprisonment. They particularly objected to what they saw as the invasion of classical criminal jurisprudence with its fixed and known penalties by practices of release and indeterminacy, based on 'pseudo scientists with broken down reputations like Lombroso's',[40] and were convinced that a very large number of petty offenders would be swept up into the new regime. Furthermore, preventive detention itself was 'monstrous' in that it inflicted 'an appalling, a terrible punishment' on those who were often victims of misfortune and would create in them 'a sense of hopelessness, and even of despair'.[41] They were unmoved by assurances that only those discovered by 'scientific enquiry' to be serious habituals would be sent to preventive detention or by Herbert Gladstone's insistence that it would only be used for dangerous professionals or by his promise that it would have a strong reformatory and training component—a statement which seemed at odds with the entire reasoning which had led up to the bill.[42]

So strong and well organised was the opposition that the government was forced to withdraw its proposal that the new sentence be imposed during royal pleasure and substituted for this provision for the judge to order a specific period of preventive detention with possible earlier release on licence. In this form the bill became law after long and angry debates, during which talk about reformatory strategies and Director of Public Prosecution's authorisation was dismissed as 'cant' with the Home Secretary the 'mouth-piece of the official machine' ever extending its executive power: members attacked the savage sentencing of poor petty offenders under present conditions lamenting that the bill gave specious scientific legitimation to even harsher disposals in future.[43] As Belloc contemptuously remarked, 'the complexities of that vast mystery' of human personality were to be subjected to the vapourings of fools like Lombroso and, as always in England, the poor would suffer these things while, in Belloc's view, the rich continued to live a life of ease funded by the undeserved and unearned profits of the stock market, unmolested by police or courts.[44] Notwithstanding, the amended preventive scheme passed into law as part two of the Prevention of Crime Act (8 Edward 7 cap 59).

Camp Hill Preventive Detention Prison for men was opened on March 5th, 1912 to receive its first batch of detainees from the convict prisons where they had served their initial three or more years of penal servitude. Within a month there were thirty three there.[45] The new prison was still in the process of building and was situated close to Parkhurst convict prison on the Isle of Wight. The detainees were divided into three divisions of disciplinary, ordinary and special and all entered the ordinary division on arrival—bad behaviour led to demotion to the disciplinary grade where conditions were more akin to penal servitude. They worked on building the prison and as bakers, cooks, gardeners, cleaners and stokers although, for around a fifth who were too old or infirm for such work, a 'knitting industry' was begun.[46] Each detainee had a cell which was 'brightly painted . . . floored with coloured tiles . . . clear glass windows'[47] and they were able to earn money to be spent on food and luxuries in a canteen established for them in the prison. Furthermore, garden allotments, the produce of which the detainees could sell to the prison, were set up; meal time and evening association was instituted; more conversation was allowed than in penal servitude. A system of certificates, each of which was earned by hard work and good behaviour, was set up and the award of each of these entitled the detainee to increased earnings and privileges. Towards the end of sentence those nearing release on licence to the Central Association were placed in one of sixteen 'parole cabins' which were self-contained units of accommodation each with its own bedroom, lavatory, kitchen with a gas stove and verandah to which the detainee had his own key as a half-way stage to freedom.[48] Smoking and daily newspapers were allowed and the amount of tobacco which could be bought at the canteen increased as privileges were earned.[49] In addition the detainees were later allowed to grow their hair longer than the 'convict crop' and to have safety razors in their cells and were all provided with suits and white shirts on Sundays, with jerseys, dungaree blouses and cord trousers on weekdays.[50] Those in the 'parole cabins' were allowed unsupervised association and to spend their entire evenings in the canteen.[51] Lastly an advisory committee was set up to report to the Home Office when they considered the detainees might be released on license.

Clearly this was a major departure from traditional prison conditions and was seen as such by the outside world. In 1914 an amazed reporter described the roomy bright cells with clear glass windows, 'a packet of peppermint drops' in one, communal meals, stews, plum duff, post prandial smoking, canteens dispensing butterscotch, strawberry jam, dates, chocolates, oranges and plum cake.[52] As one detainee put it to his wife: 'the regime here really gives one the impression that the Buddhist seventh (or eight is it?) and final stage of human existence had arrived—the stage of kindness or kindliness. One actually hears those blessed words of civilization 'please' and 'thank you'. A 'Weekly Times' and 'Weekly Mail'. A quite inoffensive costume. A canteen for tobacco, jam, sweets'.[53]

The staff were initially pessimistic and somewhat apprehensive. The chaplain at Camp Hill felt that the detainees were very unlikely to reform and, indeed, some of the new arrivals seemed hopeless. The chaplain was convinced that these were indeed the professional or habitual criminals for whom the system had been set up and he calculated that, for the first hundred detainees, the average number of previous convictions was seventeen. He lamented that 'as a class they are inflamed with a pernicious discontent, not only with prison matters but with things in general . . . coloured with a hatred of social customs and restraints . . . intellectually of a low type and physically incapable of strenuous efforts . . . morality is only noticeable because it is entirely absent . . . religion finds no place in their minds at all'.[54]

Nevertheless, the attitude to the detainees warmed. Lectures and concerts were put on and detainees regaled with accounts of 'The Humour of The Operas of Gilbert and Sullivan'[55] and the advisory committee began recommending many for license release. By 1916 the first hundred had been licensed and the Central Association assured the public that 82% of these were doing well.[56] It was said in 1919 that nearly two hundred had been placed in the parole cabins without breaking their trust.[57] Furthermore, one hundred and fifty Camp Hill detainees enlisted in the forces, of whom ten were killed, and this was seen as an indication that great hopes might fairly be placed in the detainees, who also worked on war work outside Camp Hill in parties escorted to the munitions sites by the army.[58]

This 'new departure of much historic interest'[59] was however fraught with difficulty from the start, though the Labour Research Enquiry saw much to praise in it in 1921.[60] At the beginning, before even the prison was opened, Churchill waged a campaign against what he saw as a tendency for the Director of Public Prosecutions to allow prosecution of merely nuisance-ful recidivists at the request of the police. Indeed, during February 1911, he came close to a very serious confrontation with Sir Edward Troup, his own permanent undersecretary, and the Director Sir Charles Matthews for he had in mind to publish a memorandum in which the professionalism of the Director would be impugned. Frantic flurries of telegrams were despatched and in the event he put out a strong warning to the police that this sentence was only for highly skilled, able professionals who were dedicated to their vocation.[61] Immediately the press published this in great detail and the *Spectator* urged that there was a 'vast confusion as to what preventive detention meant'. 'It may be thought a strange thing that an Act should be passed of which the meaning is not interpreted till two years later', reflected the reporter, adding that this was a typical feature of the modern era in which mere 'functionaries' decided on the meaning of statutes.[62] Further-more, Churchill came into conflict with the Treasury because he authorised payments to the detainees for their work without proper authorisation and was rebuked for this.[63]

Some Home Office officials were perturbed by the luxurious conditions at Camp Hill and H.B. Simpson commented sourly that the detainees 'had meat for dinner five days a week—cold meat or soup the other two days—pudding or cheese every day ... I am afraid that this dietary, if published, would cause some grumbling among poor tax payers who remain honest'.[64] Indeed Ruggles-Brise was against publishing too much detail about the regime because it would 'provoke criticism and needless sugges-tions for alteration in detail'.[65] Yet, despite these relaxations, the Home Office and Ruggles-Brise were puzzled by the tendency of the Camp Hill detainees to be dissatisfied and in May 1912 the governor of Camp Hill warned that even more relaxation was needed to allay discontent.[66] In June 1912 some of the detainees refused to obey orders and were sent back to Dartmoor and Parkhurst. Officials believed that this resulted from the men mistaking kindness for weakness and from disappointment that conditions were not as easy as they had been led to believe and from discontent about licensing arrangements.[67] As Ruggles-Brise explained: 'The men have been led to believe from one source or another that they had been sentenced to detention *simply* and not to punishment: that the punishment had been expiated by the sentence of penal servitude: and that their liberty would be restrained as a precaution against committing new offences if at large. They ask therefore, so far respectfully and with some reason, that the conditions of free life may be extended to them short of liberty'.[68] It was as a result of this petition, and the disobedience which occurred whilst the Home Office was considering it, that tobacco and newspapers were allowed together with other relaxations such as chess, draughts and dominoes. As Troup exclaimed in exasperation, such luxuries had been included in the scheme before Parliament modified it and 'it was only the limitation of the sentence and the introduction of the so called reformatory element that gave an excuse for omitting them. These two changes really spoiled the whole proposal'.[69] H.B. Simpson, Troup's assistant undersecretary, was sure that the system would prove 'useless for purposes of reformation or deterrence' and that, when this had become clear, the Home Office could then insist on preventive detention as originally envisaged.[70]

Indeed Ruggles-Brise and the Home Office were working a system which was theoretically indefensible and the Home Office remained convinced that the radical liberals of 1908 had ruined the scheme by destroying its indeterminacy and forcing Gladstone to commit it to a reformatory aspiration. But an even larger problem was the attitude of the courts. At first the numbers sentenced remained reasonably high and by March 1914 there were nearly two hundred in Camp Hill.[71] There had never been many women detainees who were placed in one of the wings, specially converted for the purpose, of the State Inebriate Asylum at Aylesbury. Before the war the four of these apparently found the regime too peaceful and lonely for them and asked to go back to the convict prison.[72] However, by early 1915 there were around 250 men in Camp Hill but it began to be noticed that a very large majority of these had in fact been sentenced to the minimum of three years penal servitude and five years preventive detention allowed. This tendency of judges to stick to minimum terms rather than long periods of preventive detention persisted. Furthermore, the actual numbers sentenced began rapidly to fall, perhaps as a result of Churchill's warnings, so that by 1920 Ruggles-Brise was deeply worried at the dwindling population at Camp Hill for in that year only twenty one such sentences were passed.[73] He blamed the judges for this and clearly they harboured a lasting distrust for a disposal which they had rejected after their advice had been sought. He warned that 'the principle of Camp Hill is in great jeopardy' but by the autumn of 1920 the population at Camp Hill had fallen to seventy one.[74] In December 1920 Ruggles-Brise accused Judges and Quarter Sessions sentencers of ruining the scheme and indeed had recently been reminded that from the beginning the judges had disliked it.[75] At the very end of Ruggles-Brise's time the governor at Camp Hill began enthusiastic organization of Honour Parties working under minimal supervision and remarked on the transformation in demeanour and attitude wrought by these,[76] but the preventive detention system no longer attracted the attention of the outside world.

Yet there was one more twist to the knife. By 1921 the advisory committee had recommended that three hundred and forty nine detainees be licenced and enthusiastically maintained that over seventy per cent of these had been successful and in these claims had been supported by Ruggles-Brise.[77] However, after the latter's retirement, Wemyss Grant Wilson of the Central Association argued that this figure was greatly exaggerated.[78] The Home Office became very concerned because the public message was that preventive detention did in fact reform and the officials there blamed the advisory committee for naive recommendations for release on license.[79] The chairman of the committee, a local magistrate and protege of Ruggles-Brise, Arthur Andrews, disputed this and objected vehemently to the new Home Office policy of radical reduction of the licences merely because they thought now that detainees were not reformable.[80] He also pointed out that the committee members very carefully interviewed the men under consideration and that large numbers of detainees had shown exemplary conduct during the war, but the Home Office was unimpressed. Andrews wrote a number of letters which were not answered and attended several fruitless meetings at which he told the Home Office officials that they had broken faith with the committee and detainees.[81] The new Chairman of the Prison Commission was however at one with the Home Office and he assured the officials that such detention was not reformatory and that these 'middle aged and elderly men' would be better dealt with in other prisons thus enabling 'the splendid and expensive buildings' at Camp Hill to be used as a borstal.[82] In 1931 it was so ordered.[83]

There were long and bitter memories of what was seen as the sabotage of preventive detention by Parliament, Judges, Herbert Gladstone, Churchill, and the Home Office. Dr H.B. Donkin who had been a medical prison commissioner and later sat on the local advisory committee at Camp Hill believed that Ruggles-Brise and Sir Edward Clayton, the Prison Commission Secretary, actually drafted the original bill but that Gladstone and the Home Office had altered it 'to camouflage the object'[84] when opposition arose. H.B. Simpson believed that Churchill 'hated' the 1908 Act and wished to restrict its 'scope'.[85] Ruggles-Brise himself later recalled the 'fights we had in the old days with H.O. and Judicial Authority' and remarked that Parliament was 'singularly ignorant and narrow viewed on all penal subjects'.[86] In 1920 when he was trying unsuccessfully to revise the law, after the judges had complained about the initial penal servitude which must precede preventive detention, he remarked, with justice, that he had at the very beginning been willing to be flexible and to consider alternative views but that the judges had been inconsistent: then they opposed its in-determinacy and yet now in 1920 they were opposing the severity of the initial penal servitude and demanding the right to order preventive detention in its own right.[87] Wearily he reminded the Home Office that, because of such vaccilation and misuse of the provision, habitual criminals flourished 'in abundance',[88] because the original idea to which he had given so much thought had not been properly tried.

Yet Ruggles-Brise himself had been inconsistent veering from the original pure incapacitation notion to one of enthusiastic belief in 'the reformative influence' of the system which yielded 'much more favourable results than could have been originally expected'.[89] In their hearts all who had a hand in devising this strange experiment in the years between 1895 and 1908 were, however, agreed that, in the end, it had failed as a penal project because of judicial dislike of both indeterminacy and double sentencing and of course they were right.

Preventive Detention limped on through the inter war years and after 1931 the men were sent at first to Lewes and subsequently to Portsmouth the minute number of female detainees having earlier been transferred from Aylesbury to Liverpool and Holloway. By the mid 1930s there were around one hundred and twenty male and four female preventive detainees and clearly the project of social protection from habitual criminality by a selective preventive measure had failed. In effect the strong classical traditionalism of the judiciary and, paradoxically, the tendency of some sentencers to visit it on 'petty nuisance offenders'[90] continued to dog preventive detention even though it survived the second world war by over twenty years. Its death in 1967 was unmourned.

This scheme exemplifies the type of project which Garland had in mind when he discussed the origins of modern penality. It was segregative, contained a principle of indeterminacy, was resonant to the new criminology and eugenic theory and gave the executive wide powers over the management and release of detainees. Furthermore the relaxed nature of the regime and its basis in social protection allowed the state to operate a system on the basis that it was progressive and benevolent and was rooted in the human sciences. Consequently, control of detainees during sentence and compul-sorily following release to the supervision of the Central Association allowed a substantial increase of exercise of power over them. More than any other project it exemplified a new scientific method of disposal which put convicted offenders at risk of double penalty and was at odds with the traditional classical basis of punishment for moral culpability and serious-ness of offence.

Yet it was precisely for that reason that preventive detention failed to thrive and as such warns of the danger of too great an emphasis on Garland's thesis as an analysis of penal disposal after 1895. Nor, in the wider sphere, does it stand alone. As Andrew Rutherford has remarked, other measures based upon positivistic notions of assessment of propensity and treatment or segregation on the basis of that assessment also failed as, for example, institutions for vagrants and inebriates. Both Rutherford and Radzinowicz and Hood argued that these failures to thrive after initial enthusiasm occurred because in England enthusiasm for positivistic measures was not great and that 'classical notions of justice' were too strong to be overwhelmed by such notions.[91] The history of preventive detention appears to support that view.

## NOTES

1. Report of the Departmental Committee on Prisons, PP 1895, LVI: 31.
2. RCP & DCP yr end 31 March 1902, PP 1902, XLVI: 29, 30.
3. Report of the Inspector of the State Inebriate Reformatories RCP and DCP yr end 31 March 1904, PP 1905, XXXVII: 68.
4. RCP & DCP yr end 31 March 1904, PP 1905, XXXVII: 602-3.
5. L. Radzinowicz and R. Hood, *A History of the English Criminal Law and its Administration from 1750*, vol. 5, *The Emergence of Penal Policy* (Stevens & Sons 1986): 310.
6. E. Ruggles-Brise, *The English Prison System* (MacMillan 1921): 157.
7. Aylesbury State Reformatory PRO HO 45-10284-107024/13, E. Ruggles-Brise to HO, 27 Oct. 1903.
8. R. Anderson *Criminals and Crime: Some Facts and Suggestions* (Nisbet 1907): 7, 58.
9. R. Anderson, 'The Home Office Scheme for Professional Criminals' *Nineteenth Century and After*, Jan. 1904, 55: 117-130.
10. R. Anderson, 'Our Absurd System of Punishing Crime' *Nineteenth Century and After*, Feb. 1901, 49: 268-84. R. Anderson, 'The Punishment of Crime' *Nineteenth Century and After*, July 1901, 50: 77-92. R. Anderson, 'Crusade Against Professional Criminals' *Nineteenth Century and After*, March 1903, 53: 496-508. R. Anderson, 'The Home Office Scheme for Professional Criminals': 117-130.
11. Obituary on M. Crackanthorpe, *Eugenics Review*, Jan. 1914, 5 (4): 352-3.
12. Major L. Darwin, 'The Habitual Criminal' *Eugenics Review*, Oct. 1914, 6 (3): 204-18.
13. Ibid: 215.
14. Captain A. St John, 'Crime and Eugenics in America' *Eugenics Review*, July 1911, 3 (2): 118-30.
15. H.J.B. Montgomery, 'An Ex-Prisoner on Professional Criminals' *Nineteenth Century and After*, Feb. 1904, 55: 278-87. Sir Alfred Wills, 'Criminals and Crime' *Nineteenth Century and After*, Dec. 1907, 62: 879-94.
16. Dr J.F. Sutherland, 'A Paper on the Prophylaxis and Treatment of Criminal Recidivists', read to the 15th International Congress on Medicine, *Lancet*, 19

May 1906: 1418-19.

17. Sir Alfred Wills to *The Times*, 21 Feb. 1901: 8 cols a-b.

18. *Lancet*, 6 Aug. 1904: 403-4.

19. *Law Times*, 11 Jan. 1908, 124: 240.

20. Dr J. Hall to *BMJ*, 25 May 1912: 1216-17.

21. Leading Article, *BMJ*, 20 Nov. 1909: 1491.

22. Sir Alfred Wills, 'Criminals and Crime' *Nineteenth Century and After*, Dec. 1907, 62: 879-94. H.J.B. Montgomery, 'Criminals and Crime: A Reply' *Nineteenth Century and After*, 1908, 63: 80-9.

23. R.F. Quinton, *Crime and Criminals 1876-1910* (Longman, Green and Co. 1910): 46.

24. *The Times*, 1 June 1910: 5 cols a-b.

25. C. Hopwood to *The Times*, 12 Jan. 1892: 14 col. d. Leading Article, *The Times*, 17 Dec. 1894: 9 cols e-f.

26. *Justice of The Peace*, 18 May 1895, LIX: 307. L. Radzinowicz, 'The Present Trend of English Penal Policy' *Law Quarterly Review*, April 1939, CCXVIII: 273-88.

27. Indeterminate Sentences 1906-25, PRO HO 45-14099-145740/1, HO Minute, 30 Oct. 1906.

28. Treatment of Habitual Criminals 1894-1904, PRO HO 45-10027-A56902C.

29. Ibid. /11 Lord Chief Justice to Home Secretary, 16 May 1901.

30. Radzinowicz and Hood, *Penal Policy*: 268-78.

31. PRO HO 45-10027-A56902 C/9, E. Ruggles-Brise to HO, 21 Dec. 1899.

32. Ibid. /9 E. Ruggles-Brise Paper submitted to the Brussels Congress.

33. Ibid. /11 E. Ruggles-Brise to HO, Printed 21 Nov. 1901; Radzinowicz and Hood, *Penal Policy*: 270.

34. Report of His Majesty's Judges of the King's Bench Division in Reply to the Letter of the Rt. Hon. the Home Secretary of 22 March 1902, dated 6 April 1903, PRO HO 45-10027-A56902 C/14.

35. PRO HO 45-10027-A56902 C/17, HO Minute, 15 June 1903.

36. Radzinowicz and Hood, *Penal Policy*: 272-3.

37. Permanent Detention of Habitual Criminals—Suggestions, PRO HO 45-10371-159955/1, HO Minute, C.E. Troup, 18 Oct. 1907.

38. Parliamentary Debates 4th Series, vol. 189 col. 1122.

39. Ibid. Cols 1123-5.

40. Ibid. Vol. 197 col. 237-8.

41. Ibid. Vol. 190 cols 472, 476, 482.

42. Ibid. Vol. 197 cols 254; vol. 190 col. 485.

43. Ibid. Vol. 198 cols 123-5, 121.

44. Ibid. Vol. 198 cols 166, 167-8.

45. RCP & DCP yr end 31 March 1912, PP 1912-13, XLIII, pt 2: 198.

46. RCP & DCP yr end 31 March 1913, PP 1914, XLV, pt 2: 134.

47. RCP & DCP yr end 31 March 1913, PP 1914, XLV: 139-40.

48. RCP & DCP yr end 31 March 1912, PP 1912-13, XLIII, pt 1: 23. S.A. Moseley, *The Convict of Today* (Palmer 1927): 87. S. Hobhouse and A.F. Brockway (eds.) *English Prisons Today* (Longman, Green & Co. 1922): 450.

49. B. Thomson, *The Criminal* (Hodder & Stoughton 1925): 145; RCP & DCP yr end 31 March 1914, Pt 2, PP 1914, XLV: 127.
50. RCP & DCP yr end 31 March 1912, PP 1912-13, XLIII, pt 2: 198, 201. RCP & DCP yr end 31 March 1913, PP 1914, XLV, Pt 2: 134.
51. RCP & DCP yr end 31 March 1915, PP 1914-16, XXXIII, pt 1: 21.
52. *The Times*, 16 Feb. 1914: 3 col. d.
53. G. Kennaway to Mrs. Kennaway, 22 March 1921. PRO HO 45-20332-197277/64.
54. RCP & DCP yr end 31 March 1913, PP 1914, XLV, pt 2: 136, 137.
55. Ibid: 129.
56. RCP & DCP yr end 31 March 1916, PP 1916, XV: 15.
57. RCP & DCP yr end 31 March 1919, PP 1919, XXVII: 11.
58. RCP & DCP yr end 31 March 1919, PP 1919, XXVII: 11-12. RCP & DCP yr end 31 March 1915, PP 1914-1916, XXXIII: 20.
59. RCP & DCP yr end 31 March 1911, Pt 1, PP 1911, XXIX: 16.
60. Hobhouse and Brockway, *English Prisons*: 447-8.
61. PRO HO 45-20330-197277/3. RCP & DCP yr end 31 March 1911, PP 1911, XXXIX, pt 1, App. 17a: 113-4.
62. PRO P.Com. 7/288 Preventive Detention Rules and Privileges, 1910-12, Cut. *Spectator*, 25 Feb. 1911.
63. PRO HO 45 -20330-197277/18, Treasury to HO, 29 Aug. 1911.
64. PRO HO 45 -20330-197277/20, H.B. Simpson, Minute, 9 Nov. 1911.
65. PRO P.Com 7/288, op.cit., E. Ruggles-Brise, Minute, 15 Dec. 1910.
66. Ibid. Governor Camp Hill to PC, 21 May 1911.
67. RCP & DCP yr end 31 March 1913, pt 2, PP 1914, XLV: 139.
68. PRO P.Com 7/288, op.cit., E. Ruggles-Brise to HO, 7 June 1912.
69. Ibid. C.E. Troup, HO Minute, 24 June 1912.
70. Ibid. H.B. Simpson, Minute, 22 June 1912.
71. RCP & DCP yr end 31 March 1914, pt 2, PP 1914, XLV: 126, figure is 183.
72. RCP & DCP yr end 31 March 1913, pt 2, PP 1914, XLV: 132. In fact only 11 women received this sentence up to 1921. See E. Ruggles-Brise, *The English Prison System* (MacMillan 1921): 58.
73. PRO P.Com 7/291 Review of Preventive Detention 1920, E. Ruggles-Brise to HO 6 Dec. 1920.
74. PRO HO 45 -20331-197277/40, E. Ruggles-Brise to HO, 1 Aug. 1920; /42 Report Sir John Baird Undersecretary of State HO 15 July 1920.
75. PRO HO 45 -20331-197277/43, Lord Chief Justice to Home Secretary, 29 Oct. 1920, E. Ruggles-Brise to HO 6 Dec. 1920.
76. PRO P.Com 7/293, Scheme for a Modified Form of Self-Government. Governor Camp Hill report, 27 March 1922, Governor Camp Hill to PC, 21 June 1921.
77. PRO HO 45 -20331-197277/49, Printed Memo re. Bill to Amend Prevention of Crime Act 1908.
78. PRO HO 45 -20332-197277/55.
79. PRO HO 45 -20332-197277/64, Sir E. Blackwell Memo, 19 Feb. 1923.
80. PRO HO 45 -20332-197277/66, Arthur Andrews to Home Secretary, 12 May 1923; /64 to Sir John Anderson, 8 Feb. 1923.
81. PRO HO 45 -20332-197277/69, A. Andrews to HO, 12 Oct. 1923.

82. Ibid. /73 M. Waller to HO, 5 Dec. 1923.
83. Parkhurst and Preventive Detention 1931-9, PRO HO 45 -18026-594780, PC to HO, 17 Dec. 1931.
84. PRO HO 45 -20332-197277/64, Sir H. Donkin to Mr Andrews, 1 Dec. 1922.
85. Ibid. /59 HO Minute to Sir John Anderson, no date, early 1920s.
86. PRO P.Com 7/290, E. Ruggles-Brise to Sir E. Clayton, 27 Nov. 1916.
87. PRO HO 45 -20331-197277/43, Memo, E. Ruggles-Brise to HO, 6 Dec. 1920.
88. Ibid.
89. E. Ruggles-Brise, *Prison System*: 56-7.
90. D. Walsh and A. Poole, *A Dictionary of Criminology* (RKP 1983): 175.
91. A. Rutherford, 'Boundaries of English Penal Policy' *Oxford Journal of Legal Studies* 8 (1): 134. Radzinowicz and Hood, *Penal Policy*: 287, is cited in Rutherford's article.

*Chapter Seven*

# *The Local Prisons 1895–1921*

| WEEKDAYS | 5.30 | Rise, Wash, Dress, Clean Cells |
|---|---|---|
| | 5.50 | Slop Out |
| | 6.10 | Labour In Cells For All Adults/Drill Juvenile Adults |
| | 7.10 | Breakfast |
| | 7.40 | Cellular Labour For All |
| | 8.10 | Associated Labour and Exercise For 2nd, 3rd, 4th Stagers/Cellular Labour for 1st Stagers at Hard Labour |
| | 11.30 | Chapel March |
| | 11.40 | Prayers |
| | 11.55 | Prayers Cease |
| | 12.00 | Dinner in Cells |
| | 12.40 | Cellular Labour for First Stagers begins |
| | 1.30 | Associated Labour for 2nd, 3rd, 4th Stagers begins |
| | 4.30 | Return Cells For Supper |
| | 5.00 | Cellular Labour for All |
| | 7.00 | Cellular Labour Ceases |
| | 8.00 | Lights Out |
| SUNDAYS | 7.05 | Rise |
| | 7.30 | Breakfast |
| | 10.15 | Chapel |
| | 12.00 | Dinner |
| | 2.30 | Chapel |
| | 4.30 | Supper |
| | 8.15 | Lights Out |

Such was the timetable[1] applied in 1912 to those sentenced to imprisonment in the local prisons. Those sentenced to hard labour were thus, during the first month, held in almost continuous cellular confinement with around ten hours task work per day; those in the second, third or fourth stages or in the first without hard labour were set to five hours twenty minutes per day associated labour and three hours thirty minutes per day cellular labour.[2]

In the local prisons there were in 1900 a daily average population of fourteen and a half thousand prisoners[3] and, although this figure fluctuated from year to year, there was during Ruggles-Brise's period an overall population decrease so that by 1921 the daily average had fallen to around 8.3 thousand for 1920-1921, 7.2 thousand for 1919-1920.[4] Between 1895 and 1921 men outnumbered women by never less than three to one, although the proportion of men to women could, as in the years 1910 to 1912 and again in 1920 and 1921, be six men to one woman.[5] Large numbers of prisoners were, of course, not convicted of any crime, but held on remand, or in connection with civil process, but sentences to terms of imprisonment, as opposed to penal servitude, were short: in the year ended 31.3.1907 94 per cent of men and 97 per cent of women received on sentence to a term of local imprisonment were ordered to three months or less,[6] none to over two years. The passing of the 1914 Criminal Justice Administration Act, (4 and 5 George V cap. 58) which obliged courts to consider allowing time to pay fines before committal, greatly reduced the number of very short periods of prison[7] and the average length of sentence rose to around three months for men and seven weeks for women by 1920.[8] Lastly, prisoners tended to be aged in their late teens or early twenties and by 1908 the number of under sixteens sent to prison had fallen to just over seven hundred.[9]

The Gladstone Committee had criticised the local prisons, of which in 1895 there were 57,[10] for the mechanical way in which they processed prisoners through their regimes and for a lack of individualisation and reformation. Indeed the Committee had in the first place been appointed as a result of publicity about local prisons and it had been to these that the attention of members had primarily been directed. Between 1895 and 1921, by which time the number of local prisons had fallen to forty,[11] Ruggles-Brise and the Prison Commission applied a set of policies which remained constant and which, they claimed, were designed to implement the reformatory and ameliorating spirit of the Gladstone Committee.

In the first place the Prison Commission declared unremitting opposition to short sentences, which filled the local prisons with large numbers serving very short periods of a few days or weeks. Ruggles-Brise urged that these short sentences were exceedingly harmful, because the prisoners merely lost their dread of prison without any reformatory benefit possible because of the shortness of the time served. The educational projects set up by Ruggles-Brise and described later did not begin until a prisoner had served three months and the various progressive stages, each with their attendant privileges, only operated after one month for those who had earned the requisite marks. In report after report Ruggles-Brise condemned the short sentence, lauded non custodial alternatives such as time to pay fines and probation and insisted that the system was cluttered with an army of short sentence prisoners who actually impeded the staff in their efforts at the longer term project of reforming the rest. Secondly, Ruggles-Brise aimed at full employment of local prisoners at more diverse and interesting tasks and at the abolition of unproductive or useless labour. Lastly, he urged the application to local prisoners serving longer terms of the approaches which he advocated generally—missions, visitors, instruction, exhortation, personal influence and example and access to prisons of suitably uplifting outside groups.

With regard to the first objective there was, as has been seen, a substantial fall in the local prison population and in this Ruggles-Brise played a part alongside the many theorists and practitioners who pressed for alternatives to the short prison sentence and diversion of under sixteens or first time petty offenders to other non custodial disposals. As far as those who could not pay a fine were concerned the Criminal Justice Administration Act of 1914, which obliged courts to consider allowing time to pay before committal, made a notable contribution to reduction of the population of local prisons. With regard to the second objective, it was the case, prior to 1898, that all men sentenced to hard labour and certified fit by the prison medical officer had to tread a cylindrical revolving wheel, called a tread wheel, for six hours a day (fifteen minutes on and five off) or to turn the handle, checked at twelve pounds resistance, of a machine called a crank for the same time. In addition all male prisoners sentenced to hard labour had to pick oakum or coir daily in their cells.[12] The great majority of these machines served no productive purpose, although some of the tread wheels pumped water or ground corn.

The Gladstone Committee had favoured replacement of these machines by systems of more interesting and productive labour. The Prison Commissioners, watched closely by those parliamentary critics such as Michael Davitt and Edward Pickersgill who had pressed hard for this abolition, removed the wheels and cranks from the local prisons. Some were broken up and sold as scrap, but others went for use in the military prisons, and by May 1902 all but five tread wheels used for the supply of water had been abolished.[13] Hard labour was therefore redefined and now consisted in the first one month of oakum picking, (fourteen days only) coal sack making, wood chopping and stone breaking in cells.[14] After the month the prisoner was promoted to the next stage in which he or she was allowed to work in silence in association and Ruggles-Brise's policy was to diversify the labour tasks required of prisoners and to construct galleries and workshops for them, often converting the old tread mill rooms and sheds for this purpose.[15] He energetically worked at increasing orders from government for such items as mail bags, hammocks, nose bags, fenders etc. assisted by the Controller of Industry appointed under one of the recommendations of the Gladstone Committee. Early on, he also abolished oakum picking for women and created a number of new industries, previously unknown in prisons, such as carpet weaving at Maidstone, cushion making and the 'manufacture of Japanese blinds' at Wormwood Scrubs.[16]

By 1902 there were enthusiastic reports that well over five thousand local prisoners who had progressed beyond the cellular first stage were working in associated groups, either in work shops or cell corridors, who would previously have been employed on tread wheel/crank or in cellular labour. These were said to be 'animated and alert' working with great 'interest and assiduity' and it was noted that there were at least twenty two occupations at which they laboured such as book binding, shoe making, tailoring[17] and in 1904 this rose to around sixty.[18] For short sentence prisoners the labour tended to be simple tasks which could swiftly be learned such as 'pea sorting, bean sorting, coir balling, coir picking . . . rope teasing and wool sorting' but for those serving longer sentences the policy was towards instruction in a more complex and interesting labour task.[19] As always in prisons much labour was devoted to serving the prison itself—cleaning, laundry, painting, repairing, gardening etc.

Finally Ruggles-Brise claimed to be following a policy of classification and specialisation after the spirit of Gladstone. In 1898 the new Prisons Act created three divisions of imprisonment and gave courts power to order that an offender could be placed in one of these divisions—in default of such an order or if the sentence was accompanied by hard labour, the prisoner automatically went into the third division. The second division was intended for prisoners who did 'not belong to the criminal class' or did not have 'generally . . . criminal habits' or were guilty of offences 'not implying any great moral depravity'.[20] The conditions and regime of the second and third divisions were similar, but the aim was to keep the second class apart from the more criminal third division in order to prevent corruption. The first division was a re-enactment of a similar provision of 1865 (28 and 29 Vict. cap. 126 section 67) and was intended for prisoners who had collided with the law on issues of conscience—religious objectors to compulsory education of their children or refusers of compulsory vaccination as well as those for whom prison could not be avoided, yet were seen as heroic albeit misguided —for example Dr. Jameson of Jameson raid fame. Conditions in this division were extraordinarily relaxed compared with the other two— prisoners could have their own food sent in, work at their own trades and receive full wage payment, have extra visitors, beer, wine, unrestricted conversation. This division never included more than 160 prisoners between 1910 and 1911.[21]

Earlier Ruggles-Brise, again in accordance with the recommendations of the Gladstone Committee, had transported the Star classification from convict to local sector following an experiment in the London prisons.[22] The idea was that, after careful enquiries by the police, the prison authorities might separate prisoners of 'good . . . characters' and 'respectable . . . surroundings' from 'those who are versed in crime and of corrupt habits'.[23] In fact the Prison Commission intended that the three divisions of 1898 would make the Star/Other classes redundant but the courts refused to make more than minimal use of their powers of classification so that the very great majority of prisoners ended up in the third division. Ruggles-Brise complained frequently about this frustration of legislative intentions by courts but with little success[24]—in 1910 for example only 2½ per cent of sentences passed were to the second division.

Ruggles-Brise also claimed to be introducing a greater element of institutional specialisation and therefore certain prisons were designated for particular purposes. Thus some were, in part, used for longer term modified borstal, some as training prisons for newly recruited staff (Chelmsford), some entirely for women (Holloway), and some entirely for remand prisoners (Brixton). However, this did not substantially alter the role of the local prisons which was to hold a mixed group of prisoners on remand and short sentence with provision for both male and female prisoners. Lastly the Prison Commission emphasised that they were reconstructing the local Prison Aid Societies throughout the whole of Ruggles-Brise's period and these societies will be dealt with in chapter fourteen. Overall, therefore, Ruggles-Brise claimed that he had made substantial progress with the implementation of Gladstone's recommendations in local prisons. Thus he later reflected that 'the reform or reorganization of the prison system has been proceeding in every department' and that 'very extensive and far reaching . . . changes' had been made.[25]

To the local prisons of England there trooped an army of people who had fallen into the grip of the law, for the most part very poor, often ill nourished, inhabiting the workhouses, over crowded rural cottages and urban tenements of Edwardian England. Many were convicted of the most trivial offences such as failing to obey the orders of the workhouse masters or being disobedient apprentices and some were physically ill with part paralysis, unhealed post-operative wounds or suffering from recurrent fits.[26] They were often well used to the strip searches at reception, the barked orders, the long hours of isolation in cells, the ban on conversation with other prisoners and staff, the serried ranks in chapel, the monotony. The educational programmes planned just after Gladstone were wholly discontinued during the Great War and only applied to under 25s in 1921[27] with only 12.5 per cent receiving any basic education at all.[28] In the larger prisons such as Wandsworth (with often over a thousand prisoners) or Liverpool or Birmingham the numbers were so great that chaplains could hardly hope to visit more than a fraction in their cells for, even though the daily average population in local prisons was falling, so also were the number of prisons. Despite the new access of visitors and lecturers described in Chapter 8 it is clear that the daily life of the over twenty one year old local prisoner tended to be of monotony, isolation and silence.

The governors and chaplains believed that they were doing their best systematically to teach and rehabilitate and said so in the voluminous reports which they wrote for the Commissioners. At Holloway the new thrice weekly Swedish drill for selected women 'develops their muscles, improves gait and carriage, teaches habits of alertness and promptness in obeying orders . . . and exerts a mental and moral influence'.[29] In their reports they implied that the moral, intellectual and spiritual instruction and physical development were part of the programme for longer sentenced prisoners and that concerts, missions and lectures were a feature of general prison life not merely applied to juvenile adults.

There is no doubt of the sincerity of many of these personnel nor of the enthusiasm of some of them. The governor of Warwick, Colonel D'Aeth, was active in establishing a 'labour home' at which up to six juvenile adults from local prisons could live and work on release.[30] Colonel Rich at Lewes took female prisoners who had no where to go into his home as cooks or housemaids. Rich corresponded with a number of prisoners from Northampton prison and unreservedly welcomed the new prison visitors as 'a set of thundering good fellows'.[31] The governor and chaplain at Wakefield greatly supported the establishment of a Lads' Club in Sheffield for ex juvenile adult prisoners and by March 1909 there were nearly 160 members of this.[32] At Holloway every female prisoner had an interview with a lady visitor[33] and at Wakefield the chaplain visited each prisoner in his cell at least monthly.[34] The governor of Stafford used to visit ex prisoners in Wolverhampton and the West Midlands 'in order to encourage them'.[35]

Behind the official optimism however there was considerable dispute and conflict regarding the local prisons. One issue which frequently cropped up was the tendency of the courts to under use or misuse the second division.[36] This persisted throughout Ruggles-Brise's years and, after his retirement, assistant undersecretary at the Home Office, Sir Ernley Blackwell, complained that 'the case of Rebecca Lissner . . . is a good example of a case which was not suitable for second division treatment . . . she has been associated in business with at least four young women thieves . . . a receiver can seldom be properly regarded as a first offender'.[37] Further conflicts arose with Visiting Magistrates' Committees. In 1904, for example, a visiting justice at Wormwood Scrubs complained bitterly about the restraint for three days of a man in a strait jacket, the prisoner being 'pathetically quiet and humble', in a 'pitiable condition'. The Prison Commission, however, accepted the account given by the medical officer and the magistrate was so angered by this and the failure of his committee to support him that he resigned.[38] There were also numerous disputes between visiting justices and Prison Commission over the issue of corporal punishment such as, for example, the attempt of Carmarthen justices to persuade the Home Office to suspend an order for corporal punishment given by themselves on the ground that since the order of the Visiting Justices the prisoner had been of good behaviour.[39]

Not all staff were happy to coordinate with outside agencies and this is illustrated by the local furore over the governor of Northampton prison in 1895. Captain Bell was apparently a man with 'a brusque and rather irritating manner' whom in the past the Commissioners had had to 'call . . . to order' for his 'want of tact, manner and judgement'. In mid 1895 complaints from magistrates, police, coroner, police court missions and aid societies in Northampton began to reach the Home Office and Prison Commission and the local member of parliament was recruited to get rid of Bell. Apparently he was turning the prison into a fortress into which he refused to admit external personnel and even new prisoners or to allow staff and prisoners out to attend inquests: in the end he was transferred elsewhere and warned about future conduct.[40]

Ruggles-Brise knew that, even before the war, some parts of the local prison system were not working properly. In 1912 he circularised all local prisons to the effect that for years the award of marks, by which promotion was gained to superior stages by those serving over a month, had become 'mechanical', always being awarded unless the prisoner was actually put on report for misconduct.[41] Indeed, at times, there were allegations that the system was malfunctioning to an absurd degree from outside interest groups. So just before Ruggles-Brise took over from Du Cane, a local Welsh magistrate went to Carmarthen prison and addressed officials there in Welsh. He was not understood by many and complained angrily that large numbers of Welsh prisoners, who were unable to speak English, were in the custody of those whom they could not understand.[42] In 1898 Welsh language groups pressured the Home Office to appoint Welsh speakers to the recently vacant posts of governor and matron at Carmarthen.[43]

There were also, from time to time, allegations of neglect or brutality and at the very beginning of Ruggles-Brise's time there were some very serious allegations. In late 1897, for example, it was said that an insane prisoner had died after having seven ribs broken in a struggle with officials at Manchester and that at Norwich a prisoner had died after being forced to tread the mill with a perforated ulcer.[44] Enquiries were held into both these matters by the Home Office and the public assured that all personnel had been exonerated. In fact, however, in the latter case the Home Office officials were critical of the medical officer, who had 'failed to understand the complicated nature of the disease', but directed that the Humanitarian League, which was deeply concerned about the Norwich event, should be assured that very careful investigation had established that the death was not preventible.[45]

The programmes of reformation and relaxation in local prisons were the subject of controversy at the time. Some, like Ruggles-Brise, urged that they had been successful, whilst others, such as the Labour Research group, the suffragettes and conscientious objectors to the Great War insisted that the local prisons remained harsh, unfeeling, brutalising, the reality a grim parody of Ruggles-Brise's optimistic claims. After 1898 there was introduced a modest remission for prisoners serving over six months and by 1905 this was set at three weeks on a nine month sentence, six weeks on a twelve and three months on an eighteen.[46] In 1907, at Ruggles-Brise's prompting, remission for good behaviour was allowed to prisoners serving between one month and six.[47] Clearly there was much greater access given to outside missionary and educational groups and by 1921 the treadmills and cranks had long since gone. However the impression remains, from the evidence, of a system which overall processed prisoners through the regime in a formal, distant and perfunctory manner and which at times was by no means as efficient as Ruggles-Brise claimed. Certainly some of the enquiries which Ruggles-Brise himself set in motion were bleakly critical—for example at Holloway in 1919 Adeline, Duchess of Bedford, found 'uncleanly and very ineffectual' hygienic measures, with fresh sanitary towels 'thrust into cupboards with other miscellaneous articles such as oil cans' and kept in a 'useless and unhygienic manner'.[48]

Between the high minded aspirations and world view of the new liberalism and the actual experience of the local prisoner there was a gulf. Held in these prisons the inmates watched their surroundings with intense interest, learning the strange ways of the prison from one another in secret forbidden exchanges.

'The young clerk burst into tears and buried his head in his hands. "Is prison really like this?", he asked. "Oh, say it isn't as bad as this". We were treated to the incongruous spectacle of an old lag with "slaughterer" written all over his face in great, deep, hard lines, crossing over to the lad ... bending over him and comforting him with short, silly little sentences in which there was an infinity of rough concern. "We're all in it boy", he muttered, "damn fool game. Clear out of it when you gits the chance. It ain't fer kids. Pull up yer socks. Don't let 'em see yer gives a blow or they'll larn it on yer".'[49]

The ban on communication was never wholly effective and its breaches serve as a testimony to the inventiveness and the spirit of prisoners subjected to such a regime. So they scratched messages to one another on the bottom of dinner tins and they invented a 'deaf and dumb alphabet'. They learned to speak without moving their lips and devised morse codes which could be tapped out on walls and pipes and they even operated a telephone exchange with a directory of subscribers, each with his own number of initial taps on the pipe to act as the ringing tone. In chapel behind the responses, psalms and hymns conversation was freely exchanged.

| | |
|---|---|
| And behold from henceforth | What are you in for? |
| All generations shall call me blessed | I'm in for shoplifting. |
| For He that is mighty hath magnified me | How long have you got? |
| And Holy is His name | Six months hard labour.[50] |

Workshop machinery and hammers could be used to muffle conversation and also to obstruct the talk of warders to one another[51] and in the Du Cane era Irish prisoners produced an illicit newspaper, called the Irish Felon, at the printers' shop at Chatham convict prison.[52] Later A. Fenner Brockway, imprisoned as a conscientious objector in the Great War, produced a regular prison newspaper on lavatory paper with news items, cartoons, stories and letters to the editor: the landing cleaner was the newspaper boy.[53] In the chapel it was said that chants were especially useful camouflages.

'Welcome Fenner Boy,
When did you get here,
How did you like the skilly this morn?
Lord have mercy upon us'.[54]

Yet the silence was a dominating feature of the lives of prisoners and it caused a moral and emotional deterioration. Some were actually aware of the 'driving of a man back exclusively upon himself, his own defects, his own grievances', the promotion of 'the habit of selfishness to a most grievous extent'.[55] Although many staff of all grades were kindly and sympathetic the overall memory in the minds of prisoners was of brusque demeaning orders. So when one prisoner looked around the chapel 'to get a sense of fellowship with the other faces the warder's harsh voice broke in with "Number Two Sixty Five, look to your front"' and the exercise yards resounded to the frequently barked order 'Keep that tongue quiet or you'll soon be having a change of diet'.[56] Local prisoners experienced the attitude of the bulk of the uniformed staff as constant distrust, the prisons themselves as 'stern walls, barred windows and locked door'.[57] Yet warders themselves went in fear of punishment if they relaxed the rules and one told conscientious objector, Stephen Hobhouse, that he bitterly regretted the imposition of the rule which prohibited a kiss between husband and wife at visits and begged Hobhouse to understand that it was the rules, not the man, which forbade it: a prison visitor recalled that uniformed staff were invariably punished if they spoke to a prisoner beyond an order or reproof and that one governor had told him that the regulations forced him to punish the boys for standing on their cell chairs to look out of the windows, adding that 'I know I oughtn't to do it'.[58]

Many of the prisoners experienced the local prisons of Ruggles-Brise as cold, harsh, unfeeling places with little of Gladstone's personal influence or moral inspiration. They felt 'continually in disgrace: to never hear a kindly tone or a word of encouragement is sufficient to crush those who are already weak and who have fallen in the battle of life . . . every endeavour is made to render the life dull, monotonous and dreary; all the surroundings are as hideous as human ingenuity can make them, the food unappetising and the whole tone brutalizing and hardening . . . hour after hour, day after day . . . I spent sitting on the wooden bed, doing nothing, hardly thinking, staring into vacancy . . . the horror of it is still with me and night after night, unable to sleep, I go through it all again'.[59] Others recalled the dull unpalatable diet in which porridge, bread, suet and potatoes featured heavily, the monotony of the light drab broad arrowed khaki uniform of the third division, the dark brown of the second[60] and at night 'the muffled boots of the warder as he went from cell to cell to peep in to see what the prisoner was doing, the delirious man suffering from hallucinations shouting in sheer terror and despair through being alone in the dark with the horrors of his mind'.[61]

Yet there were the contrasts. Beside the 'cold mechanical' chapel services, the 'insipid and boring' sermons which were a 'blasphemous travesty' with the visiting clergyman 'ladling out hell fire by the bucketful'[62] stood the Quaker speaker from outside who was sincere, tender, ardent and hopeful and the officer with 'cherubic smile', whose infectious laughter seemed to transfigure his face and other officers who treated prisoners 'with courtesy and kindness'.[63] Nevertheless, many realised that they must study each warder and governor's character and foibles so as to gain advantage from the knowledge, one pretending to be 'an ignoramus imbibing wisdom from a master' to win consideration.[64] Almost invariably Ruggles-Brise's local prisoners remembered a cold, distant, watchful condemnation in the manner of many of their custodians. Typically the memory of those who had gained promotion to association was of being seated in rows in galleries sewing mail bags 'with large needles which looked like skewers pressing them through the canvas by a lead knob strapped to the palms of our hands' or the 'meat safe arrangement' for visits with husband and wife in cubicles like telephone boxes separated by wire mesh[65] or the interminable cell with its 'mattress, bed, board, pillow, mug, plate, towels, blankets, soap, hair brush and comb, spoon, salt cellar, tin knife, tooth brush and paste, bible and hymn book, dish cloth . . . all in their proper places'.[66]

It was not the convict prison or the preventive detention system which became a rod for the backs of the Prison Commissioners but the local gaols. For by 1907 there had arisen a storm of protest in the English local prisons which would progressively expose Sir Evelyn Ruggles-Brise to the fiercest tests of his life and his system to prolonged public abuse. The matter of women's suffrage was the initial occasion of this.

Ruggles-Brise had had previous experience of prisoners in local prisons who had attracted the attention of the outside world. Between 1895 and 1897 he had been extensively involved in the case of Oscar Wilde, held in Pentonville, Wandsworth and eventually Reading prisons. Ruggles-Brise had carefully coordinated with the Home Office to ensure that large numbers of books and special visits from Lord Alfred Douglas, other associates, family and advisers were allowed to Wilde and his move to Reading was made after two doctors had suggested a move to a county prison with light work in the garden and library.[67] So great and intense was the public interest in Wilde that Ruggles-Brise must have felt no little relief when, after a brief return to Pentonville, on 18th May, 1897 at 6.10 a.m. 'a private conveyance containing two gentlemen arrived' at the prison, was 'admitted into the court yard and turned around. The prisoner then got into it and was driven off totally unobserved by anyone'.[68]

Ruggles-Brise also knew what was to follow, for Oscar Wilde had written two of the most swingeing and profoundly disturbing accounts of prison life to appear between 1895 and 1939.[69] These narratives of tortured loneliness, capricious and harsh treatment and foolish and petty regulations were intended to serve as a back cloth to a soldier who was executed and the dismissal of Warder Martin for his kindness to little children in a general atmosphere of callous inhumanity, with the poor mentally disabled prisoner 'grinning like an ape and making with his hands the most fantastic gestures as though he was playing in the air on some invisible stringed instrument . . . hysterical tears making soiled runnels on his white swollen face'.[70]

The suffragettes[71] and the later conscientious objectors were an altogether more intractable problem. The suffragettes began to arrive in 1906 and thereafter they increasingly threw the Prison Commission and Home Office into disarray. These were not just one individual gifted artist nor were they the destitute habitual petty offender used to obedience, judgement and severity over centuries of their history but they were a growing legion of highly skilled strategists and exceedingly determined campaigners and they had but one object in view—gaining of votes for women. Everything was subordinate to that single objective and every incident on the road to the franchise to be turned to the advantage of the cause. So the Criminal Justice System became a stage for high drama with suffragettes as martyrs in the hands of a cold, intransigent, self-perpetuating male dominated state. Thus, proclaiming the justice of their cause, they took whips to their political masters such as Churchill, threw stones at cars and buildings, set fire to deserted houses, made incendiary devices, marched in great crowds on Parliament and official residences, held orchestrated public meetings at which confrontations flared into abuse and violence, sabotaged and high jacked political meetings of their opponents and reserved their worst hatred not for the conservatives, who were at least honest in their distaste for their cause, but for the liberals, especially Asquith, who seemed to promise much but deliver nothing.

For Ruggles-Brise and the Prison Commission the results were frightful. The suffragette upheaval of English local prisons went on for over seven years, years during which prison officials worked on the edge of their nerves. For the suffragettes were demanding what the authorities would not give, the right to the status of political prisoners with consequent treatment of a far more relaxed and dignified kind. So they defied the rules at Holloway, Manchester, Newcastle, Bristol and other prisons to which they went and the staff were at times wholly unable to cope with them. They defied and slapped the warders, shouted and screamed throughout the night, flouted orders, made constant demands of the Home Office and Prison Commission. They sang the Marseillaise and The March of The Women. Then, when all this had failed, to secure a result, they devised their most effective tactic—they went on hunger strike.[72]

The Prison Commissioners were now terrified that a suffragette with a weak heart or other illness would die and the medical inspector, Herbert Smalley, careered around the country trying to assess each suffragette's state of health so as to advise the Home Secretary whether to release a suffragette early or not. The attention of Parliament and the media was riveted on the local prisons for, if there were deaths, the liberals would be condemned in Parliament and press by adversaries who seized hold of the cause of the suffragettes and used it as a stick for the back of the government.

By 1909 the hunger strike was at the heart of the matter and Smalley caught in a dilemma from which he could scarcely extricate himself. On the one hand, he and the local medical officers must not advise early release for those who pretended to ill health or were apparently fit for nasal tube force feeding and yet must bear in mind that 'anything is better than having one of these foolish women die during, or kill herself after, the forcible feeding'.[73] By late 1909, at Newcastle, suffragettes were smashing cell windows and setting fire to their bedding whilst suffragette bands played outside the prison and all hunger strikers were being force fed.[74] Some, like Lady Constance Lytton, were, however, released early because of heart disease but even this did not get the authorities off the hook. Lady Lytton, for example, at once made capital out of the argument that her kindly treatment and early release was due to her aristocratic status and promptly got herself sent to prison again under the assumed identity of an ordinary poor girl—emerging to argue that she had proved the corruption and inequity in the Home Office since her treatment had been far more severe.[75]

By the end of 1909 the suffragettes were employing the tactic of getting the oldest and sickest of their number committed, so as to embarrass the liberals even more greatly. Weary and close to despair Herbert Smalley wrote to Commission secretary Basil Thomson: 'we have had a worrying day . . . I think they must have picked out all the old crocks they could find in this batch . . . a cute move'.[76] Prison governors and medical personnel were sending daily reports about each suffragette to the Home Office with batches of sick ones being released early. All the while in prisons up and down the land, whether hunger striking or not, they waged war to gain political status. 'Vera Wentworth . . . very noisy all day . . . has broken her cell windows and is now in figure of eight handcuffs . . . Theresa Garnet . . . very noisy all day. Broke gas box and set fire to cell'.[77] As Ellen Wines Pitman declared: 'the next time I shall go for the cabinet ministers and members of parliament . . . if I can't get at them first time I shall wait until I can. They won't give us women votes. As for the punishment I shall receive I don't care two pence. If they kill me I can't die but once'.[78]

By now Prison Commissioners were in the midst of a crisis unlike anything they had known. They were accused of favouring the well born like Lady Lytton and of inflicting the cruelty of nasal tube feeding.[79] The medical officers were almost in revolt and Ruggles-Brise lamented in late 1909 that 'Dr Scott, himself one of our most self reliant and robust medical officers . . . felt that the strain and responsibility was too great for him to bear'. Indeed Dr Horatio Donkin, the Medical Commissioner, made 'the strongest possible protest' against the position of the medical officers comparing it to 'vivisection without a license . . . experiments on the living human body in order to see to what point self inflicted starvation can be carried without actual danger to life' for they must decide if and when to force feed and if and when to use early release.[80] For the next three years it went on, with force feeding the subject of bitter controversy in Parliament. As George Lansbury, the veteran socialist member, put it; 'You call yourselves gentlemen and you forcibly feed and murder women in this fashion. It is the most disgraceful thing that has ever happened in the history of England. You ought to be driven out of office' and a similar storm raged in the professional and daily press.[81] Yet the Home Office ministers and officials stood firm, for they feared that, once they allowed special conditions for suffragettes impelled by political motives, 'every kind of whipper snapper will have to be lodged in the first division and political propaganda will take a new and preposterous form'.[82]

It was Herbert Gladstone who originally devised the tactic of a special relaxed sub class of the second division to be made available to 'those who have not been guilty of offences involving dishonesty, cruelty, indecency or serious violence'[83] and Churchill who implemented it. Yet this did not meet the demand for political status and in 1912 of 240 suffragettes gaoled fifty seven were force fed with more being released on health grounds.[84] Eventually the famous Cat and Mouse Act was passed in 1913 (3 George V cap. 4) allowing release of prisoners temporarily on health grounds but requiring them to return to prison for the rest of their sentence when recovered. Plainly the situation had remained serious for so long that new law was to solve the dilemma for the government—indeed at Manchester prison earlier the Visiting Committee had ordered fire hoses to be turned on the suffragettes.[85] However, many problems resulted from the Cat and Mouse policy, as far as the police were concerned, for the suffragettes did not voluntarily return to prison and the Home Office policy was to leave 'non dangerous suffragette mice alone'[86] and to arrest the more active ones. This led to complex law cases before London magistrates who, like Curtis Bennett, were by no means happy to allow warrants under the act, with suffragettes petitioning the King and Queen against such monstrous legislation under which 'at the end of six and thirty years the Cat will still be playing with the Mouse'.[87] Basil Thomson later wrote that the Prison Commissioners believed that it would only end when the vote was given to women and that the suffragettes were 'a cross which we should be doomed to bear for ever'.[88]

But it did end, for Mrs Pankhurst put aside the issue until the Great War was won and quickly the prisons emptied of suffragettes. Then, two years later, the same process began again, this time with men. After 1916 increasing numbers of conscientious objectors were committed to prison as the last technique of an embattled state to break their wills. These were often men of high conscience and profound theological or philosophical objections to joining in the cruel and voracious death struggle being waged in the trenches of France and Flanders and in the other theatres of war. In mid 1916 the Quakers' Annual Meeting declared conscription to be a suppression of conscience and the conscientious objectors, Quaker, Socialist, Plymouth Brethren, Congregationalist or whatever, began to flow into the prisons. By November 1917 there were fifteen hundred of them and at some prisons, such as Walton and Wandsworth, there were large groups of them whilst Dartmoor was emptied of convicts to hold them: at the latter prison the

authorities set them to work to build a road which came to be known as
'Conshies' Road':[89] some who were willing to work were allowed to go
outside the prison, those who refused all work were held in ordinary prison
conditions.

Those whose sons were dying in France often hated the objectors. Soon
deputations of local people of Princetown and Dartmoor were going up to
London to complain about 'long haired idle young men wandering about
. . . with their arms about each other's necks'[90] and accusations were made
that all kinds of subversion and indecency were staining the purity of the
damsels and lads of Princetown. In Parliament a storm of hate was unleashed
against 'these cowards and shirkers' by conservative backbenchers, who
accused them of living luxurious lives, buying up all the sweets and luxuries
in local shops, accosting Dartmoor folk with disloyal and subversive views,
'miserable specimens of humanity . . . look at the countenances of these
men, their grinning faces looking like apes'.[91] Allegations of systematic
torture and medical neglect—vigorously rejected—were made[92] and both
force feeding and the Cat and Mouse approach returned, although to nothing
like the extent of the suffragette period. To his honour Labour member,
Colonel Josiah Wedgewood, who had served in 1914 in Flanders and 1915
at Gallipoli, constantly urged kindness and moderation to those who were,
for the most part, following their conscience.

A prevailing fear, especially after the creation of the Union of Soviet
Socialist Republics and the withdrawal of these from the war, was that the
conscientious objectors were Bolshevist or Anarchist revolutionaries who
waved red flags, sabotaged the war effort, walked out during the National
Anthem at Princetown church[93] and sang unpatriotic songs. Indeed, they
were banding together in some prisons and overturning the orderly discipline
of Ruggles-Brise. The latter had no doubt of the justice of a war in which
many prisoners had been released early to serve and which 'for some
mysterious psychological reason . . . is a great reforming and almost
transfiguring influence in the case of the criminal man', although the Home
Office wondered about the wisdom of putting 'criminals to train with our
clean young soldiers'.[94] Nevertheless, as with the suffragettes, prison
discipline was relaxed for conscientious objectors so as to allow the objectors
conversation and other privileges and, in general, Ruggles-Brise did not treat
them severely.

By mid 1918 the objectors had formed a Soviet collective at Wandsworth
and were dominating the prison, holding meetings and promulgating
'extreme socialistic views' to other prisoners, also singing 'the Red Flag' and
other 'revolutionary songs'.[95] Major Blake was dispatched to the prison in
February 1919 to suppress this and, on entry, marched up to them and
bawled 'you damned mutinous swine, I have come down here to restore

order and, if you do not behave yourselves, I will give you hell'.[96] The amazed objectors at once fell into line but later complained of Blake's language. At the inquiry which ensued he admitted using the word 'damned' and calling one of them a 'Bolshevist' but vehemently denied that at any time in his life he had used 'the disgusting word bloody'.[97] At the enquiry a petition from a criminal prisoner to the Home Office was produced in which he complained that the conscientious objectors were turning the prison into a shambles with 'odd refrains from old and ghastly songs . . . hideous vocal out cries of long since dead popular music hall or drinking club songs . . . shrieks and cat calls . . . revolting and loathsome conduct'.[98]

The suffragettes and conscientious objectors wrote voluminously about their prison experience and some of this literature will be referred to later. For the Prison Commissioners between 1906 and 1919 the local prisons had increasingly become a political battle ground as part of which conditions were virulently attacked by those who wished to emphasise their own unjust suffering. In the same way the Labour Research Enquiry had almost nothing good to say about the local prisons which were by 1922 an almost discredited section of the prison system.

It is, however, necessary to pause before final judgement, despite the apparently unanimous condemnation by propagandists and others. Ruggles-Brise had set himself a number of policy objectives at the beginning of his chairmanship and in all of these substantial progress had been made. He had condemned short and unnecessary sentences and they had decreased dramatically in number since 1895. He had urged the abolition of treadmill and crank and the introduction of more diverse and useful labour—by 1910 the cranks and treadmills had entirely disappeared and labour tasks were more diverse. He had aimed to open the prisons to outside missionary and religious groups and personnel and in all prisons these had access soon after the end of the nineteenth century.

Ruggles-Brise's local prisons were, as described, monotonous, disciplinary and severe. However, those who had known the Du Cane system were in no doubt that conditions had much relaxed since then. One prisoner, who knew both systems, insisted that there had been a notable improvement in education and library facilities and spoke optimistically about the direction of the local prisons in 1909-1910.[99] Another, who had served eighteen months with hard labour, complained of a tendency of prisoners to publish whinging accounts of their prison experience. He insisted that the daily labour was easy to complete and that the staff were 'a jolly decent lot of fellows' with many prisoners being better off inside the local prisons than out.[100] A conscientious objector, although in general critical, noted that many prisoners 'accept with equanimity an existence three parts of which may be spent in prison'.[101] Another wrote poetry in which he compared all prisons very favourably with workhouses and assured the British public that, as long as they clothed, fed and warmed him and his fellows so well, 'they'll never want for thieves'.[102] Another man, who served two years in 1917 and a later short sentence in Pentonville and who had served many sentences in America and Europe, casually commented that 'the English prison system of today is quite humane: men are not unduly humiliated: the food is plain but plentiful'.[103]

The suffragettes' and conscientious objectors' accounts easily sway the reader to the view that Ruggles-Brise's claims to have achieved relaxation of Du Cane's severity were mere cant and that the bleak criticisms of the Labour Research group were wholly justified. However, it is necessary to bear in mind that these accounts were intended to emphasise the cruel injustice suffered by those sacrificing themselves for the sacred causes of women's suffrage and pacifism on the one hand and to point up the injustice of the carceral institutions of the state on the other. This does not at all mean that these accounts should be dismissed for they contain a great deal of valuable material. However, there is in them a predisposition to emphasise the negative aspects of the local prisons, although it is clear that Ruggles-Brise's system was rigorous and hard—indeed he himself never doubted that severity and strict discipline should be at the heart of all prison systems.

However, it is necessary to bear in mind what had gone before in the time of Du Cane and as a comparison is drawn the relaxation of conditions under Ruggles-Brise becomes clearer. So, as Hobhouse and Brockway noted, floggings for prison offences in local prisons decreased hugely between 1895 and 1921.[104] After 1899 male local prisoners no longer suffered the 'convict crop' hair cut but might wear beards and moustaches and have longer hair.[105] Diets were greatly improved after an investigation in 1899 and to the Du Cane diet of bread, gruel, oat meal, suet, potatoes and soup were added or substituted milk, meat, porridge, cocoa, bacon and beans.[106] After 1909 the initial one month separation was abandoned for women who were thereafter allowed associated labour from the start and the mothers of new born babies, rather than the wardresses, encouraged to bathe their babies, with prison creches provided.[107] Lastly, a warder who was very critical of the prison system and who took the professional risk of giving evidence to the Labour Research Enquiry made clear that the institutionalised abuse of prisoners of many years before had by 1921 disappeared.[108]

Notwithstanding, the success of the Prison Commission fell far short of the hopes of Gladstone in the local prisons. Indeed, as far as Ruggles-Brise himself was concerned, this was not surprising for he had always emphasised that successful reformatory intervention required a lengthy period of application. Thus the local prisons with their short term population were inherently problematic so far as Gladstone's notions of personal influence and moral development were concerned. The plain fact is that local prisons, despite the amelioration of Ruggles-Brise's time in office, dispensed uniformly administered punishment on the basis of moral culpability and the requirements of deterrence. They were not influenced at all by any eugenic or other positivistic modes of analysis or disposition but intended to make punishment painful and bleak. The educational and missionary approaches described in the following chapter were thus never intended to alter the basic location of the local prison in the classical criminal jurisprudential notions of defined limited punishment, personal moral responsibility and culpability and individual and general deterrence.

## NOTES

1. RCP & DCP yr end 31 March 1912, PP 1912-12, XLIII: 113.
2. Ibid.
3. RCP & DCP yr end 31 March 1900, PP 1900, XLI: 15.
4. RCP & DCP yr end 31 March 1921, PP 1921, Session 1, XVI: 4. 1 April 1919-31 March 1920, 7205; 1 April 1920-31 March 1921, 8392.
5. RCP & DCP yr end 31 March 1912, PP 1912-13, XLIII: 5. RCP & DCP yr end 31 March 1921, PP 1921, XVI: 4.
6. RCP & DCP yr end 31 March 1907, PP 1908, LII: 8.
7. RCP & DCP yr end 31 March 1917, PP 1917-18, XVIII: 6.
8. RCP & DCP yr end 31 March 1920, PP 1920, XXIII: 5. 86 days for men, 49 for women.
9. RCP & DCP yr end 31 March 1907, PP 1908, LII: 13 Number is 728.
10. RCP yr end 31 March 1895, PP 1895, LVI, App. 2: 19.
11. S. Hobhouse and A.F. Brockway (eds.) *English Prisons Today* (Longman, Green & Co. 1922): 18.
12. PRO P.Com 7/331, Crank and Treadwheel 1878-1897, Standing Order, 5 Feb. 1895.
13. PRO P.Com 7/332, E. Ruggles-Brise to HO, 1 May 1902.
14. PRO P.Com 7/332, Standing Order, 23 April 1902.
15. RCP & DCP yr end 31 March 1904, PP 1905, XXXVII: 24.
16. RCP & DCP yr end 31 March 1899, PP 1899, XLIII: 42.
17. RCP & DCP yr end 31 March 1901, PP 1902, XLV: 55-6. RCP & DCP yr end 31 March 1902, PP 1902, XLVI: 59.
18. RCP & DCP yr end 31 March 1904, PP 1905, XXXVII: 61.
19. E. Ruggles-Brise, *The English Prison System* (MacMillan 1921): 139.
20. PRO HO 45-12905-116578, Printed Memo Prison System and Imprisonment: 3. Hobhouse and Brockway, *English Prisons*: 215.
21. Ibid: 220.
22. Star Class at Local Prisons 1895-7, PRO HO 45-9747-A57530, Circular Kenelm Digby to all Chief Constables April 1897.

23. Ibid. See also Hobhouse and Brockway, *English Prisons*: 214. So-called because they wore red stars on cap and tunic.
24. RCP & DCP yr end 31 March 1907, PP 1908, LII: 12.
25. Ruggles-Brise, *Prison System*: 77-8.
26. RCP & DCP yr end 31 March 1907, PP 1908, LII: 250. RCP & DCP yr end 31 March 1902, PP 1902, XLVI: 15.
27. Hobhouse and Brockway, *English Prisons*: 153.
28. Ibid: 156.
29. RCP & DCP yr end 31 March 1907, PP 1908, LII: 245.
30. PRO P.Com 7/592.
31. C.E.F. Rich, *Recollections of a Prison Governor* (Hurst & Blackett 1932): 62, 209. W. Blake, *Quod* (Hodder & Stoughton 1927): 141-5.
32. RCP & DCP yr end 31 March 1909, pt 2, PP 1909, XLV: 179-80.
33. RCP & DCP yr end 31 March 1912, pt 2, PP 1912-13, XLIII: 57.
34. RCP & DCP yr end 31 March 1909, pt 2, PP 1909, XLV: 178-9.
35. J.E. Thomas, *The English Prison Officer since 1850* (Routledge & Kegan Paul 1972): 136-7.
36. PRO P.Com 7/39, E. Ruggles-Brise to Chairman Illegible, Visiting Committee 31 March 1915.
37. Penal Servitude and Imprisonment Generally, PRO HO 45-12905-116578, E. Blackwell to Sir Leonard Kershaw, 8 July 1927.
38. Means of Restraint 1904-1940, PRO HO 45-18366-122929/1, W.S. Gilbert to A. Akers-Douglas Home Secretary, 18 Oct. 1904. /4 W.S. Gilbert to HO 22 Nov. 1904.
39. Gross Personal Violence 1900, PRO HO 144-280-A561703/3.
40. Criticisms of Magistrates at Northampton Prison 1895, PRO HO 45-9745-A56682/7, PC obs. to HO, 27 June 1895. /7 Mayor of Northampton to Sir Philip Mansfield M.P., 11 May 1895.
41. PRO P.Com 7/303, PC Circular Local Prisons, 29 Feb. 1912.
42. English Officials in Welsh Prisons, PRO HO 45-9974-X42020/1.
43. Welsh Officials at Welsh Prisons 1893-1899, PRO HO 45-9737-A54590/4,/5.
44. Death of Edward Cox—Inquiry 1897-8, PRO HO 144-513-X66658, Treatment of a prisoner on the treadmill, PRO HO 144-514-X66675/1,/2,/3.
45. PRO HO 144-514-X66675/3, HO Minute, 18 Dec. 1897.
46. Penal Servitude and Imprisonment Memorandum, PRO HO 45-12905-116578.
47. Remission of Sentence PRO HO 45-11050-153582, H. Sec to E. Ruggles-Brise, 20 June 1907; circular to police 23 Aug. 1907.
48. Enquiry into Holloway Prison by Adeline Duchess of Bedford 2 May 1919, PRO P.Com 7/57-2a.
49. S. Scott, *The Human Side of Crook and Convict Life* (Hurst & Blackett 1924): 22.
50. B. 2.15 *Among the Broad Arrow Men: A Plain Account of English Prison Life* (A. & C. Black 1924): 43, 78, 90.
51. J.S. Balfour, *My Prison Life* (Chapman & Hall 1907): 80.
52. T.J. Clarke, *Glimpses of an Irish Felon's Prison Life* (Maunsel & Roberts 1922): 39.

53. A.F. Brockway, *Inside the Left. Thirty Years of Platform, Press, Prison and Parliament.* (Allen & Unwin 1942): 99.
54. Ibid: 92.
55. S. Hobhouse, *An English Prison from Within* (Allen & Unwin 1919): 21.
56. Ibid: 21, 23.
57. Ibid: 24, 25.
58. Ibid: 26; T.E. Harvey, *The Christian Church and the Prisoner in English Experience* (Epworth 1941): 67.
59. H. Blagg and C. Wilson, *Women in Prison.* Fabian Tract no. 163, 1912: 11-12.
60. E.W. Mason, *Made Free in Prison* (Allen & Unwin 1918): 203-5, 208.
61. Ibid: 139.
62. Ibid: 146-7.
63. Ibid: 152, 154, 148.
64. Ibid: 153-4.
65. A.F. Brockway, *Inside the Left*: 93.
66. E.W. Mason, *Made Free*: 159.
67. PRO P.Com 8/432, Oscar Wilde. P.Com 8/433, Oscar Wilde. HO to PC 29 Oct. 1895, Governor Reading Prison to Capt. Stopford PC, 9 Nov. 1895.
68. PRO P.Com 8/434, Governor of Pentonville to PC, 19 May 1897.
69. C. 3.3. (Oscar Wilde), *The Ballad of Reading Gaol* (Smithers & Co. 1899); O. Wilde, *De Profundis* 2nd edn. (Methuen 1905).
70. O. Wilde to *Daily Chronicle*, 28 May 1897, cut. PRO HO 144-271-A58947/3.
71. It is impossible to write on this subject without urging the reader to study the very detailed account of state policy regarding suffragettes in prison in L. Radzinowicz and R. Hood, *A History of the English Criminal Law and its Administration from 1750*, vol. 5, *The Emergence of Penal Policy* (Stevens & Sons 1986): 439-61.
72. For the suffragettes see PRO HO 45-24630-223849 (Imprisonment of the Pethick Lawrences) PRO HO 45-10345-141956 (Suffragists in Prison—General) PRO HO 45-10418-184276 (Suffragists in Newcastle) PRO HO 45-17879-237531 (Cat and Mouse Act 1913-39) PRO HO 144-552-185732 (Suffragists in Bristol Prison) PRO HO 144-891-171454 (Suffragettes 1908).
73. PRO HO 45-10418-184276/2, E. Troup to H. Gladstone, 12 Oct. 1909.
74. Ibid. /13,/17,/23.
75. C. Lytton, *Prisons and Prisoners: Some Personal Experiences* (Heinemann 1914).
76. PRO HO 45-10418-184276/31, H. Smalley to B. Thomson, 13 Oct. 1909.
77. PRO HO 144-552-185732/6, Suffragettes at Bristol, Memo Governor Bristol Prison, 17 Nov. 1909.
78. Ibid. /21 Report Det. Con. H. Slade on E.W. Pitman, 22 Nov. 1909.
79. Troup denied this in a letter to *The Times* of 23 Nov. 1909: 9 col. f, in which he argued that no more was being done than happened in lunatic asylums and that Lady Lytton was in fact released early because of a weak heart.
80. Prison Treatment of Persons Convicted for Crimes Not Involving Moral Turpitude 1908-1914, PRO HO 144-1042-183256/17, E. Ruggles-Brise to HO 14 Oct. 1909.

81. Quoted in E. Pethick-Lawrence, *My Part in a Changing World* (Gollancz 1938): 275. Examples from the press and journals: *Lancet* 24 Aug. 1912: 549-51; *BMJ* 22 Nov. 1913: 1393; 9 Oct. 1909: 1089; *The Times* 21 Dec. 1909: 10 col. d, 22 Dec. 1909: 8 col. d.
82. PRO HO 144-1042-183256/17, H. Gladstone HO Memo, 5 Feb. 1910.
83. Ibid.
84. Prisoner's Temporary Discharge for Ill Health Bill (Cat and Mouse) 1913, PRO HO 45-10699-234800/9, HO Memo to Lord Haldane, April 1913.
85. PRO HO 144-552-185732/15, HO Minute C.E. Troup, 20 Nov. 1909, in an aside about Manchester.
86. Prisoners' Temporary Discharge for Ill Health Act (Cat and Mouse) 1913-1939, PRO HO 45-17879-237531/23, C.E. Troup to B. Thomson, 26 Jan. 1914.
87. PRO HO 45-17879-237531/7, Inspector Parker report, 16 May 1913. /9, Women Writers Suffrage League, Petition to King and Queen May 1913.
88. B. Thomson, *The Scene Changes* (Collins 1939): 225.
89. A.J. Rhodes, *Dartmoor Prison: A Record of 126 Years of Prisoner of War and Convict Life, 1806-1932* (Bodley Head 1933): 2.
90. B. Thomson, *The Scene Changes*: 122.
91. Parl. Deb. 5th Series, vol. 92 col. 1822, vol. 93 col. 185.
92. Parl. Deb. 5th Series, vol. 93 col. 500, vol. 103 cols. 259-61.
93. Parl. Deb. 5th Series, vol. 92 col. 1822.
94. Release to Join the Army, PRO HO 45-10995-158871, E. Ruggles-Brise to HO 23 Feb. 1917, HO note scribbled on this letter dated 26 Feb. 1917.
95. Report to the Secretary of State ... on an Enquiry into the Allegations Made Against the Acting Governor of Wandsworth, PP 1919, XXVII: 3.
96. Ibid: 5.
97. Ibid: 5, 6.
98. Ibid: 11, 12.
99. A. Cook, *Our Prison System* (Drane *c.* 1911).
100. F. Martyn, *A Holiday in Gaol* (Methuen 1911): 176, 193-4, 278.
101. E.W. Mason, *Made Free*: 143.
102. Found on a slate in prison, Quoted in *The Times*, 30 May 1910: 4 col. c.
103. E. Guerin, *Crime: The Autobiography of a Crook* (Murray 1928): 297.
104. Hobhouse and Brockway, *English Prisons*: 241. 1901-2, 32 floggings, 1920-21 1 only.
105. Ibid: 138. Various Relaxations, PRO HO 45-11033-428541, M.L. Waller to HO 9 Nov. 1921.
106. Report of the Departmental Committee on Prison Dietaries, PP 1899, XLIII: 7-12.
107. Hobhouse and Brockway, *English Prisons*: 341, 346-7.
108. Ibid: 615.

# Chapter Eight

# Chaplains, Educators and Visitors in English Prisons 1895–1921

The Prison Commission claimed that between 1895 and 1921 it was putting into practice a project which was intended to improve prisoners morally, spiritually and educationally. This project had a great deal in common with similar endeavours in the prisons of the early Victorian era and the central concept underlying it was that under the supervision of each prison chaplain a cluster of morally improving influences would be brought to bear on the individual prisoner. It was intended that this would result in a deeper knowledge and love of God and rested on an assumption that the chaplain and those he brought into the prison as visitors and other prison established educational staff were dedicated to the wellbeing and improvement of the prisoners, fostering gratitude and awareness of the prisoners' true spiritual destiny and moral obligations. The Prison Commissioners persistently maintained that a great deal of progress was being made with this project in their very long annual reports and indeed after 1895 included much material about the work of chaplains, visitors and educators in these reports.

There was a Church of England chaplain at every prison, either full or part time, depending on prison size, and indeed at some large prisons the full time chaplain was served by an assistant and by scripture readers. Furthermore it had long been established that at convict and local prisons salaried Catholic priests would serve prisoners of their faith either on a part or full time basis with chapel provided where daily average numbers of Catholics justified this as at Wandsworth but, where numbers were smaller, Catholic priests would be employed as need arose to minister to prisoners, most salaried on a per capita basis, some however not salaried.

The role of the Church of England prison chaplain was to hold the compulsory Sunday and daily services, to superintend the work of schoolmaster/mistress and schoolmaster/mistress warders, to participate actively in the work of the Discharged Prisoners Aid Societies, to minister individually to the prisoners by means of cell visits and to administer the prison library. Catholic chaplains, when fully established as at Parkhurst or Liverpool, carried out the same functions with their own prisoners.

The Gladstone Committee was clearly critical of the way a number of these functions were carried out, in particular the exercise of personal influence over prisoners, the quality of teaching and instruction by prison educators and the maintenance of libraries and made recommendations for substantial improvement. Ruggles-Brise and the Home Office almost at once set up an enquiry to consider the implementation of the recommendations regarding education in 1895 and this was undertaken by a committee including Robert Mitford Prison Commissioner, George Merrick the Visiting Chaplain and Charles Sim a representative of the London School Board.[1] The Committee found that prisoners in local prisons were receiving fifteen minutes instruction in reading, writing and arithmetic twice a week if they were serving four months or more and were under 40 (36 in the case of women). In local prisons the schoolmaster warders passed from cell to cell to give this instruction. In convict prisons each convict under 40 received half an hour education per week in classes, apart from those undergoing the initial nine months separation who were instructed in their cells; all schoolmasters and mistresses in the convict service were certificated by the State education authority and did not wear uniform.[2]

This committee recommended that a more efficient examination system be introduced alongside instruction of prisoners to a higher standard of proficiency and also suggested that outside lecturers and visitors be given access to prisons to participate in a more substantial attempt at 'arousing a dull intelligence, exercising the receptive and reasoning faculties and creating an interest in new subjects together with the raising of the prisoner's self respect that always results from showing him that his intelligence is worth cultivating'.[3] In particular it was suggested that historical or biographical stories were highly suitable for prisoners, over and above basic literacy and numeracy, as a vehicle for moral development, for prisoners had a low 'average mental density' and it was better to help them to draw out the moral of a story than to engage in 'discussion of an abstract subject even though illustrated by anecdote'.[4] In addition, the enquiry disapproved of the tendency to sacrifice education whenever it seemed to staff that it was in competition with prison labour and learned that there were a great variety of opinions and practices among chaplains, some chaplains advocating class teaching, others swearing by cellular instruction, some bringing in outside clergy to bring moral influence to bear on prisoners, some not, some having assistance of scripture readers to visit and counsel prisoners, some having no help.

Although under Du Cane the Prison Commission had tried to standardise practice so that all within the age and sentence length qualifications received instruction according to the elementary standards laid down by the state as desirable for education in schools, there was obviously great diversity in practice in prisons. However, all agreed that the education of prisoners ought to be part of a more general attempt to uplift the prisoner morally and spiritually. Thus, apart from schoolmasters' instruction in basic skills of literacy and numeracy, which was intended to increase capacity to cope with life's social and economic demands, contact with chaplains, school-masters and outside lecturers was intended to show prisoners the wonderful complexity of God's universe and to demonstrate the power for good of God's ministers' and teachers' concern for them. As the Chaplain of Winchester put it: 'in going into their cells I teach those that are willing to learn . . . I have taught them astronomy or physiology. I find that, if I can show these men that I take an interest in them and let them see that I wish to do them good, then I can lay hold of them'.[5] Prisoners were now encouraged to reflect upon a particular subject and by use of new visual and other teaching aids to learn to appreciate the wonders of the least parts of God's world: as one young prisoner later commented; 'the schoolmaster is giving some very good lectures all about living creatures in the ponds and ditches and it is very interesting. He explains everything about them, how they live and all and he has taken the trouble to magnify and photo them on glass and shows them on a lantern'.[6]

There had been much criticism of the basic education of the schoolmaster and schoolmistress warders at the time of the Gladstone Committee. Some doubted that these were competent to teach, assess and examine in accordance with the requirements of a reformed prison education system. So, the Chaplain of Liverpool complained that their general standard of practice 'would be laughed at' if applied 'in any dame's school'[7] and other critics reported that schoolmaster warders were often deployed on other work by those governors who gave education low priority.[8] A persistent complaint was that, because of the four month sentence qualification, only a small proportion were eligible for instruction—at Knutsford Prison in 1895 only 25 men out of 370 and 9 women out of 69 qualified.[9] Others complained that classes for convicts had been relegated to the evenings and that after the daily labour the convicts were too tired to participate.[10]

The Prison Commission decided that their educational system must be brought into line with the code of precisely differentiated standards applied in English schools so that more prisoners would be, at the very least, enabled 'to read and write easily' and to do 'simple calculations in money'.[11] Therefore the four month sentence qualification was reduced to three and it was resolved that all candidates for the post of schoolmaster/mistress warder must henceforth be certified as suitable by the State Education Authority and that the post itself should be upgraded.[12] It was accepted that numbers taught would remain small for 62 per cent of men and 70 per cent of women were in fact serving very short sentences of two weeks or less, 94 per cent and 98 per cent respectively three months or less. Consequently by 1900 all local prisoners who qualified were divided into one of four educational groups (illiterate, standard 1, 2 and 3) and taught either in cells or in groups up to fifteen in number, all being tested periodically for progress. All prisoners whether convict or local who were under 16 were to be taught in class for one hour a day and every convict of whatever age who was not competent to standard three was to receive cellular individual instruction twice a week.[13] In 1900 the Visiting Chaplain reported that nearly four thousand prisoners had improved by one standard, over two thousand by two and nearly seven hundred and fifty by three.[14]

As indicated, between 1895 and 1914, the overall aim was a wider improvement by instruction and education than just literacy and numeracy progress. The Gladstone Committee had believed that prisoners should be uplifted morally by earnest, reflective and knowledgeable discourses both by prison governors and chaplains and by outside philanthropically minded experts on particular subjects. A major part of the endeavour was instruction in Christian truth and theology which again came to the fore and which was carried out by chaplains and outside clergy invited in by them. Throughout the prisons a much more systematic and confident exposition of Christianity was apparent between 1895 and 1914 with chaplains giving courses of lectures on all manner of Christian subjects. Furthermore, chapels were beautified and a greater emphasis put upon Holy Communion, confirmation, music and liturgy. Prisoners' responses to all these things were carefully noted and reported. Thus the Visiting Chaplain claimed that they were 'exceedingly fond of the singing and musical portions of the service . . . hearty in their responses and following with close attention the reading of the biblical lessons' and outside clergy were regularly called into the prisons throughout England to supplement the work of the chaplains. As the chaplain of Canterbury prison explained: 'the giving of ghostly advice from a prison chapel pulpit by clergy other than the chaplain, if only from its freshness, is highly appreciated by prisoners and . . . is, in the case of some attentive listeners, highly resultful'.[15] Another chaplain of Cambridge enthusiastically reported great interest one Ash Wednesday when 'I tried the experiment of having the Commination Service'![16] In many prisons weekly classes of instruction were held on the Creed or the Gospels and great thought was given to the sermons preached. So, at Leeds the chaplain 'preached three courses of sermons on Coming to Christ, My Duty Towards God and My Duty Towards My Neighbour. At other times I have taken courses on the Sacraments, the Lord's Prayer, the Parables, the Lessons of Our Lord's Life and Ministry and The Lives of The Apostles'.[17] At Oxford on Good Friday the chaplain used a magic lantern to show pictures of Christ's passion.[18]

Chaplains also, as in the early Victorian era, again gave lengthy courses of lectures on temperance, virtue, the evils of gambling, industry and sexual morality. At Liverpool therefore the chaplain lectured on 'fresh air, bad language, food, the origin of life, unselfishness, the Gift of Life, Truth, Honesty, Courage, Manliness, Energy, Perseverance, Books, Politeness' and other subjects[19] and in this connection chaplains generally began to bring in outside lecturers as Gladstone had recommended. So in 1900 at Aylesbury female convict prison the chaplain on the staff of Field Marshal Earl Roberts in South Africa 'gave a most touching account of aspects of the soldiers' religious life at the front which greatly pleased, as some of the women have sons and near relatives in the field'.[20] At Dartmoor the assistant chaplain brought outside lecturers into the prison to address young convicts so as to promote 'the mannerly and proper expression of ideas, thoughts and opinions'. The lectures were followed by discussion between young men and the chaplain and after one lecture on digestive processes 'Tetlow . . . and Page both gave personal experience of hypnotism and effect on mind and digestion' whilst another 'spoke of a human case of chewing the cud and desired to know if such would have any effect on progeny'. The chaplain in such situations was on guard for the introduction of ideas by outsiders which might call into question theological truths. So, at Dartmoor the assistant chaplain pointed out to the young convicts that 'the lecturer's remark that appendix in man is a relic of pre-animal existence need not necessarily mean man rose from an animal as Darwin put it'.[21]

Indeed, the Prison Commission kept anxious watch on the moral content of all lecture courses whether by chaplains or outside speakers and the chaplain of Knutsford was gently rebuked on Ruggles-Brise's instructions because he began to give resumes of outside news to prisoners: 'the problems of Persia' and 'the Chinese Loan' did not seem to the Commissioners to fulfil the condition of a 'useful moral lecture on the duties of self respecting men and good citizens'. The rueful chaplain replied that he had better henceforth 'turn my energies in another direction . . . I had better start golf to keep me out of mischief'.[22] Notwithstanding, by the end of Ruggles-Brise's period of office there was more encouragement to freedom of expression among prisoners. At a number of prisons organised debates were held on such subjects as 'state education, the war and class distinctions, professionalism in sport, trades unions, prohibition, gambling, will and fate' and the chaplain of Maidstone believed that these were 'of great value to a prisoner as a means of self expression and an opportunity of heading him away from excessive self-introspection'.[23]

The introduction of outside lecturers and visitors to English prisons was to have profound effects on prisons in the inter war years but even in these early days it was a change which was designed to bring the outside world into closer more paternal and inspiring contact with prisoners as the Gladstone Committee and the New Liberal philosophers desired. Perhaps the most striking change was the creation of 'Lady Visitors' who were intended to bring to bear on women prisoners, and later young males, educational instruction, moral exhortation and sympathetic understanding so as to inspire and improve. These 'Lady Visitors' were in part a response to Gladstone's criticisms about a lack of female presence at the Commission Headquarters for Ruggles-Brise relied heavily on the voluntary services of Adeline, Duchess of Bedford, to set up a nation wide system of these. By early 1897 there were nearly seventy of them in local and convict prisons and 'they cannot fail to produce excellent results among the outcast and unfortunate class, who, in the absence of such encouragement and advice, might lose the means of being saved from a life of crime and of being restored to an orderly and decent life'.[24] Furthermore, Ruggles-Brise used Adeline as a voluntary female advisor at headquarters: so she produced a report on inadequate nursing at Holloway prison in 1919 which had led to the deaths of a young girl and her baby, the girl having been left alone in Holloway and giving birth unexpectedly.[25]

In 1900 an association of these Lady Visitors was formed under the Presidency of The Duchess of Bedford and nearly every prison where women were held had a contingent of them working closely with chaplain and governor. At Aylesbury they provided materials to the women convicts out of which 'they dress dolls, make children's garments, petticoats and fancy articles' which were then sold and the money given to the convict on discharge.[26] By 1905 they were visiting many thousands of women annually and in nearly half the prisons of England were running lecture courses on 'temperance, domestic economy, hygiene, morality, self respect, intemperance, training of children': as one explained 'the women seem to follow every word you say and it is delightful to see them smile sometimes and still more delightful to hear them laugh. The women all sat on their stools in the corridors . . . I talked rather than lectured to them'.[27]

Lady Visitors' chief function however was to become a valued adviser and counsellor of individual women and to improve them by earnest and moral conversation, visit their families and bring news of these to the women. They also instructed women in their cells and some saw their prisoners weekly to discuss progress and corresponded with them on release.[28] They also made assessments of the women to the authorities and thus played a large part in placing of female convicts who were often sent to 'refuges' as preparation for final release from Aylesbury. So 'Jane Jones mother of four illegitimate children' was 'placed in St. John Baptist's Home for Fallen Women' whilst Kate Thorne, 'an intelligent young woman', who was allowed to return home was said by her parish priest to be 'doing well in a situation'.[29] So well known were these Lady Visitors by 1909 that the new Lady Inspector, Mary Gordon, was often mistaken for one by prisoners who asked her for clothes and money or began to tell her tearfully their life stories.[30]

Another example of the wider access to prisoners was the rapid growth of missions to prisons by the Church Army and other missionary bodies after 1895. So in November 1897 the Gloucester Diocesan Mission held a ten day mission at the local prison and in 1899 the Church Army sent a missioner to Dartmoor for eight days whose sermons, it was claimed, were listened to with 'marked attention' being 'much appreciated for their earnestness and intensive sympathy'.[31] By 1914 these lengthy missions were annual events at almost all prisons. The missioners such as Captain Hanson of the Church Army emphasised a vital passionate Evangelical appeal to the spirit, redemption from sin, the universal love of God and went to the prisoners in their cells as well as held revivalist services in the prison chapel.

Gladstone insisted upon moral improvement and spiritual growth by personal example and influence and it is clear that chaplains, scripture readers, visitors and missioners were encouraged to establish this by the Prison Commission which began to print lengthy reports of individual chaplains in their annual reports, which now grew to an immense length. The theme of these reports was that a moral and spiritual crusade was under way in the prison system with newly reconstituted services, visiting choirs to give concerts, courses of instruction, cellular visiting by chaplains and earnest philanthropists, teaching of Christian doctrine. So 'on Palm Sunday one church choir generously lent itself for the singing of Stainer's Crucifixion and a very impressive effect was produced. The kindness of the choir greatly pleased and touched the prisoners'; choirs of prisoners themselves sang at services and to prison hospital patients; prayer groups were formed 'for those who are in spiritual or mental trouble ... prisoners have learnt how to pray, to take an interest in the work of God in others and to find out their own stumbling blocks to repentance';[32] carol services were held; temperance pledges taken. As the chaplain of Nottingham reflected 'I was deeply impressed with the way in which they sang the Story of The Cross on Good Friday ... far more beautiful sights of penitence have been witnessed in prison ... than I, for one, ever experienced in parochial life': (in my cellular visits I find them) 'extremely sensitive of any kindness shown to them' possessed of 'sterling good qualities' which the world refused to see because the prisoner 'is deemed so black and so hopeless of reformation'.[33] In 1913 the chaplain of Wandsworth, who had joined the service in 1877, reflected that in his young days penal servitude had been so severe as to drive convicts to acts of self-mutilation or brutishness: now 'their intellectual, moral and spiritual welfare is anxiously studied' and 'gentle and more humane methods' and 'greater attention to the temperament and peculiarities of the prisoners' prevailed.[34]

There were very striking similarities between all this and the early Victorian prison discourses and indeed the Lady Visitors' Association brings to mind the work of Elizabeth Fry and her associates. Another similarity was the publication by the Prison Commission of letters sent to prison chaplains and missioners—something which had been last done by the Convict Prison Directorate in the 1840s and 1850s. So one prisoner wrote 'I was a miserable wretch through my own fault, without a friend, my home sold, my character gone, my wife nearly leaving me and all through the accursed drink ... listening to you morning after morning ... I began to look at things a little different ... so I determined by God's help to make another start'.[35] Another wrote that the chaplain had reconciled him and his wife and wished to express gratitude.[36] Another commented 'I often think of you, particularly on those dark evenings when you will be taking your classes; in fact I sometimes wish I was back with you and often hum over the old tunes I learned there'.[37] After the outbreak of war letters arrived from soldiers in the trenches. 'I can assure you that I always think of the good advice you gave me. I have been having a very rough time ... they have chipped a lump out of me'.[38] Another wrote 'a few lines to let you know that I am A1. I am here now and I am trying to do my very best for my King and Country. Hoping to hear from you as early as possible ... I am a bit of a devil when I am drunk. But I am teetotal now'.[39] Another sent a photograph of himself and 'a few shillings' as a contribution to prisoners' aid.[40]

The Gladstone Committee had urged that the supply of books to prisoners be improved and in this endeavour also the earnest moral approach was plain as the prison libraries, of which each prison had at least one, were expanded. In the first place in every cell was placed a bible, prayer book (for Catholics The Garden of The Soul) and hymn book together with at least one text conducive to spiritual and moral uplift—for Roman Catholics 'Think Well On't', for Anglicans 'The Narrow Way', for non conformists 'Pilgrim's Progress' as well as a book given to every prisoner called 'The Healthy Home and How to Keep it'. Secondly there were manuals of instruction and text books used in connection with education.[41]

However each prison also maintained a library of novels and bound journals which was superintended by the chaplain who, after 1898, decided upon acquisitions. Access to this was restricted because no local prisoner was allowed such literature during the first twenty eight days, thereafter permitted one book a week rising to two. Since 81 per cent of prisoners in

1911 were serving one month or less such books did not reach the great majority.[42]

For convicts and longer sentence local prisoners these novels and journals were a very important relief from the monotony of long periods of cellular confinement. Indeed in local prisons two hours a day were available for reading, in convict prisons three. Chaplains were particularly concerned that no book which glorified vice or crime or explained criminal methods should get into the library. So, they and the schoolmaster and librarian warders who assisted them spent much time removing from the regular journals any material deemed unsuitable. Some less cautious chaplains, who asked whether they might purchase 'Raffles' or 'Robbery Under Arms' 'on the ground that the evil doer comes to a bad end', were reminded by the Chaplain Inspector that these books were most unsuitable in that they portrayed 'the singular picturesqueness of the antecedent career of successful crime'.[43]

Some of the books most commonly found in these libraries had a plain moral message such as Charles Reade's 'It's Never Too Late To Mend'. There was also a tendency to stock 'stories of a healthy bracing outdoor kind'[44] such as the Henty sagas of derring do and imperial mission and large numbers of such books found their way to prison. For the highly educated prisoners historical and philosophical works by such as Macauley, Burke, Gibbon, J.S. Mill were often available and for illiterate prisoners 'pictorial magazines and catalogues, maps and puzzles' were provided, some of which were scrap books made up of illustrations cut out of condemned volumes.[45]

There was a belief that fiction could have a particularly profound effect upon prisoners in their separate cells, a 'vivid reality', and the aim was to capitalise on this by providing 'descriptions by good novelists of the incidents of a society in which certain standards of manners and conduct are habitually observed' so as 'insensibly to elevate the mind'.[46] Indeed Dickens, Thackeray, Scott, Shakespeare, Pope and Chaucer were in the libraries of many prisons: presumably the behaviour of MacBeth or Richard III did not count as a bad literary example. The most popular writers apparently included Dickens, Henty, Haggard, Scott, Wilkie Collins and Dumas; Boys' Own Paper was also popular.[47]

In the convict prisons by 1911 catalogues of the books were made available and the convict noted regularly on the slate kept outside the cell the books wanted. In the local prisons it was more haphazard and as late as the 1920s some libraries were crammed with 'dull, closely printed, out of date educational and scientific works' dumped on the prisons by schools no longer wanting them.[48] Not all prisoners were inclined to the moral or dull reading experience planned for them and on the slates at some convict prisons would appear demands for 'a book about pirates', 'plenty of female pictures' and 'plenty of murders'.[49]

The reality was often very different to the official version of a crusade for mind and soul and the nature of the actual engagement between chaplains and prisoners will be discussed in chapter 9. However, for the officials the difficulties were great and much conflict was generated over the many profound issues raised by the new approach.

In the first place it proved difficult to create and maintain the kind of personal sympathetic relationship envisaged because there were too few chaplains. Even in Parkhurst convict prison with a long term population the chaplain was only able to visit each convict five times a year and at Dartmoor in 1910 Ruggles-Brise was angered by the failure of the chaplain to carry out his visits thoroughly. 'I am not sure', he wrote, 'if Mr Pigott has the energy or power for a large convict pr. tho'. no doubt he means well. I think D'moor is too big and important for him'.[50] Furthermore, many prisoners seemed to chaplains hopelessly ignorant or spoiled by environment. These the chaplain at Leeds described as characterised by 'utter absence of spiritual sense due to utter neglect of religious education in childhood, the in-numerable temptations to drink, dishonesty and immorality'.[51] Others were defiant or contemptuous seeing religion as a 'thing invented by the clergy to get a tit-bit for themselves' appearing wholly materialistic in outlook, embittered against society for 'their present trouble' and determined to return to crime on release.[52] On occasion there were also complaints from the Lady Inspector that the Lady Visitors often tended to visit the women towards the end of their sentence rather than, as had been intended, throughout it.[53]

As religious and voluntary bodies became more deeply involved between 1895 and 1914 disputes increased. The established Discharged Prisoners Aid Societies which had been working for many decades and which will be discussed in chapter 14 often resented the new prison visitors and felt, as at Wandsworth, that these creamed off the most hopeful prisoners and acted without reference to the older aid societies.[54] Furthermore there were at times disputes between religious organizations and the Prison Commission. So in 1899 the Catholic chaplain at Parkhurst complained that he was underpaid and in 1910 the Catholic chaplain at Manchester threatened a public scandal over his remuneration ultimately complaining to the Home Secretary and his bishop of 'cruel and irreligious persecution' by the Commission and sending to the Home Secretary copies of his rates demands and bank overdrafts.[55] Ruggles-Brise indeed feared that the Catholic bishops would cease to sanction appointments[56] and in March 1910 the Treasury agreed to increase the salary of five full time Catholic chaplains to the same level as the Anglicans.

The non conformist groups observed the rebirth of the prison crusade with keen interest. The policy of the Commission under Du Cane had been to allow ministers of such churches access on the specific request of a prisoner only, but not to allow the holding of services or more general entry for purposes of proselytisation. Non conformist prisoners were therefore deemed Anglican for the purposes of moral and spiritual care and the Home Office emphasised in 1900 that 'it is not desirable to multiply these prison ministers. There are sects innumerable and, even among the methodists, there are many sub (and antagonistic) divisions . . . if we allow one we have to allow them all'; indeed there were '360 religious bodies who individually claim to be the sole possessors of divine truth'.[57]

Between 1900 and 1914 the Methodists and the Free Church Council campaigned vigorously for increased access and false claims in the *Methodist Recorder* that such access had been granted angered the authorities greatly.[58] By 1913 the Wesleyans had set up a Prison Committee to press the issue and the Free Churches demanded that certain nominated ministers be allowed more general access. Questions were frequently asked about this in Parliament and eventually in 1913, under pressure from Ruggles-Brise, a scale of payment was agreed for those non conformist ministers visiting prisoners who asked for them.[59] In 1905 Wesleyan ministers had been allowed to address small groups of prisoners who asked for their ministry but not to hold services and indeed the governor of Parkhurst was earlier reprimanded for allowing one Wesleyan minister to hold a service.[60]

Another dispute developed over the pressure for access brought to bear by the Salvation Army. In the time of Du Cane a number of Salvationists had defied the law about public meetings on conscientious grounds and had been sent to prison. Du Cane and Godfrey Lushington therefore viewed them as anarchists and refused them the same access as had been agreed, on an individual basis, with the St. Giles Christian Mission which specialised in aftercare. There followed a long and confused dispute during which Herbert Gladstone as under secretary of state gave a consent, which he later had to retract, but eventually the Salvation Army was placed on the same basis of access allowed to any prisoner who asked for it as the other groups.[61]

With Jewish prisoners matters were easier, because the Commission recognised their status as it did Anglicans and Catholics. Nevertheless in 1894 pressure was exerted when Jewish convicts, who had been collected at Portsmouth for over thirty years, were moved to Parkhurst. Lord Rothschild and the Council of the United Synagogue sought to achieve a replacement of the unsalaried visiting rabbi at Portsmouth with a more permanent arrangement.[62] Eventually a full synagogue and a salaried rabbi came into being at Parkhurst, but generally relations between Ruggles-Brise and the Council of the United Synagogue were close—in 1901, for example, after consultation between the two, unleavened bread and roast beef were given to Jewish prisoners during passover.[63]

The new policy of wider access to outside educational groups also brought tension in its wake, for Ruggles-Brise was cautious about the granting of permits. So he only reluctantly admitted the Liverpool School of Cookery after the Home Secretary insisted, and nursing education groups found a similar reluctance.[64] Certainly later on he was suspicious that suffragette groups might gain access by posing as women's education groups but earlier he felt that there were insufficient staff to supervise all the classes now requested by voluntary groups: indeed there was an angry dispute between him and the Home Office when encouragement was given to the London School Board request to give evening lectures on 'commercial, scientific or other subjects' during his absence.[65]

Lastly there were of course occasions when the behaviour of personnel did not match the earnest, philanthropic and zealous image so vividly portrayed in the annual reports of the Commissioners. In the early 1920s the chaplain of Shrewsbury was forced to resign for 'supposed abominable and disgraceful indecency towards two boys' who were prisoners.[66] Around the same time a male prison visitor had to be refused further access to Birmingham prison after sensational newspaper reports of his adultery and violence to his wife together with a police report to the Home Office that he had called a constable 'the scum of the earth'.[67] A female voluntary teacher of typewriting to male and female prisoners at the same prison was banned following the discovery of 'a rubber appliance which is known as a French letter in (her) bag after she had visited the prison and . . . this letter had been apparently recently used'.[68]

By 1921 the work of chaplains, teachers and outside clergy and lecturers had become a stronger feature of the system and a few education groups of a more secular nature had gained a somewhat reluctant admission even though their teaching was not obviously moral or spiritual. Indeed, aware of Ruggles-Brise's caution regarding such groups, applicants for access learned to sway him with claims of likely moral improvement. Thus nursing educators successfully justified their appeal for access to women prisoners on the basis that nursing 'had a wondrously humanising result and rouses all that is best in a woman's nature'[69] and the Prison Commission were even prevailed upon to allow the use of 'the cinematograph' by the Church Army as part of its 'methods of spiritual warfare' in 1918.[70]

There had therefore been some success in mounting an improved reformatory system of spiritual address, moral uplift and educational work. There were however also fundamental problems with these educational and moral reformation projects. Chaplains were in the main unable to get to know each prisoner intimately because of the large number of prisoners for whom each chaplain was responsible. Furthermore at local prisons a high turn over rate increased this difficulty. Secondly, although the perception of chaplains among prisoners will be discussed in detail in chapter 9, it has to be said that the task itself was a very daunting and difficult one requiring great sensitivity and commitment. Clearly, many chaplains fell below the standard in the eyes of prisoners, some of whom remembered particular chaplains as judgemental and centring their sermons and individual admonitions on the imminence of hell fire for criminals, a version of religion described by one prisoner as a 'Mosaic conception of religion . . . divine morality of social vengeance . . . cold, formal and pharasaical . . . dead and powerless by virtue of the unbridgeable gulf which separated the warm patient love of Christ from its official caricature in prison'.[71] It must, however, be added, as will later be shown, that many prisoners regarded their chaplains with great fondness.

Thirdly it was clearly the case that the educational programme of the Prison Commission fell a long way short of the initial hopes. The Prison Commissioners devoted a great deal of effort to this between 1895 and 1914 and indeed in 1906 agreed that local prisoners eligible for education could be taught in associated classes rather than in cells. However the outbreak of the Great War led to reductions of male staff and, apart from younger prisoners, the educational classes given by schoolmaster warders were 'almost entirely discontinued'.[72] In 1919 the educational system was revived but education then was only granted to those up to the age of 25 (instead of 40 as before) although the three month sentence qualification was reduced. In general there was a great deal of concern about the work of schoolmaster/mistress warders/wardresses despite the Commissioners' insistence that these should be tested by the state. In late 1921 the Board of Education were highly critical in reports to the Home Office of what the Board saw as the unacceptably low standard of their work.[73] There were also concerns about out of date, dull, inappropriate library stocks and defective allocation of books to prisoners.[74] Lastly it was clearly the case that financial and manpower resources devoted to these projects were insufficient for their successful operation and that requirements of security, order and discipline at times led to education being set aside in their favour: indeed Ruggles-Brise was himself very insistent that security should not be disrupted by outside education groups.[75] The kind of chaplain who disliked and distrusted prisoners in any case[76] was scarcely likely to fight to protect such projects although others stood their ground more forcefully.

These theological and educational endeavours as well as the substantial problems with them have been described in detail because the Prison Commission consistently emphasised that these projects lay at the heart of their reformatory endeavours. Indeed the priority attached to them illustrates plainly the highly traditional approach to reformation advocated by the Commission for these projects irresistibly remind the writer of the early Victorian reformatory endeavour with its emphasis an evangelical chaplains, education, the British Ladies Association and so forth. In point of fact therefore the Prison Commission were seeking to resurrect old methods and indeed the Gladstone Committee itself had supported the idea that the old methods tried at Pentonville model prison in the 1840s should be re-introduced.[77] The advocacy of these approaches, the methods applied and the problems encountered with them and even the phraseology employed in fact show that these projects were as much a revival of old approaches as a new departure. Furthermore they graphically illustrate the truth of the emphasis of Radzinowicz and Hood on the traditional classicism of penal policy making during the Ruggles-Brise era.[78] Indeed these endeavours depended upon the notion of moral and spiritual rebirth through divine grace and revelation, of enlightenment, knowledge and progress through education and of gratitude, uplift and determination to make a new beginning through the example and earnest exhortation of pious and worthy visitors. These notions were the very soul of early Victorian reformatory projects before the scepticism of the Du Cane era all but overwhelmed them.

## NOTES

1. Report of the Departmental Committee on the Education and Moral Instruction of Prisoners in Local and Convict Prisons, PP 1895, XLIV.
2. Ibid: 6-10.
3. Ibid: 13.
4. Ibid: 13.
5. Ibid. Minutes of Evidence: 37.
6. RCP & DCP yr end 31 March 1907, PP 1908, LII: 264.
7. Committee on the Education and Moral Instruction of Prisoners, PP 1895, XLIV, Minutes of Evidence: 33.
8. Ibid: 53-4, 115.
9. Ibid: 27-8.
10. Ibid: 79.
11. Statement of the Prison Commissioners of the Action which has been taken up to January 1898 to carry out the recommendations of the Departmental Committee on Prisons, PP 1898, XLVII: 13-14.
12. RCP & DCP yr end 31 March 1898, PP 1898, XLVII: 24-5.
13. Ibid. App. 25: 154-6.
14. RCP & DCP yr end 31 March 1901, PP 1902, XLV: 43.
15. RCP & DCP yr end 31 March 1899, PP 1899, XLIII: 31. RCP & DCP yr end 31 March 1901, PP 1902, XLV: 217.
16. RCP & DCP yr end 31 March 1901, PP 1902, XLV: 210.

17. RCP & DCP yr end 31 March 1902, PP 1902, XLVI: 371.
18. RCP & DCP yr end 31 March 1907, PP 1908, LII: 320.
19. RCP & DCP yr end 31 March 1907, PP 1908, LII: 289.
20. RCP & DCP yr end 31 March 1901, PP 1902, XLV: 540.
21. PRO P.Com. 7/281, Class for Mental Intercourse Among Juvenile Adults, Oct. 1910.
22. PRO P.Com. 7/317, PC Minute Capt. Wilmot, 3 Oct. 1912. Chaplain Knutsford Prison to Chaplain Inspector PC, 25 Oct. 1912.
23. RCP & DCP yr end 31 March 1921, PP 1921, XVI: 21-2.
24. RCP & DCP yr end 31 March 1897, PP 1897, XL: 29.
25. Nursing Staff in Prisons, PRO HO 45-10429-A53867. E. Ruggles-Brise to HO 18 June 1919. Enquiry into Holloway Prison by the Duchess of Bedford 1919, PRO P. Com 7/57.
26. RCP & DCP yr end 31 March 1901, PP 1902, XLV: 33.
27. RCP & DCP yr end 31 March 1905, PP 1906, L: 46. *Law Times,* 17 Nov. 1906, 122: 67.
28. PRO P. Com. 7/595.
29. Report of the Lady Visitor to Aylesbury 1897-8, PRO HO 45-9750-A58684.
30. Lady Visitors, PRO P.Com. 7/174, PC Minute, Dr M. Gordon to Chaplain Inspector, 9 Feb. 1909.
31. RCP & DCP yr end 31 March 1898, PP 1898, XLVII: 246. RCP & DCP yr end 31 March 1899, PP 1899, XLIII: 496.
32. RCP &DCP yr end 31 March 1904, PP 1905, XXXVII: 45, 46.
33. Ibid: 429-30.
34. RCP & DCP yr end 31 March 1913, Pt 2, PP 1914, XLV: 95-6.
35. RCP & DCP yr end 31 March 1909, Pt 1, PP 1909, XLV: 38-9.
36. RCP & DCP yr end 31 March 1898, PP 1898, XLVII: 350.
37. RCP & DCP yr end 31 March 1914, Pt 2, PP 1914, XLV: 125.
38. RCP & DCP yr end 31 March 1915, PP 1914-16 XXXIII: 35.
39. Ibid.
40. Ibid.
41. Report of the Departmental Committee on the Supply of Books to the Prisoners in HM Prisons and Borstals, PP 1911, XXXIX.
42. Ibid: 5-6.
43. Ibid: 15.
44. Ibid: 25.
45. Ibid: 18, 7.
46. Ibid: 8.
47. Ibid: 33. RCP & DCP yr end 31 March 1899, PP 1899, XLIII: 32.
48. L. Le Mesurier, *Boys in Trouble* (Murray 1931): 98.
49. J.S. Balfour, *My Prison Life* (Chapman & Hall 1907): 346.
50. PRO P.Com. 7/437, PCMinute, E. Ruggles-Brise to Chaplain Inspector, 16 April 1910.
51. RCP & DCP yr end 31 March 1904, PP 1905, XXXVII: 362.
52. RCP & DCP yr end 31 March 1899, PP 1899, XLIII: 486.
53. PRO P.Com 7/174, Minute Dr M. Gordon to Chaplain Inspector, 9 Feb. 1909.

54. PRO P.Com 7/590, Wandsworth DPAS to R. Mitford, 13 Nov. 1901.
55. PRO HO 45-10431-A58001 Parkhurst Catholic Chaplain petition to PC 10 Oct. 1899. PRO HO 45-10431-A58001, Manchester Catholic Chaplain Petition to Home Secretary, 16 Feb. 1910, 29 Jan. 1910.
56. PRO HO 45-10431-A58001, E. Ruggles-Brise to HO, 30 Jan. 1900.
57. PRO P.Com 7/445, G.P. Murdock to E. Ruggles-Brise, 21 March 1900.
58. PRO P.Com 7/445, PC Minute, 12 Sept. 1902.
59. PRO P.Com 7/446, E. Ruggles-Brise to HO, 23 Dec. 1913.
60. PRO P.Com 7/445, E. Ruggles-Brise to R. Mitford 5 Aug. 1903.
61. PRO HO 45-9739-A54979, Salvation Army Officers Visiting Prisoners.
62. PRO HO 45-9743-A56064/1, Allowances to Jewish and Roman Catholic Chaplains 1894, PC obs no date, referred by HO 5 July 1894; A.L. Emmanuel to Treasury 21 June 1894, /2 Council United Synagogue to Lord Rothschild, 26 July 1894.
63. PRO P.Com 7/443, Jewish Prisoners PC Circular 22 Jan. 1901, Council of United Synagogue to PC 3 Sept. 1900.
64. Evening Schools at Prisons, PRO HO 45-9751-A59262/1, PC obs, 22 Sept. 1897, HO Minute 30 Nov. 1897. /2 Miss Honnor Morten to HO, 27 March 1898.
65. Ibid. /5 HO to Clerk to London School Board 5 Sept. 1899. /6 E. Ruggles-Brise to HO 13 Dec. 1899. /8 Clerk London School Board to H.Sec., 7 March 1900.
66. PRO HO 45 -24729-406711/1.
67. Two Unsuitable Visitors at Birmingham, PRO HO 45-12119-479817. Cut. *Evening Dispatch* 20 Feb. 1923. Chief Constable Birmingham to HO, 20 June 1925.
68. Ibid. Chief Constable Birmingham to HO, 2 June 1925.
69. PRO HO 45-9751-A59262/2, Miss Honnor Morten to HO, 27 March 1898.
70. PRO P.Com. 7/444, Church Army Missions to Prisons 1915-18. PC Minute, 27 Nov. 1918.
71. S. Wood, *Glorious Liberty: Dartmoor to Calvary* (Hodder & Stoughton 1933): 67-8.
72. Hobhouse and A.F. Brockway, (eds.) *English Prisons Today* (Longman, Green & Co. 1922): 153.
73. Education in Prisons, PRO HO 45-24800-447129/7, Board of Education to Home Office, 20 Oct. 1921.
74. Hobhouse and Brockway, *English Prisons*: 160-1
75. Evening Schools at Prisons, PRO HO 45-9751-A59262/6, E. Ruggles-Brise to Home Office, 13 Dec. 1899.
76. Viscountess Rhondda, *This Was My World* (MacMillan 1933): 157. C. Lytton, *Prisons and Prisoners* (Heinemann 1914): 120-1.
77. Departmental Committee on Prisons, PP 1895, LVI: 28.
78. L. Radzinowicz and R. Hood, *A History of the English Criminal Law and its Administration from 1750*, vol. 5, *The Emergence of Penal Policy* (Stevens & Sons 1986): 598.

# Chapter Nine

# Staff and Prisoners 1895–1921

Prison chaplains were aware of the mental scientific and social diagnostic concerns of eugenists and positivist criminologists, although their own approach centred upon a theological view of environmental temptation of the individual towards the stumbling blocks of sin such as intemperance and lasciviousness. Their theological emphasis upon sin inducing environment incidentally played a part in paving the way for the secular social diagnosticians of the inter war years in the same way as the redemptionist police court missionaries laid the foundation for their successors, the more secular probation officers.[1] However, as far as positivist constitutional criminology was concerned, very few prison chaplains were persuaded by the Lombrosian view that many criminals were prenatally fixed in their criminality and detectable by their appearance, although one chaplain was convinced that criminals were born with a predisposing 'anatomico-pathology' and could be detected on sight by their 'cat like, cold, glassy, fixed, ferocious ... penetrating gaze'.[2] The great majority of chaplains dismissed Lombroso's theories as 'tommy rot', but many of them, at the time of the Great War, did take seriously later constitutional psychological theorising, such as that of Charles Goring, that criminals tended to have a lower intelligence and 'physical, mental or moral' characteristics of a lower order.[3] The chaplain of Parkhurst described most of the convicts there in terms similar to those used by eugenists—'social derelicts to a great extent, physically and mentally unfit'.[4]

Notwithstanding, up to 1921 the overall tendency of the work of chaplains was traditional evangelical redemption based on a view of environment inducing sin. So the chaplain must try to excavate 'the underlying better part which has been so thickly bedded over with evil for so many years' and must believe that there was good within each, even though 'the filth and dirt of years of a sinful, careless and self indulgent life may need much shovelling away in order that the smothered germ of good may be brought to light and air'.[5] Here was represented the belief in the satanic cunning by which evil triumphed, the idea that Lucifer led the sinner progressively into a deepening mire of sin, fostered by parents who encouraged sin or did not check it, and the vicious self indulgent neighbourhoods in which such things flourished. So the child began to miss Sunday school to join bad company, was invited to see petty pilfering as 'a smart bit of business', began to steal, was sent to a Reformatory, learned more criminal attitudes and skills from the other boys or girls and so at last came to a life of prison and penal servitude as the habit of crime became fixed.[6]

With this dramatic albeit sombre news chaplains confronted prisoners in sermons, lectures and individual encounters and urged upon them that descent into the kingdom of Lucifer was inevitable to all men unless they reached out to tap the boundless waters of God's mercy and love and begged for the redemption promised to all through Christ's sacrifice. This survival of the universalism of the Wilberforcean evangelicals was of great importance to some prisoners who were very aware that they were not the only sinners: Jock of Dartmoor particularly valued a Church Army Captain who helped him to reflect that there were many worse sinners outside the prison than he.[7]

Many chaplains were aware that large numbers of prisoners initially saw them as merely another group of paid officials of the penal system and they tried hard to convince their prisoners that theirs was a spiritual mission concerned with the value of each individual. One Dartmoor chaplain spent most of his evenings visiting convicts in their cells to 'hear a good deal concerning the past and advise as to the future' and was struck by their openness and honesty.[8] From some he got gentle sarcasm as they wondered what would become of prison chaplains if convicts did all suddenly reform and was regaled with vast knowledge by others—Pliny, Sallust, Horace, German, French, one who could translate Vergil 'better than I could have done myself'.[9] From some he got despair: 'I don't want to leave . . . I dread what I shall have to face if I am discharged. No work for who will employ me? No home, no money, no friends. What can I do but starve or steal and that will be my fate. I dread it'.[10]

The arrangements in prisons scarcely conduced to a close and intimate relationship. For example, in the chapels the warders and wardresses sat closely watching the prisoners from 'box like contraptions set on stilts' listening and waiting for breaches of the rules, ready to bundle out those who, like some suffragettes, launched into their own prayer 'O Lord Save Emmeline Pankhurst. Give her strength to endure and bless her'.[11] Nonetheless chaplains thought deeply about the best way to appeal in their conversations and sermons. Some of them knew that prisoners had often been subjected to huge quantities of religious discourse over the years and had been told about hell fire or the prodigal son over and over again.

Furthermore, they knew that prisoners found many chaplains impossible to understand. So the Dartmoor chaplain argued to an outside colleague, about to speak to the prisoners, that they would not understand the word 'felicity'. He had to prove his point by the two men asking a Dartmoor farmer if he understood it. 'I don't rightly know', said the man, 'but I know its something inside a pig'.[12] They also realised that apparently very suitable anecdotes could have unexpected results: so the story of the King of France pardoning the only prisoner who admitted the justice of his sentence prompted a long letter to the Home Secretary in the same vein from one hopeful convict![13] Furthermore, tales from the bible had to be selected with great care. One elderly outside clergyman was greeted with roars of disbelieving laughter when he said that Daniel actually put his hand in the lion's mouth[14] and chaplain Rickards of Dartmoor always tried to illuminate biblical passages with reference to the experiences of the prisoners—so the text in St. James' third epistle, 'we put bits in the horses' mouths and we turn about their whole body also', was related to control of horses on the prison farm by prisoners.[15]

At the heart of all this was the urgent call of God to the suffering sinner, a God who would shoulder the despair and misery of a sinful life if only the penitent would knock upon the door; and the message that, without enlisting God in the war against sin, all were lost, for the temptations of the world were too full of lascivious attractions to be resisted by unaided mortal man. In particular chaplains called to the feelings of prisoners for themselves and their loved ones, the years of betrayed beloved parents, wives and children and urged the personal love of Christ for each, the Christ who died a rejected criminal. Indeed, at times, poems and writings of prisoners showed that the words had not been in vain.

> 'Now to Calvary mount,
> Ah! must it be
> That Jesus there must die
> All for me.
> Yes there between two thieves,
> My Saviour hangs
> For my sins he bears those
> Bitter pangs'.[16]

or another

> 'And Jesus who came down and died
> For such a one as I
> Will take me from the mire of sin
> And save me ere I die'.[17]

Chaplains also called upon the rationality of prisoners in an attempt to enable them to see that the actual steps of their lives could logically only end in the prison cell. This was a somewhat hazardous enterprise, for many prisoners were adroit at logical analysis of criminality. So chaplain Rickards urged that honest labour earned more than crime, a view indignantly disputed by convicts urging examples of burglars of their acquaintance living in luxury at home.[18] Another urged that God's law was against theft and was told that the prisoner did not believe that God existed and thus was free to do as he pleased.[19] Another pointed out that all that was needed was to desist from pick pocketing and was told 'Lor' bless you chaplain, we don't pick pockets; we take them as they come! We've all got to get our living somehow; if it wasn't for us chaps you'd lose your job'.[20]

Prisoners reflected on what they had heard and came to a decision about it but there was much humour and folk lore about chaplains in prisons. Oscar Wilde apparently overheard the prisoner in the cell below him expressing the hope that the ravens which fed Elijah (as described in the day's sermon) would feed him also. Wilde lowered some fruit and sweets on a string and was delighted to hear the prisoner below exclaim 'Blimey . . . the bloomin' dickey's darn well come'.[21] Others recalled a convict who had worked out various statistics about the bible, such as that there were 181,258 words in the New Testament of which the shortest verse was John 11 v 35 'Jesus Wept', adding 'with a sidelong look at the screw . . . and well he might if there were people about in those days like there are now'.[22]

Prisoners carefully assessed their chaplain as to the relevance of his words to them and his ability to speak plainly and simply. On this latter score prisoner Frederic Martyn believed that most prison chaplains were 'round pegs in square holes' with tendencies to incomprehensible doctrinal exposition, but he recalled one who spoke 'very straight to the prisoners' about the harmful results of theft with the outcome that one prisoner said to him that 'thieving was about as mean and unmanly a game as the parson . . . said it was'.[23] Others dismissed the chaplain as speaking 'such bloody nonsense' and complained about 'the same blasted 'ymns every week—why can't 'e give 'em a rest'. An elderly female recidivist reflected, 'they mean well but, as far as actions go, it is years since they have given a person anyfink to go out with. Let 'em jore . . . after all . . . they're paid for it and 'e 'as a family at 'ome'.[24]

Prisoners overwhelmingly praised chaplains who spoke directly, sensitively, simply and sincerely and whose attitudes to prisoners were consistent with their words, who did not side with the staff against them but who were able nevertheless to be blunt and firm in the face of trickery or deception. They even singled out such men as very important to their mental and spiritual survival of the sentence and the standard set by prisoners was clearly exceedingly hard to reach. Frederic Martyn said that many prisoners were ashamed to return to Wormwood Scrubs because their reconviction so obviously distressed the chaplain there.[25] Another recalled that the Catholic chaplain at Parkhurst was greatly respected as 'genial and cheery' but also as one who would confront misconduct 'in a very straight forward manner'.[26] Governor Major Blake recalled that one chaplain was respected for his refusal to put up with hypocrisy and, when a prisoner tried to wheedle his way into the man's favour by claiming that during the sermon 'I could feel the 'oly spirit descending', the chaplain, 'a look of intense annoyance on his face, interrupted him' and exclaimed "Oh chuck it" . . . and passed on'.[27] Jock of Dartmoor considered that chaplain Beckett there had saved 'not only my reason but also my soul . . . he gave me the impression that for two pins he'd knock hell out of me unless I was prepared to become a man again . . . I told him my story and of the canker eating into my soul'.[28]

Chaplains worked in their most difficult ministry entirely untrained for prison work and largely unsupervised by the outside church. At times, they were abused and insulted sometimes as a result of a thoughtless word or phrase. One visiting preacher was astonished in the midst of his sermon when a bomb maker suddenly roared out 'vive l'anarchie, à bas la religion'.[29] A chaplain at Wormwood Scrubs had a boot thrown at his head in chapel after admonishing a prisoner.[30] Another reflected in a service that Britain ruled a free and just empire and was nearly attacked by a Polish prisoner who roared at him that there was no law or justice in England.[31]

Prisoners also recorded in great detail those who were severely judgemental or condescendingly pious for they regarded these attitudes as a departure from true Christian spirit. Suffragettes recalled that one chaplain refused books to hunger strikers and was 'the only unpleasant person in the whole prison . . . and began not merely by abusing me and all suffragettes . . . but by abusing my father too'.[32] Constance Lytton recalled a chaplain who emphasised the wickedness of prisoners in his sermon. 'At this remark, an old woman stood up. She was tall and gaunt, her face seamed with life, her hands gnarled and worn . . . the tears streamed down her furrowed cheeks as she said in a pleading, reverent voice. "Oh Sir, don't be so hard on us". The wardresses at once came up to her, took her by the shoulders and hustled her out'. Lytton contemptuously contrasted this with the same man's unctuousness to herself as an aristocrat asking for library books. 'Your Ladyship is such a good judge of literature. I shall leave the choice of books entirely to you'.[33] In another prison she was appalled when the chaplain confessed to her that he saw female prisoners as unreformable and indeed elsewhere communion was peremptorily denied to suffragettes who would not admit the evil of their conduct: other prisoners recalled chaplains generally perceived as ignorant and condescending with some as callously insensitive, preaching at prisoners condemned to death that 'the wages of sin is death'.[34]

The missionary project also included an emphasis on forgiveness by prisoners of those who had trespassed against them and the urging of a constant comparison between the self and the perfect Christ. So, chaplains quoted case examples of those prisoners who had learned to forgive drunken violent fathers and unyielding severe mothers[35] and published letters of ex-prisoners whose view of themselves had changed. 'I thank God that through your teaching and advice I have been led to think and meditate and rightly understand what I ought to be . . . since I have been in prison God has blessed me beyond all I could have dreamt of'.[36] Some chaplains withheld the sacraments until reparation was made. Thus an Exeter chaplain refused to admit a man and woman to communion until they had authorised the governor to repay the money in his possession to the victim of their deception.[37]

Plainly chaplains were more optimistic about young prisoners and first timers but, nevertheless, at Dartmoor with its recidivist and intermediate convict classes the chaplains insisted that convicts were more 'to be pitied than blamed'[38] as victims of bad parents, slums, unemployment and drink and emphasised the wonderful power of God to transform human life. Indeed, this optimism had to be transmitted to those in the most hopeless prison situation, that of those awaiting execution, for the chaplain at local prisons where executions occurred, must minister to them and attend at their death.

It is difficult to conceive of the impact on all concerned of this, yet prisoners, governors and chaplains were precise about it. Prior to an execution 'an atmosphere of silent brooding' would often spring up among 'officers and men alike'[39] as the entire institution concentrated on two matters, the likelihood of reprieve and the preparations for the death sentence to be carried out. As each day passed there increased a 'dreadful consciousness' of the approaching execution[40] and there was a tendency for the 'silent brooding' to be interrupted by sudden outbursts for prisoners became 'restless and undisciplined' and warders 'ill tempered and bullying'.[41] On each Sunday the condemned attended chapel and sat in a red curtained pew beyond the sight of the rest,[42] the subject of intense concentration among them. The night before the execution was often disturbed, for many prisoners were deeply distressed or moved, and in the morning all prisoners were kept in cells for at least two hours extra until the death sentence had been carried out.[43] During this period a silence reigned over the prison as some watched every movement outside from their cell windows and others paced up and down deep in thought so that all that could be heard was the sound of footsteps.[44] Although the prison authorities tended to say that 'the man walked firmly to the scaffold' prisoners noted that this was not always the case and reported sounds of terror and struggle at the last moment as the offender was carried to the execution chamber.[45] At last amidst the 'dread silence . . . suddenly the hush is broken by the faint thud of the traps'.[46]

Not only prisoners were profoundly distressed by this but also staff. One principal warder told a prisoner that he could not sleep for many nights before and after an execution, because the face of the man appeared in the night to him and because he often became fond of the prisoner during the weeks of intimate involvement up to the execution.[47] Some chaplains, such as the one at Liverpool, found capital punishment a horrifying thing and the latter 'a sincere sensitive man . . . for days before an execution . . . went about with pain on his face and in his bearing'.[48] Yet the chaplain must minister to the prisoner to the end. Although some reported 'inhuman and unsympathetic' ministry and angry warders reproved such chaplains for their unchristian behaviour,[49] the general impression is that chaplains took their ministry very seriously. So, a curate who replaced the man referred to above 'was brotherly and humane and quite melted the negro, addressing him by his Christian name'[50] and in conversation with governors and others they pondered over the morality of capital punishment. The governor and chaplain at Pentonville visited a young man daily and after his execution admitted that each felt 'a bit of a murderer'.[51] Indeed governor Major Blake felt capital punishment to be 'morally and inherently wrong' and both he and his chaplain noted the simple gratitude expressed by a man actually on the way to the scaffold for their kindness to him.[52] Chaplains at times arranged for condemned prisoners to be confirmed by the local bishop and for special parental visits. As one mother wrote to a chaplain; 'You were a great comfort to him in teaching him the right way to save his soul . . . Oh how I should like to have had his body and buried him in our quiet church yard . . . Oh my trouble is hard to bear. Please again accept my thanks for your kindness to my darling boy'.[53] It is important to note that there was a spiritual reformatory mission at the heart of such involvement, that the sinner might repent and turn to Christ and his soul fly to the eternal bliss of the Heavenly Kingdom.

Turning now to warders it needs to be said that throughout Ruggles-Brise's period there were recurring tensions between the Prison Commission and the uniformed grades divided into chief, principal, ordinary and assistant warders. This was because hours of work were long and poorly paid and because warders of the lower grades were often severely punished by fines, reprimands and dismissal, without sufficient opportunity to defend themselves. Between 1895 and 1910 they were in effect dependent upon the fairness of superior staff and the Commissioners but in 1910 the Prison

Officers' Magazine was founded in part to express their discontent and in 1915 a Prison Officers' Federation was established. Three years later this body amalgamated with the National Union of Police and Prison Officers and the Commissioners sought to cut off this movement towards unionisation by setting up a Prison Officers' Representative Board, which had regular access to them to discuss pay and conditions of service. The Police and Prison Officers' Union refused to recognise this and in early August 1919 sixty eight warders at Wormwood Scrubs and six at Birmingham were accused of refusing to come on duty. All were dismissed and the entire warder staff warned by telegrams to all prisons that any refusal to come on duty or obey orders would be met with instant dismissal. So, between 1919 and Ruggles-Brise's retirement the sole recognised representative body of Prison Officers was the Representative Board elected by warders at each prison.[54] As records show this Board was no mere lapdog, but pressed the case for better conditions and reinstatement of the dismissed warders very hard.[55]

The Board was not only concerned with such things as a forty eight hour week, increased holiday leave, quarters and pensions, at times threatening to dissolve if the Commissioners did not respond to them more positively and swiftly,[56] but also after 1921 increasingly began to urge the adoption of reformatory measures. However, the difficulty for the historian is that warders individually, unlike chaplains and governors, did not tend to record their thoughts and aspirations in books or articles or even in prison records and it is thus harder to excavate precisely their role in the process of relaxation and reformation prior to 1921. J.E. Thomas studied warders between 1850 and the outbreak of the Second World War and he maintained that the Ruggles-Brise era placed them in an unenviable position. On the one hand, the official emphasis tended to be on cautious relaxation and reformatory projects, whilst on the other staff were increasingly tightly regulated so as to ensure that they carried out the more complex tasks required of them. He believed that, in general, prison warders were hostile to the reformatory project because they felt that they were increasingly unfavourably treated, as the emphasis in official reports came to be on the treatment of the prisoners.[57] Furthermore, he suggested that the bulk of the reformatory project was carried out by non warder grades such as governors, chaplains, borstal tutors, as well as by prison visitors and that in the educational field schoolmaster warders were never regarded as an acceptable alternative to certificated teachers. He argued that warders aimed to improve their position vis à vis these personnel and it is the case that in late 1921 the Prison Officers' Representative Board successfully persuaded the Commissioners to ask the Home Office to agree a change in title from warder to officer. This was reluctantly agreed by the Home Office although there were grumbles there that 'the next step wd. be for privates in the army to claim to be called officers, privates being a derogatory description for those who are doing public duty'.[58] In January of 1922 the change was made.

The fact of the matter is even more brutally simple in that warders, apart from schoolmaster/mistress warders and task instructors, were positively prohibited from conversation with prisoners except to give an order or deliver a rebuke. This policy had been in force in Du Cane's time and had not applied in the prisons run by the local magistrates before 1877 nor in the convict prisons before Du Cane. Despite Ruggles-Brise's claims to the contrary it is quite obvious that the authorities did not view warders as having the wisdom, knowledge or skill to participate substantially in the reformatory programmes which, of course, heavily depended upon word of mouth. Du Cane had not deemed it worthwhile to train warders, believing that they learned best by doing and seeing after appointment but Ruggles-Brise introduced training in accordance with Gladstone, initially at Chelmsford and Hull for men and Wormwood Scrubs for women. During the four month training warders heard lectures from governors and chaplains and had to pass examinations on standing orders as well as receiving instruction in the basic tasks of warders' work.[59] However, they were viewed as strictly regulated subordinate operatives of a system run by their superiors, the commissioners, governors and chaplains, and any discussion or intimacy with prisoners was severely punished. Indeed it has already been noted that warders often feared their principals more than the prisoners and they were at all times under close regulation. As Annie Kenney, the suffragette, remarked, wardresses led a 'dull, dreary, uneventful, enervating life' in an atmosphere of 'too much discipline, too little companionship, too much gloom, too little laughter'.[60]

The result of all this was that the interaction between warder and prisoner was a peculiar one with verbal deliveries similar to barked military command with explanations given where necessary as a slowly intoned simply expressed formula. Given that large numbers of male warders had come from the army, this was not difficult to learn. However, Constance Lytton reported that it was also characteristic of the speech of wardresses and described a typical exchange. She had asked for better fitting shoes and waited for the reply. 'She seemed not to have heard what I said, did not look my way, but shouted past me into the air, speaking in a loud voice without any variety of intonation in a way that sounded strange and unnatural, as if she were proclaiming an edict written by another person: "Its—no—good—complaining—about—those;—they're—the—largest—size—in—stock—you—can't—have—any—others—so—you'd—better—make—the—best—of—them".'[61]

Constance Maud based a novel called *No Surrender* on suffragettes' experience and she has one of the wardresses abusing suffragettes as "ooligans . . . disgraceful unsexed creatures . . . I never knew such magpies as you Suffragitts. Get on with yer work now and 'old yer jaw'[62] and doubtless there were warders and wardresses, as there were governors and chaplains, who were tyrannical and bullying. However, a great deal of the literature suggests that many warders and wardresses were adept at breaking the rules and holding secret conversations with prisoners. So, one spoke to Constance Lytton ' "I have never been angry with you yet". I looked up into her eyes. They were lit with kindliness and her whole face beamed on me with genial good will . . . the personality was the same but the mask was off and I realised something of the sacrifice it must be to this woman continually to conceal her good nature under so forbidding a manner'.[63] Viscountess Rhondda described the wardresses as 'all pleasant, kindly folk though they were supposed not to be'.[64] Ex-prisoners giving evidence before the Labour Enquiry believed that the harshness was in the system, not the warder, and longer term ex-prisoners 'constantly speak highly of them . . . ordinary men, some hardened by the system they have to apply, but kind underneath'.[65] There were reports that a small number were brutal.

Overall, the personality of the governor was a deciding factor in the nature of the regime, for the Prison Commissioners were often far away in London and the inspectors' visits, although regular, were not frequent. At times, the stratified disciplinary structure of Ruggles-Brise was seriously disturbed and enquiries had to be made. This happened at Parkhurst in 1900 when the general body of warders became agitated because the governor was led to believe by a cabal of warders that other warders were trafficking with prisoners. The governor them employed one of the convicts to spy on the warders suspected and 'urine letters' were discovered in the lavatories anonymously substantiating the governor's fears. The warders as a body suggested that these 'urine letters' were plants by the cabal which named names in them in order to destroy promotion prospects of warders outside the cabal. Ruggles-Brise was deeply angered by the weakness and stupidity of the governor and lamented to the Home Office that 'the discipline of the Prison has been seriously jeopardised and a spirit of suspicion, unrest and disloyalty created among all ranks'.[66]

In both Du Cane's and Ruggles-Brise's time there was a careful process of vetting suitable personnel for governor careers outside the interviews which were held of prospective candidates. So, social status and previous relationships were important. Basil Thomson, appointed to deputy governor rank in the late 1890s, was the son of the archbishop of York, a friend of the Home Secretary's private secretary and a school fellow of Ruggles-Brise.[67] Colonial and military experience was seen as highly suitable and detailed references of colonial governors and military commanding officers carefully studied. Basil Thomson who, as secretary to the Commission had much to do with selection, considered his own Boer War experience to have been 'a useful training for a man when dealing with criminals'.[68] Another well known governor, Colonel Rich, had also served in that war. Rich had met Ruggles-Brise who impressed him as 'an absolute sahib . . . clever and an autocrat, accustomed to make up his mind and sweep all obstacles out of the way of his will'. Clearly the respect was mutual for Rich was later appointed.[69] Another governor, Major Blake, had served as acting governor of Jubaland in East Africa and his father knew well Clare Garsia the Prison Commissioner who spoke up for Blake's appointment.[70] There was thus an established custom of choosing a recognised type of man with military or colonial experience, whose previous conduct could be clearly vouched for and it was helpful to have an ally at headquarters: so Major Clayton, who had been secretary of the Commission, and was a close friend of Ruggles-Brise, successfully urged his son's appointment to the service in 1920.[71] All successful candidates then went on the training course at Chelmsford for governors set up by Ruggles-Brise, performing the duties of each grade, assistant warder, warder, principal, chief, clerk and storekeeper and so forth,[72] receiving instruction generally before being posted as deputy governors.

There was snobbery among many of these ex colonial and military personnel of public school background in regard to the smaller number of governors who had been promoted up from chief warder. Blake rather condescendingly described this when he reported as the new deputy governor at Borstal Juvenile Adult prison and was greeted by the ex-warder governor. 'Very 'appy to make your acquaintance, Sir . . . I 'ope we shall get on well together. Captain Heccles, whose place you are taking . . . 'ad one big fault. He was a bit 'aughty. I hope you are not 'aughty. I am not an 'ard task master. I conceal the iron 'and beneath the velvet glove but I'm not hard on them as does their best and gets into my ways'.[73] It might be added that there was always a sense among convict prison staff of all grades that they were superior to the local prison service.

This type of governor tended to be clear about what they believed conduced to the reform of prisoners. A clear eyed, smart, soldierly bearing, an interest in the well being of the men, no nonsense from them, an alert and dutiful attention to conditions, a vigilance for abuses and brisk activity, if possible of an athletic type, were the essentials of a good reformatory regime. They had little interest in theory and judged warder and prisoner according to experience and a plain view of what was right and wrong, fair and unfair. So, Blake was outraged by a chaplain who wished to put a young girl, who had gone joyriding with her fiance on stolen bicycles, into a home for fallen women and lambasted the chaplain (later receiving a piece of wedding cake from the happy couple)[74] and Rich, as earlier noted, set up out door camps for borstal boys 'early morning parades for physical drill . . . fatigue parties for wood carrying, all beds neatly made up to pattern and kit inspection'.[75]

These governors were intolerant of those whom Rich saw as 'soft and sentimental extremists', who did not see the need to put 'the fear of God' into warder and prisoner alike before anything could be achieved.[76] Major Blake sarcastically described Winston Churchill as 'a most energetic and zealous Home Secretary' who thought he knew more about prisons than anybody else and had earned the undying hatred of one old convict 'who was perfectly happy in tending flocks on Dartmoor'!'[77] Basil Thomson was always sceptical of reformatory theory with older prisoners and through his work emphasised the importance of firmness, justice and humanity as the most important ingredients of successful management of prisoners.[78] Indeed, Rich reported, almost in disbelief, a conversation between a female prisoner and a prison visitor during which the woman thanked the visitor 'with a forlorn smile' saying 'it's something memorable on the long road of prison life to speak to a man like you, if only for a few minutes. Thank you so much. Good bye. God bless you'.[79] The woman, he expostulated, was reconvicted within days of her release.

Yet these governors greatly valued the realistic, down to earth, reformatory agent and Blake recorded his approval of an aid society agent, confronted with a request for a grant of £2 to buy a barrow and vegetables to sell, in order to support his old mother. The agent replied 'when you were sent to the reformatory you were an orphan, when you were in Borstal you had no relatives except a respectable sister . . . where do you get this poor old mother from'? Yet he noted with great approval and admiration the Prison Visitor who promised to visit a man's wife and the genuine relief of the prisoner: 'would you, Sir, what, you mean you'll go and see 'er and tell 'er I'm alright. I'd take that very kind of you . . . tell 'er the only thing that's fretting me is that I've brought this trouble on 'er'.[80]

They were often conservative men who hungered for a return to the imagined old bucolic England of stratified classes cemented together by mutual respect in place of 'a dissatisfied, unstable populace, shunning hard work, seeking only pleasure and begetting a race of undisciplined and do-as-little-as-you-can young wastrels'. They wanted a nation of men who 'rode straight and shot straight with the almost certain addition of living straight'.[81] For what they saw as a genuine trier they would take immense pains, often being disappointed by the outcome, and in general aimed at an atmosphere of activity and energy instead of apathy and slouch. Furthermore, many prisoners saw governors like Rich, Blake and Thomson as essentially humane men who spoke straight and made few petty demands.

As one professional Anglo American criminal wrote of Blake; 'he was a thorough gentleman in every possible way . . . what I liked about him was the kindly way he greeted you, no animosity, no official frills, just plain man to man talk'. He was glad that Blake had left the service because 'I would have hated to have gone back and met that silent reproach which does more to shame a man into righteousness than all the lectures in the world'.[82]

It remains to discuss some of the stereotypes about gender, race and prisoners as a group which were held amongst staff between 1895 and 1921, for these influenced the ways in which prisoners were treated. As has already been noted, Ruggles-Brise was against the appointment of a female Commissioner and was not keen to appoint female governors and medical officers of prisons. He was put under great pressure on this issue during the last ten years of his career for women's organizations lobbied members of parliament to demand change.[83] Ruggles-Brise argued that all women prisoners were under control of wardresses and their superiors, lady superintendents and matrons, and that there was a Lady Inspector and Lady Visitors. However, in the end he yielded on the matter of female doctors at Holloway and Aylesbury and conceded that an honorary seat could be provided on the Prison Commission, a suggestion that did not bear fruit. The Home Office supported his reluctance viewing such matters as merely 'a question of satisfying a feminist demand' which 'would not promote efficiency'.[84]

However, the issue of female governors, which had been a major one since the suffragettes, who had experienced male governors as a particularly blatant example of the male domination of women, was also hard fought and in the post war era suffragist organizations, such as the Women's Freedom League, mounted very strong and well orchestrated protests, based on the pre war suffragette experience, to the Home Office.[85] Limited success was achieved for a month before Ruggles-Brise's retirement it was announced that a female governor had been appointed to Aylesbury borstal.[86]

Throughout the period prison staff tended to accept the prevailing assumptions about women offenders and women in general. In 1895 Edmund Spearman articulated some of these. A woman, he suggested, 'differs from (man) in moral strength' and she rarely took the initiative in crime: often, when concerned in an offence, she was involved because she had been coerced or influenced by a lover or husband and her crimes, apart from this, tended to be crimes of passion fuelled by 'love, hatred and revenge'.[87] So, one assumption was that women were more at the mercy of emotions than their more rational male counterparts and another was that their crimes were extensions of male criminality or the result of male exploitation. However, because it was believed that women were so vulnerable to emotion, it was also believed that they were more difficult to manage in prison, liable to remorseless revengeful cruelty, driven by 'mortal hates', extreme jealousies and selfish egocentric thirst for attention, prone to deep resentments and uncontrollable frenzied outbursts.[88] Rich described this with regard to female preventive detainees who had been by then removed from Aylesbury to Liverpool. He saw them as driven by their own feelings and emotions, quarrelsome with each other, vilely abusive when thwarted and liable to turn on him with 'all sorts of blasphemy and general obscenity'.[89]

Paradoxically, however, women prisoners were also seen to be capable of extreme craftiness and cunning if the objective in view was sufficiently attractive to motivate self-control. Rich described the cunning of a woman who dressed up as an aristocrat to steal jewellery from hotels and recited other examples of theatrical camouflage. Nevertheless, underneath the exterior, the volcano seethed ever liable to erupt if the act were detected or the motive challenged. One prisoner would thus change 'in a trice from a nice mannered woman into a fiend incarnate' and another 'would refuse to work but would lie on the floor and do absolutely nothing but hurl abuse at any one who came near her'.[90] Alongside this stereotype of emotionality, either uncontrolled or fostered in order to obtain advantages,[91] there lurked medical speculations about the link between 'aberrant uterine and sexual functions' and crime and earnest admonitions from doctors that gynaecological considerations must always be taken into account when assessing a female criminal.[92]

The overall vulnerability to despair, rage or whatever was one of the reasons for the emphasis on lady visitors, for these would please the women by their close personal attentions and still the troubled heart with quiet, peaceful, hopeful conversation so that by soft persuasive words the prisoner might be wooed from her mischievous conduct. They even tried this on the suffragettes and sent Adeline, Duchess of Bedford, to see Mary Richardson imprisoned for damaging the Venus Velasquez in the National Gallery: 'in a low crooning voice' Adeline talked of 'sin and suicide. If you had a correct spirit, a right spirit, your sacrifice would call for Divine assistance. In some way you would be miraculously enabled to break your prison bonds to walk freely from your prison as St Paul and Silas did'.[93] This cut no ice.

The worst of the female prisoner was the wholly lost and befouled, drunken, lewd recidivist lag, old long before her time, and in every particular an obscene reverse of all that a feminine daughter and mother of the race should be. Indeed, Lombroso had believed that such female criminals reflected the survival of masculine qualities of the worst type in the born female criminal—the idea that the born female criminal had not evolved in such a way as to differentiate organically from masculinity, the notion of the born woman criminal as no more than half a female. Yet at the other extreme was a stereotype of the fragile, naive girl, victim of men, her offending the mere instrument or result of men, perhaps sexually exploited and brought to desperation by pregnancy and disgrace or hurled into crime by the bringing to bear of more instrumental calculative male minds upon her. Ruggles-Brise believed that it was particularly hard for women 'who have fallen from their high estate of probity and virtue' to regain their position, the idea being that the chastity and honour of a woman was always assessed to be beyond question by a gentleman: once its loss was known the woman was all but a social pariah.[94] Another stereotype was the introverted, moonstruck, isolated, unwed girl, hardly knowing what she did, in need of supervision and care, agitated by strange fears. So, Churchill strove to secure the release of one who was frequently sick and vomited blood after a music lesson and whose behaviour seemed to him bizarre and to the mother incomprehensible. 'Some time ago I got her a donkey and a little trap . . . I have since learned that she cut up a number of blankets for the purpose of making night dresses which were made to fit and button round the donkey'.[95]

Because Ruggles-Brise felt that women's criminality was essentially different from that of men[96] in that they were dependent on others and vulnerable to emotion, he was sure that they were less able to cope in society if cast adrift with no recourse save theft or prostitution. For this reason he particularly fulminated against repeated short sentences for women, because, in his view, they needed long term supervisory care either by Police Court Missionaries or the prison system. He therefore emphasised training homes as the penultimate stage of a penal servitude sentence before licence and as part of the actual experience of license for borstal girls. So, women and girls tended to be placed in the network of training and rescue homes mentioned earlier in this work.

Women were seen as emotionally and physically more frail than men and the system was not as severe for them. So, initial convict separation was not enforced, the silence rule was relaxed, convict remission increased to one third of sentence instead of the quarter for men. They were not flogged for prison offences nor subjected to oakum picking and, indeed, long ago in the years 1815 to 1825 there had been a successful campaign to prohibit treadmills for them. The work which they did rested on another assumption about them, namely that they should be trained for their inevitable role in life as mother and homemaker and thus sewing, laundry work, knitting, cleaning, cookery classes, needlework and nursing and hygiene training were particularly suitable for them. So, at Aylesbury borstal laundry work, housework, needlework and cooking were to be at the centre of the training as well as gardening, care of 'poultry and cattle'.[97]

That there was an ignorance about women among prison chaplains, theorists and practitioners was pointed out in 1898 by Eliza Orme, the female member of the Gladstone Committee, who complained about man made rules about baby care in prisons and the regulation that after nine months the baby must be sent to the work house (subsequently relaxed). She urged that this was 'torture' of women by men and ought not to be tolerated[98] and this theme of domination and misunderstanding was reiterated by suffragettes. So, Constance Lytton reflected of a chaplain who sermonised that human beings were all born helpless and ignorant into the world that 'there was apparently no mother to thank who, through nine months, had tended the little one in her body and through pain, sometimes excruciating, brought it to birth'.[99]

Many male officials seemed at a loss when confronted with women prisoners and were reduced to pleading with them. As the governor of Newcastle begged the suffragettes: 'Don't break your windows, please don't break your windows'.[100] Yet at the heart of the assumptions was the belief that women were not as fully responsible for their criminality as men and had to be cared for rather than treated as more instrumental males. So the relaxed conditions reflected a belief in lower culpability and it was of course just this attitude which so angered the suffragettes. As one put it, a female child and adolescent in Britain 'was more protected, less was expected of one in very many directions . . . a girl in innumerable subtle indirect ways is taught to mistrust herself. Ambition is held up to her as a vice—to a boy it is held up as a virtue. She is taught docility, modesty and diffidence . . . lack of courage and self confidence'.[101] Obedient to such assumptions the prison system was thus less severe to women and in its wider attitude was one of the myriad of institutions which implicitly denied that women were as responsible or as capable as men and in its dealings with them reinforced the structure of a society dominated by men.

There was also a tendency to racial stereotypes in the prisons. Eustace Jervis, who had been a chaplain for twenty five years, referred to 'the chosen people whom we seem to allow to flood this country from every part of the world to the detriment of our own people . . . engaged in Fagin's occupation'[102] and the idea of the lazy, cunning Jew as organiser of thieves, taking his luxurious ease whilst English lads took the risks of thieving for him as receiver, was commonly believed. However, black prisoners were also stereotyped. These were seen as prone to sudden frenzied outbursts whilst normally being indolent and of a low childish mentality, at times of frenzy requiring to be subdued by the superior stern warder. So a prison visitor reflected, 'I could see from the state of the room that "Sam", as they called him, had been mischievous again'.[103] Jabez Balfour remarked that a negro prisoner was 'incorrigibly idle justifying all that has ever been said (and often said most unjustly) about the innate laziness of the negro race. On one occasion he threw down his work and refused snarlingly to pick it up again until he was cowed into obedience by the stern and resolute action of the warder'.[104] Often a black prisoner would be called 'The Nigger' and at times, this, when combined with an order, resulted in the prisoner refusing to have 'white bastards' ordering him about in such fashion.[105]

Staff expected other races to be more difficult to control than English prisoners and one prison officer, a good while after Ruggles-Brise's time, reflected that some foreign black and brown skinned prisoners were more troublesome because they were in prison among a strange people and they believed that staff took advantage of them.[106] Prisoners themselves often shared the stereotypes and Jabez Balfour for example, although quick to defend black prisoners against accusations of laziness, was sure that Jewish prisoners were 'most difficult to manage ... aggressive, cunning and ungrateful'.[107]

The prisons were saturated with assumptions about the moral and social behaviour of prisoners as a group and this linked into the belief that such approaches as instruction and supervision were vitally necessary for young offenders. Superior staff tended to see inmates as a group as simple minded people, who were of low moral capacity and tended to gratify their desires heedless of consequence to self or others. Constitutional and positivist criminology reinforced this and there was always a doubt about the ability of many prisoners to take responsibility for their lives. The labour systems made little demand of them and the approach emphasised the paternal and supervisory control of warders and the superior staff. As one official noted: 'the strongest factor in the reformatory work has been the tact and fatherliness of the officers; the boys ... invariably speak of them in terms of gratitude'.[108] Furthermore, the educated elite were amazed by the ignorance of prisoners: 'the ignorance of so many ... on the subject of religion is pitiful, indeed almost incredible. They are unable to answer even the simplest questions'.[109] Of course lectures and lantern slides on 'perseverance, books, politeness' and 'A Visit to Japan' or 'A Visit to China'[110] said more about what their social superiors thought they needed to know than about what they actually did know and the gulf was great between the lecturer regaling the prisoner with tales of South African wars and mysterious far Eastern lands and the prisoners with their knowledge of, say, survival and poverty in the warrens and rookeries of Bethnal Green or Tiger Bay.

There was an overwhelmingly strong view among prison officials that the great bulk of prisoners were used to deprivation and severity and that they did not find prison hard to cope with. This is in contrast to the anxiety felt by chaplains and governors when offenders of their own social standing were sent to prison, for they felt that these experienced prison as more painful than the others. In particular, they feared that such prisoners of a higher status would not be able to get used to the severe conditions, such as the basic diet, and would be deeply pained by the criminal crowd amongst which they must live. Major Blake was obviously deeply concerned about a young doctor, who had been to his public school and had subsequently aborted the child of a desperate friend and showed great sensitivity to the feelings of the man, visiting him in his cell for long conversations.[111] William Morrison, somewhat unnecessarily, worried that Oscar Wilde was 'quite crushed and broken' and 'in an excited flurried condition'[112] as a result of the initial prison experience, and part of the rationale for relaxing conditions for both suffragettes and conscientious objectors was that these were often of higher social status and therefore, it was believed, would find conditions of prison more painful than the rest.

## NOTES

1. W. McWilliams, 'The Mission Transformed: Professionalisation of Probation Practice between the Wars' *The Howard Journal*, 1985, 24 (4): 257-74. W. McWilliams, 'The Mission to the English Police Courts' *The Howard Journal*, 1983, 22 (3): 129-47.
2. J. Pitkin, *The Prison Cell in its Lights and Shadows* (Sampson Low, Marston & Co, 1918): 23, 21.
3. C. Rickards, *A Prison Chaplain on Dartmoor* (Arnold 1920): 67-8.
4. RCP & DCP yr end 31 March 1912, pt 2, PP 1912-13, XLIII: 192-3.
5. A Half Timer, *Prison Reminiscences* (Stock 1917): 82, 125.
6. Ibid: 45; Rickards, *A Prison Chaplain*: 248.
7. Jock of Dartmoor, *Dartmoor from Within* (Readers Library Publishing Co. 1933): 139-40.
8. Rickards, *A Prison Chaplain*: 11, 61, 125.
9. Ibid: 101, 30, 107.
10. Ibid: 102.
11. M. Richardson, *Laugh A Defiance* (Weidenfeld & Nicholson 1953): 83.
12. Rickards, *A Prison Chaplain*: 156.
13. Ibid: 131-2.
14. Half Timer: 106.
15. Rickards, *A Prison Chaplain*: 139.
16. Ibid: 173.
17. Pitkin, *The Prison Cell*: 135.
18. Rickards, *A Prison Chaplain*: 60.
19. Half Timer: 80-1.
20. E. Jervis, *Twenty Five Years in Six Prisons* (Fisher Unwin 1925): 54.
21. S. Scott, *The Human Side of Crook and Convict Life* (Hurst & Blackett 1924): 87.
22. F.W. Harland-Edgecumbe, *Lord High Executioner: An Amazing Account of*

*Prison Life in England and America* (Long 1934): 260.

23. F. Martyn, *A Holiday in Gaol* (Methuen 1911): 69-70.

24. F.W. Harland-Edgecumbe, *Lord High Executioner*: 192, 194. M. Gordon, *Penal Discipline* (Routledge & Sons 1922): 147.

25. Martyn, *A Holiday in Gaol.*

26. W.B.N., *Penal Servitude* (Heinemann 1903): 95.

27. W. Blake, *Quod* (Hodder & Stoughton 1927): 271.

28. Jock of Dartmoor: 16, 40.

29. Rickards, *A Prison Chaplain*: 127.

30. Jervis, *Twenty Five Years*: 19.

31. W.B.N., *Penal Servitude*: 98.

32. Viscountess Rhondda, *This Was My World* (MacMillan 1933): 157.

33. C. Lytton, *Prisons and Prisoners* (Heinemann 1914): 120-1.

34. Ibid: 266. Richardson, *Laugh a Defiance*: 84. E. Browne, *Road Pirate* (J. Long Ltd 1934): 63-4. H. Pollitt, *Serving My Time* (Lawrence & Wishart 1940): 251. Cited P. Priestley, *Jail Journeys: English Prison Experience 1918-1990.* (Routledge 1989): 133-4.

35. Pitkin, *The Prison Cell*: 90.

36. Ibid: 111.

37. Ibid: 153.

38. Rickards, *A Prison Chaplain*: 247.

39. A. Cook, *Our Prison System* (Drane 1911): 377.

40. B.2.15., *Among the Broad Arrow Men: A Plain Account of English Prison Life* (A. & C. Black 1924): 43, 142.

41. A.F. Brockway, *Inside the Left: Thirty Years of Platform, Press, Prison and Parliament* (Allen & Unwin. 1942): 74.

42. Scott, *The Human Side of Crook*: 57-60.

43. Ibid.

44. R. Calvert, *Capital Punishment in the Twentieth Century* (Putnams & Sons 1927): 106, Calvert quoting B.2.15., *Broad Arrow Men.*

45. Scott, *The Human Side of Crook*: 63.

46. H.U. Triston, *Men in Cages* (The Book Club 1938): 108.

47. S. Hobhouse and A.F. Brockway (eds) *English Prisons Today* (Longman, Green & Co. 1922): 248.

48. Brockway, *Inside the Left*: 103.

49. Hobhouse and Brockway, *English Prisons*: 247.

50. Ibid: 247.

51. Blake, *Quod*: 62.

52. Ibid: 319, 322.

53. Pitkin, *The Prison Cell*: 127

54. PRO P.Com 7/713, A. Paterson, Memo to the Committee to consider claims of men dismissed the Prison and Police Services as a result of the 1919 strike 13 March 1924.

55. PRO P.Com 7/719, 720, 721, Representations of the Prison Officers' Representative Board (PORB).

56. PRO P.Com 7/719, Resolutions of the PORB 1919.

57. J.E. Thomas, *The English Prison Officer since 1850* (Routledge & Kegan Paul 1972): 140, 142, 147.

58. Substitution of Officer for Warder. PRO HO 45-11082-427916, HO Minute, 13 Jan. 1922.

59. Blake, *Quod*: 147.

60. Annie Kenney, *Memories of a Militant* (Arnold & Co 1924): 96.

61. Lytton, *Prisons*: 82.

62. Maud, *No Surrender* (Duckworth & Co 1911): 266, 268.

63. Lytton, *Prisons*: 160.

64. Viscountess Rhondda, *My World*: 157.

65. Hobhouse and Brockway, *English Prisons*: 369.

66. Trafficking at Parkhurst 1900, PRO HO 144-526-X78840/2, Clare Garsia and Major Clayton to E. Ruggles-Brise 16 May 1900, E. Ruggles-Brise to HO 21 May 1900.

67. Thomson, *The Scene Changes* (Collins 1939): 183.

68. Ibid: 224.

69. Rich, *Recollections of a Prison Governor* (Hurst & Blackett 1932): 19.

70. Blake, *Quod*.

71. Clayton, *The Wall is Strong* (Long 1958): 32.

72. Rich, *Recollections*: 23.

73. Blake, *Quod*: 71.

74. Ibid: 121-4.

75. Rich, *Recollections*: 101.

76. Ibid: 48.

77. Blake, *Quod*: 132.

78. Thomson, *The Criminal* (Hodder & Stoughton 1925).

79. Rich, *Recollections*: 174.

80. Blake, *Quod*: 215, 246-7.

81. Rich, *Recollections*: 58, 59.

82. E. Guerin, *The Autobiography of a Crook* (Murray 1928): 307-8.

83. Female Governors and Medical Officers 1913-1938, PRO HO 45-24643-234940/1, Federation of University Women to R. McKenna, 25 Feb. 1913. /2 *Hansard* cut. 10 April 1916. /5 Sundry news reports in *Manchester Guardian*, 1 Aug. 1921, *Daily Herald*, 29 July 1921.

84. Appointment of Women as Prison Governors and Commissioners, PRO HO 45-16184-424021. PC obs 17 April 1919, 20 June 1921. HO Minute, 22 April 1919.

85. PRO HO 45-16184-424021. Resolutions of 23 organisations sent to HO, 24 May 1923.

86. PRO HO 45-24643-234940/5.

87. E.R. Spearman, 'Women in French Prisons' *Nineteenth Century*, 1895, 37: 798-812.

88. Pitkin, *The Prison Cell*: 27. Rich, *Recollections*: 160.

89. Rich, *Recollections*: 151.

90. Ibid: 160, 163, 165.

91. Hopkins, *Wards of the State* (Herbert & Daniel 1913): 229-58.

92. *Lancet*, 11 Aug. 1900: 446.
93. Richardson, *Laugh a Defiance*: 171.
94. Ruggles-Brise, *The English Prison System* (MacMillan 1921): 116.
95. A Woman Sentenced to One Month Imprisonment and Mr Churchill 1911 PRO HO 144-1144-209195. /4 Mother's Account of Beatrice Carter sent to HO 1 June 1911.
96. Ruggles-Brise, *Prison System*: 122.
97. Prison System and Imprisonment 1904-1928, Borstal Rules for Females, Rule 16 Industrial Training, PRO HO 45-12905-116578.
98. E. Orme, 'Our Female Criminals' *Fortnightly Review*, May 1898, 69: 793.
99. Lytton, *Prisons*: 285.
100. Ibid: 225.
101. Viscountess Rhondda, *My World*: 231.
102. Jervis, *Twenty Five Years*: 85.
103. S.A. Moseley, *The Convict of Today* (Palmer 1927): 7.
104. J.S. Balfour, *My Prison Life* (Chapman & Hall 1907): 176.
105. Triston, *Men in Cages*: 14, 70.
106. Ibid: 70-1.
107. Balfour, *Prison Life:* 291
108. RCP & DCP yr end 31 March 1907, PP 1908, LII: 414.
109. RCP & DCP yr end 31 March 1909, pt. 2., PP 1909, XLV: 136.
110. RCP & DCP yr end 31 March 1907, PP 1908, LII: 289, 422.
111. Blake, *Quod*: 261-7.
112. PRO P Com. 8/432 Oscar Wilde, W.D. Morrison to Mr Haldane, 11 Sept. 1895.

# Chapter Ten

# Mental and Social Diagnosis in English Prisons 1910–1939

Under Sir Evelyn Ruggles-Brise there were well established prison medical officers at each prison appointed by the Prison Commissioners and at some of the larger prisons, such as Brixton, there was a Senior Medical Officer leading a small team. The task of these was to treat prisoners who were sick, assess the capacity of prisoners to undergo corporal punishment, attend at executions and supervise the prison hospital. After 1898 one member of the Prison Commission (with one short hiatus) was always a medical man who had been promoted from prison medical officer to inspector and thence to commissioner. The medical commissioner, assisted by a medical inspector, was responsible for supervising the prison medical staff and for advising the Home Office and Prison Commission about all matters which had a bearing on the physical health of prisoners.

In Du Cane's time the prison medical staff had restricted themselves largely to such matters as diet and medical treatment of sick prisoners although a number of them, on evolutionist grounds, had been pessimistic about the reformability of most prisoners. Between 1900 and 1910 they naturally began to explore the truth of the claims of eugenists and others who were more generally concerned about national efficiency. So, they began to study the physical and psychological capacities of prisoners as a whole, their intellectual level, the tendency of prisoners to be feeble minded, their physical comparability to non prisoners and so forth. They proved to be somewhat uncertain about eugenic claims. On the one hand they wanted to avoid any theoretical erosion of the notion of criminal responsibility and yet most of them believed that there were many vagrants, inebriates and feeble minded in prisons who were defective as a result of heredity and environment and desired these to be placed under long term supervisory or medical control. So, a number of medical officers and other Prison Commission medical personnel measured the physical and mental capacities of prisoners and concluded, firstly, that there were indeed anomalies and defects amongst many, but that these were less common than eugenists suggested. Therefore, although attentive to eugenic arguments, the Prison Commission nevertheless urged caution about their extreme claims whilst acknowledging that many prisoners did show signs of deficiencies in physique, intellect and affect as eugenists claimed.[1]

Prison medical staff had thus been drawn into the debate about the eugenic and national efficiency discourse and their investigations between 1900 and 1914 were very largely intended to discover the truth or otherwise of various parts of that discourse as far as prisoners were concerned. The research of Dr Charles Goring, deputy medical officer at Parkhurst, was encouraged by the Prison Commission to extend knowledge about the existence or otherwise of innate defects among prisoners and was published in 1913.[2] Goring concluded that convicts tended to be effected by hereditarily transmitted inferior intellect and inherited inferior physique and his research methods were based on the biometric method of analysis favoured by the leading eugenist, Dr Karl Pearson, whose biometric laboratory played a significant part in formulating and supervising the design and execution of the project.

Ruggles-Brise was at first enthusiastic about Goring's report but this enthusiasm began to wane as he realised that there was a danger that Goring's findings about inherited low intelligence and inferior physique among criminals might well be taken to imply that they were innately predisposed to crime and were thus not able to control their behaviour. The Prison Commissioners at first tried to argue that Goring's findings merely reinforced the need for close supervisory and reformatory approaches to all offenders who clearly required control and guidance, given their constitutional and inherited weakness and incapacity. However, in 1917 Dr Horatio Donkin, retired Prison Medical Commissioner, challenged Goring, arguing that post natal environment played a great part in fostering criminality and he insisted that the majority of prisoners were entirely capable of exercising free will, rather than merely hereditarily programmed to criminality.

At this time Donkin was a member of the Local Advisory Committee at Camp Hill Preventive Detention Prison and was enthusiastic about reformatory endeavours with preventive detainees. It was therefore in his interest to narrow the importance of hereditary transmission and he emphasised that 'the only important link between the study of crime and that of biological heredity is the fact that a considerably larger minority of persons with clearly appreciable mental defect, apparently of congenital nature, is found among convicted criminals than in the population at large'.[3] Goring at once riposted that Donkin was inherently prejudiced against the biometric methods pioneered by Karl Pearson, upon which Goring had based his analytical method, and professed himself astounded by what he saw as an ill informed attack. Unrepentant Donkin again attacked biometrics and hereditary transmission of criminal propensities and urged that most preventive detainees were just as bright and alert as non criminals and could be successfully reformed.[4] For the minority of prisoners who were certifiable mental defectives, he urged treatment and maintenance in hospitals and asylums.

Donkin had forceful allies outside the Prison Commission in his crusade against the erosion of the classical view of legal responsibility, in the absence of which criminals 'with the assurance of a Hyde Park lecturer' would insist that their 'long course of misconduct was due to the inheritance of . . . constitution from a drunken father'.[5] So, Charles Mercier, President of the Psychological section of the British Medical Association, and well known lawyers interested in medical forensic problems vigorously attacked eugenists such as Edgar Schuster who were around this time considering the implications of complex experiments in plant hybridisation and publishing the demands of the American Breeders' Association that 'the defective germ plasm in the human population' should be identified and neutralised.[6]

Donkin was not arguing for a purely environmental approach but rather seeking to emphasise the importance of environment. He, in fact, had the last word because Goring died at the height of the dispute, and so he insisted that although human beings came into the world with 'innate capacities', these were 'developed by the innumerable influences which act upon those capacities' subsequently.[7] He urged that culpability should remain at the heart of criminal jurisprudence undiminished and, with Charles Mercier, swung the opinion of the British Medical Association towards his views, a matter of great importance since in the early 1920s there was much pressure to revise the M'Naghten rules of 1843 which laid down a very strict definition of the mental state which would exculpate the accused person from the death penalty.

Along with Donkin and Mercier the tendency of prison medical staff was to narrow the definition of irresponsibility to traditional insanity and severe mental defectiveness and they were therefore distrustful of eugenists or others who urged inherited predisposition as the major cause of behaviour. Thus William Norwood East, now senior medical officer at Brixton, warned against 'hyper-enthusiasts' who saw the great majority of criminals as victims of inherited mental deficiency and he insisted upon the need to distinguish between mere mental and social inefficiency, common among prisoners, and mental defectiveness, a much rarer and more serious thing.[8] More generally than prisons and prisoners the human sciences in the inter war years were aiming to integrate the environmental and constitutional explanations of the formation of attitude and conduct. Although Cyril Burt, the London County Council psychologist and prolific writer on psychological matters, was steeped in Darwinian and eugenic theory and firmly maintained that innate factors determined intelligence and influenced temperament, he also insisted upon the great importance of 'social and environmental forces' in shaping conduct.[9] As far as crime was concerned Burt explained that, although certain character weakness might be inherited and would strengthen tendencies to delinquency, this by no means implied an inevitable outcome, but rather made clear the importance of family, neighbourhood, education and so forth in turning the youngster away from such a life. So, Burt began to analyse the kinds of environment which were undesirable in that they conduced to crime amongst congenitally weakened young people and pointed up the evils of chronic poverty, overcrowding and a lack of warm spontaneous joy in the home, 'a joyless home' where 'leisure hours are vacant' and where 'life is too stern for the father to waste strength in making or mending his children's playthings, or for the mother to smile upon their noisy racketeering'.[10]

Like Norwood East, Burt insisted upon the distinction between backwardness and mental deficiency and depended upon detailed tests of intelligence to argue that the majority of young offenders were merely backward intellectually. However, he also began to reveal novel and arresting details about the emotional lives of children, for he wished to find out about their attitude to their environment, their relationships with their parents, even their sexual lives, and to describe this in a way which gave an idea of subjective feeling rather than relying only on theoretical and objective analysis. So, readers were presented with the way some children saw their parents and step parents: 'I am going to see my mother on Munday I am going to tell her a lot of lies about you and rotten cow wife and I will put that dam kid on the fire or out the winder and you just wate when I am grown up I will be werse you old *swine and devil* I will never call you father again'.[11]

So the message urged was that heredity did indeed lead to a dull intelligence or excitable temperament but environmental conditions, especially those in the family, would usually determine whether such predispositions broke out in crime. The search must therefore be for ways of measuring intelligence and personality and assessing hereditary and environmental individual influences on the individual child in agencies strengthened for the treatment of the youngster at risk of delinquency.

In America this mental and social diagnostic endeavour was also under way. For example, William Healy, director of the Psychopathic Institute of Chicago, emphasised very detailed assessment of each case[12] and prepared long reports about the origin of delinquency in each.[13] At other clinics the psychological and social progress of those under treatment was carefully noted—'at the end of a year during which unhygienic attitudes to self criticism were corrected, a serious mother fixation dispelled and other emotional speech blocks removed, the Bernreuter scores indicated an improvement of from 10 to 15 per cent'.[14] Lastly, as with Burt, these clinicians and analysts emphasised subjective feelings towards parents and family.[15] Overall in America analysts such as the Gluecks or clinicians like Healy painted a general picture of alcohol abuse, sexual promiscuity, habitual petty crime, parental neglect, rootlessness and so forth. Indeed, the mental scientific and diagnostic language of their writings scarcely concealed a highly judgemental attitude to the subjects of their analysis and treatment, the revelation of an underclass of immoral and destructive beings damaged by heredity and poor environment, a menace to the stable and industrious classes upon whom they preyed.

In Britain and America the aim was to fuse the eugenic and environmental approaches to delinquency to produce a mental hygienist approach to diagnosis and cure which took account of both heredity and environment, categorised in terms of necessary treatment measures and emphasised the importance of parental nurturing of the child. The objective was to bring to bear on the family and individual a battery of tests and therapeutic measures designed to treat and improve—better physical care by the family, cleanly homes, appropriate nurture by the mother—and essentially the prevention of later delinquency and 'major mental disturbances' by 'early recognition and treatment of all the minor troubles from which they grew and by promotion of correct habits of mental hygiene in the family'.[16]

These approaches both in America and Britain led to an emphasis on treatment and improvement. So, in America experiments in rehabilitation of young offenders outside the walls of traditional institutions became much more common and self governing communities for young offenders, children and prostitutes were set up along the American lines at Batcombe in Dorset, Newbury and St Pancras.[17] It might be noted that interest in foreign experiments in the rehabilitation of offenders was marked during the inter war years and eulogistic accounts were given in Britain of Soviet education in prisons[18] and the mixed sex self governing collective at Bolshevo where, it was said, ten thousand Soviet offenders lived and learned responsibility and duty.[19]

Although English prison medical staff did not deny the importance of heredity as a factor in criminality they came into open conflict with eugenists during the inter war years. Eugenists continued to urge that 'in any large city was to be found a social problem group, the source from which the majority of criminals and paupers, unemployables and defectives of all kinds are recruited' by biological transmission[20] and, as a result of their skilful advocacy, in 1932 a departmental committee was set up to examine the desirability of sterilization of mentally disordered or deficient people. It did not recommend compulsory measures but rather that sterilization should be made available as a voluntary measure.[21]

For over twenty years Prison Commission medical personnel had opposed all forms of sterilization. Horatio Donkin duelled with Alfred Tredgold, a leading eugenist and later member of the Sterilization Committee, in the press[22] and others of them attacked sterilization on various grounds. Donkin urged that the sterilization of sex offenders did not alter the strength of sexual desire, and the superintendent of Broadmoor urged that the effect of such treatment on other mental patients would be catastrophic: '. . . there are a number of highly dangerous lunatics in confinement whose delusions are based on sexual subjects, and they declare that the medical staff by means of drugs, chemicals, electricity etc. are engaged in torturing them and causing their nature to run away from them as they put it . . . if it were once bruited about that doctors were actually mutilating patients . . . these ideas would assume a concrete form and would be fraught with very serious consequences indeed'.[23] Norwood East, who had been appointed medical commissioner in 1929, memorialised the sterilization committee to the effect that no scientific basis existed to justify such a measure and that opinion in America, where over three thousand habitual criminals had been sterilized,[24] had now decisively turned against the practice which had been abandoned. East insisted that both castration and sterilization often exacerbated sexual desire, and concluded that 'eugenic sterilization' was 'previous, unwarranted and possibly harmful to the race. As a punitive measure it is outrageous. As a therapeutic measure it is otiose, may incite to sexual crime and lead to a false sense of security in the public mind'.[25] So, under East's influence, the Prison Commission opposed this eugenic idea no matter how many judges, bishops and journalists supported it, or lunacy experts demanded a 'national lethal chamber' insisting that the state should 'concentrate our social, educational and financial efforts at well doing on nature's noblest work—the normal human intellect'[26]

In their determination to restrict the notion of criminal irresponsibility to traditional insanity and severe mental deficiency the medical personnel of the Prison Commission were concerned in laborious attempts to define the exact nature of the various insanities which they entirely accepted should exculpate the offender from punishment. Thus, prisoners remanded for trial and suspected to be insane, were analysed and described in detail, so that the symptomatology might be understood and located within the classifications which made up insanity and severe deficiency. So, a man who murdered and sexually mutilated an elderly woman was a moral imbecile, having a long history of cruelty to animals, lacking remorse, of low intelligence, habituated to sexual vices and, after his crime, wandering unconcernedly back to rejoin the game he had been playing with his friends.[27] Many books and articles were written to analyse the relationship of each case to classifications such as psychosis, general paralysis, senile dementia, moral insanity, moral imbecility and so forth but, despite disagreements about details, prison medical staff agreed that the proportion of insane or certifiably defective prisoners was very small—around one in eighty seven according to Norwood East.[28] Compared with the horrific eugenic claims of widespread degeneracy, lunacy and deficiency among the lower orders during the pre war era these estimates were reassuring. However, Norwood East and his colleagues were not prepared to leave the matter entirely as one of insanity definition and certification under the M'Naghten rules and in venturing further they played their part in widening the boundaries of mental treatment and diagnosis to include large numbers of people who were never considered to be either insane or certifiably mentally defective.

In line with the mental hygienism, which Cyril Burt and William Healy were playing a large part in systematising, Prison Commission medical staff were well aware that they were leaving open a wide ground between certifiability and normality, an area, as noted, of great interest to American and British clinicians. This area of psychological peculiarity or abnormality, a disorder of mind rather then insanity, was agreed by most professional opinion to result from the influence of environment upon inherited personality weakness. However, given that eugenic measures of sterilization or other means of eliminating such transmissions were seen by them as scientifically flawed, the question remained as to how these disorders should be analysed and treated. The American clinicians were certainly pointing a way through this, and the Great War with its psychological casualties of shell shock and 'neurasthenia' also emphasised the potential of the environment to contribute to mental aberration or disorder. Indeed, just after the war there was a great deal of pressure to establish clinics in Britain to treat such people who came before the courts and these offenders were called at the time 'psychopathic'.[29] The Prison Commission noted approvingly that the Birmingham Justices had asked for a special diagnostic facility, to be set up at Winson Green prison in early 1919, so that courts could be guided as to disposal in such cases.[30] The Medical Officer at Portland convict prison, Hamblin Smith, was duly dispatched to assess such persons, and by October 1920 'besides an attempt to overcome nervousness and lack of confidence by conversation each day, a series of mental tests are applied'.[31] Two years later Dr. W.A. Potts, 'psychological expert to the Birmingham justices', was publicly praising the application of such methods which were closely modelled on the work of Healy in Chicago.[32]

The appearance of psychoanalysis in the criminal justice field gave impetus to the work of some English prison medical staff in their approach to the middle ground between insanity and normality. Psychoanalysis had been established as a theory and practice in Britain just before the Great War when its devotees had set up an association in London and opened a clinic for its practice. However, it was not until 1922 that the Home Office began to take a wary interest in the work of Freud and Jung. Puzzled officials there were ordered to make painstaking collections of published letters from archdeacons expostulating about sacrilegious claims that Christ wanted all to have sexual fulfilment, and from Cambridge professors condemning psychoanalysis as unscientific. Somewhat bemused they concluded that Freud was 'obsessed by sex ideas, reference to the anus and such like' and that 'psychoanalysis is still in its infancy ... psychotherapy must be mere guess work'.[33]

There was certainly much hostility to this version of mental hygienism. It was accused by eminent men of producing 'morbid ideas' and it was said that it 'induces and aggravates introspection'.[34] Journalists alarmed the public with stories about its potential to cause suicide: 'DANGERS OF PSYCHOANALYSIS ... FATAL INTROSPECTION AFTER VISIT TO EXPERT'.[35] Fierce prolonged disputes erupted in the medical profession as one group attempted to influence the British Medical Association to condemn its practitioners, who at once retorted that closed minds and 'heresy hunts' had not only occurred in the Middle Ages: in answer to this came cries of quackery and charlatanism and dark allegations that the youth of England would be corrupted by such vile ideas about sexuality and desire.[36]

The walls of the penal city had, however, already been breached for Hamblin Smith was a convert and Norwood East, during his time at Brixton, had been impressed by the potential of psychoanalysis.[37] Before long Hamblin Smith was extolling the new approach: 'Freud's theory of the unconscious with its hidden complexes leading to mental conflicts' made clear the need to attend to 'proper treatment of the repressed conflict which causes the complex' and soon he was telling Chief Constables about the importance of 'mental conflicts', 'unconscious conflicts' which required detailed assessment and treatment by the psychoanalytic method.[38] In 1923 he persuaded the Prison Commission to appoint Dr Grace Pailthorpe to carry out 'intensive investigations' of the female offenders at Holloway under his guidance.[39]

Hamblin Smith and Grace Pailthorpe proved to be determined and skilful advocates and made grand claims which tended to ignore the fact that psychoanalysis required long application for successful outcome and that it was based upon a voluntary notion of patient participation and unforced cooperation. They also overlooked the unproven nature of Freudian theory, and that, what had on face of it been successful with aristocratic or bourgeois Viennese during the last years of the Austro-Hungarian Empire, might not be entirely suitable for British criminals. Nonetheless, Hamblin Smith insisted that 'by psychoanalysis we are able to discover the ultimate origin of much of our unconscious mental life' and assured his listeners and readers that 'in the majority of cases a repressed complex will be found to have a sex basis'.[40]

Hamblin Smith argued that there was a theoretical problem which all previous explanations of crime had not resolved. Therefore previous diagnostic approaches had not explained why only some of the unintelligent, unemployable, poor general capacity group, at risk of delinquency according both to eugenic and more general psychology, in fact, committed crimes. This failure of explanation was, he said, inevitable because previous enquirers had not grasped the psycho dynamic process. The missing factor was thus the impact of environment, in particular the nurture of parents, upon the unconscious of the individual, the creation of complexes and repressions which must express themselves in crime. So, psychoanalysis alone had made possible an understanding of why only some at risk in fact offended. As he urged: 'the sleeping princess of psychology found her deliverer in Sigmund Freud . . . we are all under bondage to our personal complexes'. Indeed, 'when we say that it is necessary to punish an offender we are influenced to a great extent by our personal sense of guilt and the demand of that sense of guilt for punishment'.[41]

There was a sense in which this was hack to full blown irresponsibility, for the emphasis was upon the personality of the offender, who was not responsible for the kind of care given by parents when he or she was a baby or for repression of complexes into the unconscious, which would later be expressed in crime. Indeed Hamblin Smith wanted prisons to be seen as hospitals, for crime was the result of psychodynamic process,[42] and, in emphasising family and environment as the procreators of neurosis, conflict and repression, he was insisting not only on an environmental analysis of mental process but optimistically pointing to the probability of cure by psychoanalysis. Consequently it was not long before the public began to hear accounts of assessment and treatment from Grace Pailthorpe. There was Nora, whose phobias were traceable to a traumatic event in her third year of life, Mrs Brown, whose 'unresolved Oedipus conflict' was re-enacted in her relationships with men, Rose whose persistent habit of biting into apples on shop counters resulted from the fact that the apples symbolised her mother's breast.[43]

These prison psychoanalysts were fully aware that not all prisoners were suitable for treatment by their method. Grace Pailthorpe devised a tripartite classification of prisoners, those of low intelligence lacking capacity for insight, those showing no symptoms of repression and those showing clear symptoms of repression, apparently trapped in mental conflict, exhibiting feelings of shame, self-disgust, rage and so forth.[44] On this basis she proposed an entirely new penal structure with a central assessment station and differential facilities for treatment of each category in a separate block on an appropriate programme. Those with neurosis or mental conflicts could be treated by individual and group analysis in one block; those without conflicts could be educated and trained to self-government in another; those of severely deficient intelligence or insane should be permanently segregated in another. These blocks would be called hospitals and to each would be attached research laboratories.

As with the American and British clinicians working with juvenile delinquents and their families each prisoner surveyed and treated must be dealt with on an individual basis and the operation required most intimate knowledge of mind and body. So, prisoners were induced to confess that they were 'horrified and disgusted at the idea of sexual congress' or alternatively 'overridden by sexual desires' or had 'delusions about . . . excretory functions'.[45] Concerning the importance of this endeavour both Pailthorpe and Hamblin Smith skilfully educated the public and in their writings and official reports great quantities of case material were included to show the effectiveness of this new approach. With regard to sexuality it should be added that the work of Pailthorpe, like that of Cyril Burt, was often heavily influenced by moral preconceptions or indeed 'moralistic perceptions'.[46] Certainly Pailthorpe, Burt and the American diagnosticians and clinicians played a part in emphasising a link between sexual activity of women, reported to be high among many female delinquents, and their offending as well as other links between women's bodies (e.g. the onset of menstruation) and crime.

Outside the prisons clinics to treat delinquency psychotherapeutically sprang up in London in 1920 at the Tavistock Institute and in 1933 set up by the Institute for the Scientific Treatment of Delinquency. In the provinces courts also became most interested and in Bradford, for example, magistrates and doctors began to identify 'Woolworth Jackdaws' (said to be often menopausal) and mothers whose 'thwarted mother love' and 'sexual excitement' following marriage of daughters preceded their offences.[47] Home Office officials dourly discouraged publication of this kind of explicit sexual material, fearing that reports about such cases would be sold in pornographic bookshops 'along with the History of The Rod and the works of Krafft-Ebing'.[48] These clinics also differentiated treatment, psychotherapy according to analytic principles to some such as sexual offenders and 'psychoneurotics'; explanation of the meaning of symptoms and 'suggestion with or without hypnosis' to others; mere re-education and persuasion to others.[49]

Norwood East was determined to extend psychotherapeutic assessment and treatment of prisoners, although he always emphasised in the annual reports of the Prison Commission that very great caution should be adopted towards wide claims by psychotherapists to cure large numbers of offenders. However, East wanted the psychoanalytic method tested more widely than had been done by Hamblin Smith and Pailthorpe, not only because he was himself impressed by its potential, but also because he feared that the Prison System would be accused of outdatedness if the new method were not more widely applied. Therefore in late 1933, calling in aid the successful clinic set up by the Institute for the Scientific Treatment of Delinquency, the Prison Commission, prompted by East, urged the Home Office to allow a major experiment of psychoanalysis in the prison system. So, in early 1934 a part time psychologist, Dr W. De B. Hubert, began work at Wormwood Scrubs and all medical officers were circularised to the effect that selected prisoners under forty years of age and serving over six months, especially those with sex and arson convictions and those whose offences were due to 'obsession or hysterical reactions' should be considered and if suitable sent to Wormwood Scrubs.[50]

The report of this experiment was submitted to Home Secretary Samuel Hoare in December 1938. In its pages appear a long line of prisoners, each tagged according to personality,—hysteric, depressive, obsessional and so forth—to whom were differentially applied either the simple method of discussion about past lives and difficulties, or the complex method of full blown psychoanalysis during repeated meetings, so that the prisoner might come to know that he was 'repeating in his reaction to the therapist, prison officials and other persons, a form of behaviour which is specifically related to the behaviour he has shown in the past'.[51] By 'transference', use of 'phantasy ... dream material ... free association', the prisoner would 'under psychotherapeutic influence ... live through a situation safely and satisfactorily, which corresponds as exactly in form as is possible, to those in the past which have been dealt with by psychoneurotic reactions or other forms of abnormal behaviour'.[52]

Some of these prisoners were openly hostile to this intervention in their lives. One would do 'little more than grunt in reply to questions and not infrequently spit upon the floor'; others were not keen to answer the questions of the psychotherapist and preferred to tell him about 'adventures of rum running, gun running and shipwreck'.[53] Some quickly picked up the jargon and began to talk about 'uncontrollable impulses'.[54] A good many were dismissed as unsuitable for treatment on account of their love of crime or resentment of the therapist or their wish to exploit him to gain advantage. Dr De B. Hubert wanted in particular to identify those whose crimes were the result of 'a particular morbid pattern of thought and behaviour' or resulted from odd or unusual circumstances or were the result of conflicted or otherwise problematic relationships.[55] In particular sex offenders were very carefully scanned.

Altogether around 80 per cent were dismissed as unsuitable for treatment of whom some were judged too close to clinical insanity to be helped by the method. One who had a history of suicidal attempts, violent attacks on his father and transvestism was seen as unsuitable and another, who had conversations with God and the Devil, was seen as a very poor prospect and dismissed as unsuitable.[56] Others, however, were better prospects seen to be of good intelligence and victims of environment. 'His early life had proved unhappy, his school days and later his experiences at work had confirmed his belief that he was different to other people and would never get on. He appeared to gain considerable relief and encouragement from a discussion of his difficulties'; another who had lost all confidence as a result of his experiences and stammered badly 'was able to understand examples of these reactions as they appeared in the therapeutic situation'.[57] However, some had backgrounds and patterns of behaviour which seemed too damaging or intractable for effective treatment. One whose homosexuality was thought to be based upon deep rooted fear of woman as 'a dangerous object' was believed to require more intensive therapy than could be offered in the prison[58] whilst another who had been sexually active since childhood with men, boys and prostitutes was judged to be too fixed in his behaviour for it to be modified by therapy.[59]

Norwood East was enthusiastic about the outcome and entirely accepted that only a minority could be successfully treated. In particular he and De Burgh Hubert were sure that the treatment would benefit offenders of average or high intelligence who were in the 'mentally inefficient and psycho neurotic groups', in other words those who had the capacity for insight into the purposes of the Freudian project and who were possessed of the conflicts and other mental stresses of which Pailthorpe and Hamblin Smith had spoken; for those of defective intelligence or close to insanity East was sure that the approach would not work.[60] Overall it is obvious from their report that those who were seen by the therapist as genuinely participating in the programme and had a combination of high intelligence and problematic family background were positively assessed for treatment.

The mental hygienism of the inter war years also required detailed assessment of the family and general environment of the individual at risk of developing the mental or social problems believed to be precursors of delinquency. As the pessimistic eugenic view of a hopelessly unreformable mass of defectives, paupers, insane, unemployables and criminals receded, psychological diagnosticians continued to see heredity as but one element in behaviour outcome, albeit a significant one, and the objective was now to discover the aetiology of the pathology which had come to the notice of the authorities. So, armed with the new analytic understandings and the kind of knowledge revealed by Healy and Burt, a range of new workers came into being informed by these hygienist approaches and, in particular, the emphasis on the origin of criminality as being within the home.[61] Consequently, the project of social diagnosis rapidly made progress during the inter war years, an attempt to analyse family, neighbourhood influences and environment in order to discover their impact upon the psyche of the individual.

Doubtless the growth in number of Child Guidance Clinic workers, probation officers and psychologists was implied by some of the Liberal reforms in social policy between 1906 and 1914 and by the Fabian recommendations of Beatrice Webb in the Minority Report of the Poor Law Commission of 1905-1909 for a much stronger interventionist welfare system. Be this as it may, during the inter war years the poor of Britain were the subjects of close attention and their social environment and intimate feelings were probed by various professionals seeking to understand the particular pathology of the family which had come to the notice of the authorities in connection with one problem or another. There is more than a grain of truth in Rose's remark that 'to be delinquent or withdrawn, to lie or bite your nails, to not sleep or wet your bed was to be the victim of the emotions of your parents',[62] The British Medical Association extolled the new Child Guidance Clinics[63] and Dr Letitia Fairfield insisted that 'behaviour and conduct difficulties . . . were superimposed by bad training or external environment' and that great attention must be paid to the 'development of the child's love life—its libido', 'real or imaginary harshness and repression', 'dream interpretations' and 'play activities of the child especially with dolls and puppies'; not without some truth did another doctor exclaim that the old foundations of will, knowledge and reason had been shaken to their core by these new illuminations of the mainsprings of human conduct.[64] Such groups as the National Council for Mental Hygiene (which had a somewhat eugenic orientation) and The People's League of Health advocated painstaking assessments of physique, mentality, family and environment, taking full account of theorists, and urged wide scale curative and preventive programmes of treatment and improvement, whether the need for better nutrition, more sunlight and air, recognition of sleepy sickness in children as effecting mental condition and so on.[65]

During the 1920s social diagnosis entered the prison system and was held up as a great advance on the missionary and temperance chaplains and visitors of the early twentieth century.[66] A group of volunteer women led by Lilian Le Mesurier assessed young men at Wandsworth and later Wormwood Scrubs in order to guide courts as to disposal and the Prison Commission as to allocation to one of the borstal regimes. These were clearly greatly influenced by mental hygiene and worked in accordance with its methods. So they saw delinquency often as the result of unconscious process, a symptom of neurosis, and detailed guidelines shaped their assessments: 'mental tests' must be used, the importance of 'nervous symptoms' assessed, physiological matters suspected by scientists to have relevance such as 'endocrine glands' must not be overlooked.[67] The interviewer must self-critically attend to interview style, must offer 'friendship' as a 'welcome aunt', and on no account take notes during the interview, only afterwards. The assessor must avoid an interrogatory 'official catechism' and gently guide rambling distressed parents back to the habits and feelings of their wayward son, for 'there are so many things to be known about him'. Disappointed ambitions, domestic unhappiness, a sense of inferiority, the need to compensate, must all carefully be tracked and charted in 'intimate private talk', and the need was paramount for more clinics, insights and workers. The project appeared to have almost limitless scope for 'any signs of strong feeling, whether of attachment or secret hatred or resentment are always of deep significance . . . innumerable questions will at once occur to any thoughtful visitor'.[68]

The Prison Commission saw the 'professionalisation' of lady visitors as a most important part of the adaptation of prisons to the new era of social diagnosis and mental hygienism. So, the Commissioners devoted great care to the preparation of long and detailed formats according to which reports on the boys and their homes might be more effectively researched. Behaviour at home and at school was to be analysed, work history surveyed, wishes for the future discovered, health checked. Was he affectionate towards his parents? Did he tell the truth? Was he generous? Are the parents well disposed or hostile to him in his present trouble? Are there any peculiarities about the boy? Is he repentant? Is he stubborn? Does he see himself as the victim of bad luck in being found out?[69] So, there was Tom, 'a reckless rollicking lad' with no conscience or scruples, wedded to crime, bitter towards his stepmother whom he believed was against him. There was Harry, brought up by indulgent 'Grannie and Grandad' and resentful when moved back to his more disciplinary mother and stepfather and falling into bad company. There was one unnamed who reflected that 'what you said in the prison that day, Miss, made a lot of difference to me. I seemed to think about it afterwards'.[70]

Many contemporaries lavished praise on these endeavours and believed that the treatment of crime by mental and social diagnosis and treatment would result in progressive strides away from an outdated system of criminal disposal. So the medical press strenuously argued that more doctors, psychologists and workers were needed to examine children to detect and treat 'all character deviations and mental abnormalities' in order to prevent 'the waste of good citizens' by an effective 'prophylaxis' of mental hygiene and child guidance.[71] Others were more sceptical and journalists grumbled that Norwood East was undermining 'the sense of moral responsibility' among the people, 'the rule that a man is responsible for his actions'.[72] Writers in magistrates' journals lugubriously pointed out that 'precocious young Americans' glibly attributed all their faults to 'unc' (unconscious).[73] Women Justices were appalled to hear that tiny children had such libidinous desires: 'but Doctor', exclaimed one, 'the dear babies, how could you say such awful things about them?'[74]

To many the age of D.H. Lawrence, Havelock Ellis, Freud and Jung, with its insistence upon self-expression and the central importance to human development and happiness of intimacy, emotion and sexuality, seemed to be the dawn of a new aeon in human affairs in which war would be outlawed, cooperation between men and women of all creeds and nations be characteristic, and human beings would express their emotions and satisfy their mysterious sexual desires unfettered by the shackles of the old social and intellectual order. To some, however, it seemed that 'the old beliefs . . . old props were gone; first religious faith, later faith in reason'[75] and that the psychologist was a major actor in that tragedy of dissolution.

On the face of it these trends among medical officers, in particular, suggest a radical shift towards positivistic determinism, even management of prisoners according to the theories of psychologists and psychotherapists. However, a number of points must be made about this. In the first place psychotherapy was only practised with a very small minority of prisoners. Secondly, although, for example, Grace Pailthorpe desired an entirely new penal system allocating its inmates to treatment programmes on the basis of selective psychological assessment, this view was not generally held by prison doctors. Apart from the theorising of Pailthorpe and Hamblin Smith about Freudian deterministic ideas, the great majority of Prison Medical Officers were, like Norwood East, unwilling to see radical changes in the classical basis of sentencing practice and prison discipline in punishment and culpability.

There is, however, no doubt that between 1910 and 1939 medical officers in prisons increased their role in the diagnosis and mental treatment of prisoners and that they depended upon contemporarily growing psychological theories to establish this greater significance. They did not dominate reformatory theory but rather achieved a greater credibility and influence. After 1945 psychiatric personnel would increase their effect on sentencers and the opening of Grendon Underwood psychiatric prison in 1962, as a result of the East / Hubert report, showed also the growth of their influence over actual management of prisoners. Between 1910 and 1939, however, medical officers and social diagnosticians had done no more than establish themselves as a significant part of a more aggressive correctional emphasis on the part of the Prison Commission. It is to this more general approach that we must now turn.

## NOTES

1. RCP & DCP yr end 31 March 1904, PP 1905, XXXVII: 42. yr end 31 March 1905, PP 1906, L: 38-9. yr end 31 March 1906, PP 1906, L: 37-8. RCP & DCP yr end 31 March 1908, PP 1908, LII: 34-5. W. Norwood East, 'Physical Moral Insensibility' *Criminal Journal of Mental Science*, October 1901, XLVII: 737-58.
2. The original vast document may be consulted by the heroic at Kew Public Records Office in: *The English Convict*, a Study by Dr. C. Goring, Deputy Medical Officer, Parkhurst PRO HO 45-10563-172511.
3. H.B. Donkin, 'Notes on Mental Defect in Criminals' *Journal of Mental Science*, Jan. 1917, LXIII: 23.
4. C. Goring, 'The Aetiology of Crime' *Journal of Mental Science*, April 1918, LXIV: 129-46. H.B. Donkin, 'The Factors of Criminal Actions' *Journal of Mental Science*, April 1919, LXV: 87-96.
5. H.B. Donkin, 'Notes on Mental Defect': 19.
6. *Lancet*, 9 Aug. 1913: 400. E. Schuster, *Eugenics* (Collins 1912): 105, 243.
7. H.B. Donkin, 'Mental Defect and Criminal Conduct' *Lancet*, 13 Nov. 1920: 985.
8. W. Norwood East, 'The Incidence of Crime and Mental Defect' *BMJ* 11 Aug. 1923: 228-9.
9. L.S. Hearnshaw, *A Short History Of British Psychology 1840-1940* (Methuen & Co. 1964): 205.
10. C. Burt, *The Young Delinquent* (University of London Press, 1925): 91-2.
11. Ibid: 386.
12. W. Healy, *The Individual Delinquent: A Text Book* (Little, Brown & Co. Boston 1922, 1st edn. 1915).
13. Ibid.
14. S. and E. Glueck, *Preventing Crime: A Symposium* (McGraw Hill 1936): 394.
15. S. and E. Glueck, *500 Delinquent Women* (Kraus Reprint Co. New York 1971): 142-57, cases of Marie, Alice, Grace.
16. N. Rose, *The Psychological Complex: Psychology, Politics and Society in England 1869-1939* (RKP 1985): 159.
17. Cecil Chapman, *The Poor Man's Court of Justice* (Hodder & Stoughton 1925): 287, 295. W. Clarke Hall, *The State and the Child* (Headley 1917): 172, 179.
18. *Justice of the Peace*, 12 Dec. 1931, XCV: 780.
19. *Lancet*, 22 Aug. 1936: 451-2.
20. Caradog Jones, *The Social Survey of Merseyside*, vol. 3 (Liverpool University Press 1934): 546. Cited J. MacNicol, 'In Pursuit of the Underclass' *Journal of Social Policy*, July 1987, 16 (3): 311.
21. Departmental Committee on Sterilization, PP 1933-4, XV: 55.
22. H.B. Donkin to *The Times*, 19 Dec. 1923, 11 col. e, 26 June 1924: 12 cols c-d.

23. Expert Opinions on Sterilization, PRO HO 144-1088-194663/4. H.B. Donkin to HO 20 July 1910, /5 J. Baker to HO, 7 Jan. 1911.

24. R.A. Gibbons, 'The Treatment of the Congenitally Unfit and of Convicts by Sterilization' *Eugenics Review,* July 1926, 18 (2): 100-9.

25. PRO P Com. 9/123 Memo W. Norwood East to Dept Cttee on Sterilization, 27 March 1933.

26. Sterilization 1931—4 PRO HO 144-19779-197900/69, /72, /77. Sterilization and Mental Deficiency 1911-1930 PRO HO 144-19778-197900/30 cut. Dr R. Berry to *The Times,* 6 Feb. 1930: 10 col. b.

27. W.C. Sullivan, *Crime and Insanity* (Arnold, 1924): 195.

28. W. Norwood East, *Medical Aspects of Crime* (Churchill 1936): 387-8.

29. *Lancet,* 25 Jan. 1919: 143-4.

30. RCP & DCP yr end 31 March 1920, PP 1920, XXIII: 19.

31. *Lancet,* 23 Oct. 1920: 873.

32. *Lancet,* 23 Dec. 1922: 1365-7.

33. Psychological Treatment of Crime 1921-41, PRO HO 45-18736-438456/9, HO Minutes, 3 and 7 Nov. 1922.

34. Ibid. /7 cut. *Daily Mail,* 17 Oct. 1922.

35. Ibid. /17 cut. *Evening News,* 28 Dec. 1925.

36. Ibid. /21 cut. *BMJ,* 27 July 1929.

37. Hearnshaw, *British Psychology:* 291.

38. PRO HO 45-18736-438456/14, cut. *Manchester Guardian,* 29 Nov. 1923 Hamblin Smith to Annual General Meeting of Chief Constables Association 1 June 1923.

39. Ibid. /16 Report Hamblin Smith to Birmingham Justices, 10 Sept. 1924.

40. M. Hamblin Smith, *The Psychology of the Criminal* (Methuen 1933, 2nd Edition): 78, 101.

41. M. Hamblin Smith, *Prisons and A Changing Civilization* (Bodley Head 1934): 60, 61

42. Ibid: 145-6.

43. G.W. Pailthorpe, *What We Put in Prison* (Williams & Norgate, 1932): 47, 62, 72.

44. G.W. Pailthorpe, *Studies in the Psychology of Delinquency* (HMSO 1932): 14-22.

45. Ibid: 52, 94, 22, 54.

46. R.P. Dobash, R.E. Dobash and S. Gutteridge, *The Imprisonment of Women* (Blackwell 1986): 121.

47. PRO HO 45-18736-438456/37, Report by F Coddington Stipendiary Magistrate, Bradford, to Sir A. Maxwell 1 July 1938.

48. Ibid. /39 HO Minute 12 Oct. 1938 in reference to Norwood East's reports.

49. Ibid. /33 J.R. Rees, Medical Director, Tavistock Clinic to Sir A. Maxwell 8 Feb. 1937, Accompanying report p. 5.

50. Treatment of Sexual Offenders 1932-54 PRO HO 45-No Box Number-24955/2, PC to HO 2 Nov. 1933; /1 HO Memo, 30 Dec. 1932. Psychological Treatment of Crime 1932-8, PRO PC 9/186/1, Norwood East to PC Chairman, 24 Oct. 1932, /3 Circular PC, 1 March 1934.

51. W. Norwood East and W.H. De B. Hubert, *Report on the Psychological Treatment of Crime* (HMSO 1939): 37.

52. Ibid: 37.

53. Ibid: 58, 69.

54. Ibid: 71.

55. Ibid: 36.

56. Ibid: 60, 43.

57. Ibid: 63, 78.

58. Ibid: 101.

59. Ibid: 95.

60. Ibid: 6, 8.

61. N. Rose, *The Psychological Complex: Psychology, Politics and Society in England 1869-1939* (RKP 1985): 174.

62. Ibid: 207.

63. *BMJ*, 12 July 1930: 68.

64. *BMJ*, 28 Nov. 1931: 1002. *BMJ*, 19 Oct. 1935: 735.

65. G. Jones, *Social Hygiene in Twentieth Century Britain* (Croom Helm 1986): 82-3.

66. For development of prison assessments of young male prisoners see V. Bailey, *Delinquency and Citizenship: Reclaiming the Young Offender 1914-1948* (Clarendon 1987): 175.

67. L. Le Mesurier, *A Handbook of Probation* (NAPO 1935): 2, 12, 15, 216.

68. L. Le Mesurier, *Boys in Trouble* (Murray 1931): XIII, 103, 104, 140, 192, 260.

69. Lady Visitors At Wandsworth 1924-7, PRO P Com 7/176.

70. Le Mesurier, *Boys in Trouble*: 102.

71. *Lancet*, 2 June 1928: 1129-30.

72. Psychological Treatment of Crime, PRO P Com 9/186 /26, cut. *Daily Sketch*, 8 March 1939.

73. Justice of the Peace, 18 July 1925, LXXXIX: 419.

74. Hearnshaw, *British Psychology*: 291.

75. C.L. Mowat, *Britain Between The Wars* (Methuen 1955): 202.

## Chapter Eleven

# Relaxation and Reformation – A Radical Policy 1921–1939

Ruggles-Brise's departure was attended by protest at his system from those who insisted that it fell far short of what he claimed for it. In early 1922 the Labour Research Committee report appeared. During its preparation there had been prolonged dispute, for George Bernard Shaw had wished, against the views of the editors, to insert a preface in which he would urge euthanasia by 'lethal chambers' for unreformable criminals; furthermore, one of the editors, Stephen Hobhouse, had come close to collapse as a result of the immense labour of preparation for publication.[1] In the event the report was a swingeing attack on Ruggles-Brise's prisons which it claimed to be places of monotony, misery and despair where individualisation and reformation were notable chiefly by their absence.[2] Some of Ruggles-Brise's own people turned on his system and his Lady Inspector of Prisons, Mary Gordon, at the same time publicly insisted that the prison system demoralised women and was out of step with modern theory. So, she argued that the woman offender was often 'exhausted and neurasthenic', hysterical, self-destructive, an abused tool of men, progressively demarcated as a criminal by a harsh system of criminal justice, ultimately deteriorating into a habitual prisoner, the victim of 'conflicting emotions of shame and self justification, depression and bravado, inferiority and defiance at war within her'.[3] Gordon was sure that the prison system had utterly failed and demanded that the woman prisoner be handed over to the expert in instinct, emotion and mental conflict, 'the doctor . . . the man of science . . . the student of the whole man'.[4] At present it merely exacerbated criminality, for it shut down expression of emotion and denied human warmth, leading to an unhealthy disassociation between inner feeling and outer world thus inflaming the very mental conflict which had created the criminality in the first place.

The new chairman, Maurice Waller had joined the commission long before in 1910, after Rugby and an Oxford first, followed by thirteen years at the Home Office: indeed, between 1906 and 1910, he had been Herbert Gladstone's private secretary. Waller was aware of the general contents of the Labour report before publication and discussed it with two members of the Labour Committee who were well known contributors to penological discussion, William Clarke Hall, a London magistrate and expert on Juvenile Courts, and Margery Fry, a Quaker magistrate and secretary of the Howard League. Waller's attitude to the report contrasted with the distrust of Ruggles-Brise towards the editors and researchers and the result of this change of view was swiftly apparent. In February 1922 Alexander Paterson took post as a third prison commissioner alongside his Chairman and Dr. S. Dyer the Medical Commissioner.

Alexander Paterson was born in 1884 of a well to do Cheshire family and educated at Bowden College and Oxford. He thereafter went to work in one of the settlement foundations at Bermondsey which were set up as a practical response to T.H. Green's and Canon Samuel Barnett's calls for a voluntarist social and moral crusade of rescue and during his first term at Oxford he was deeply affected by an appeal from John Stedwell who addressed the students about his work at the Oxford Medical Mission in Bermondsey.

Paterson devoted himself to working, at first as a teacher in Bermondsey, and then as a 'voluntary officer for boys at the Tower Bridge police court' and after 1906 organised clubs and outdoor camps for these and other poor young people as well as helping Bermondsey Juvenile Adults coming out of Borstal.[5] He subsequently attracted the attention of the Home Office and was asked for advice about the new Children's Courts and the probation system. He was also invited to become assistant director of the new Central Association for discharged convicts set up in Churchill's Home Secretary-ship. Apparently his interest in prisoners had been awakened by the sentence of ten years penal servitude on a young man whom he knew well in Bermondsey and who killed his wife and Paterson had been accustomed to cycle to Dartmoor to see the man. In 1914 Paterson led a contingent of Bermondsey men to volunteer for military service and for a time he refused a commission, preferring to fight alongside his men. He was wounded, twice recommended for the Victoria Cross and decorated with the Military Cross. After demobilisation he worked with the Ministry of Labour prior to his appointment as Prison Commissioner.

The basis of Paterson's theoretical approach was set out in 1911 in a book which he wrote called 'Across The Bridges'.[6] Here he vividly described a harsh, poverty stricken neighbourhood of exhausted and ill mothers, unhappy alcohol abusing fathers, listless despairing marriages between couples who, like robots, went through the motions of a joyless harsh life. Their babies died in very high numbers, their children were malnourished and sickly, their teenaged offspring lived off flourishing street crime and much of their existence was a wastage of their humanity. Paterson therefore demanded a vibrant self-critical commitment from the well to do and a new social crusade to create dignity and purpose amongst the poor. Surmising that the classes had been geographically and socially pulled apart by industrial change, he argued that the rich lived complacently and comfortably, knowing little, and caring less, about what happened in places like Bermondsey and often exploiting the poor by erecting and profiting from the foul tenements and bad housing.

Paterson, like Ruggles-Brise, based his vision on the new liberal tradition of T.H. Green and those who came after him at Oxford. In addition, again like Ruggles-Brise, Paterson was convinced of the value of the public school model for training a social elite by 'building up discipline from within, by encouraging . . . social instincts of loyalty and esprit de corps and stimulating latent capacity for leadership'.[7] He emphasised strongly the commitment of the public school/university elite to the communities of the poor. So, he urged that public school and university men should live among the poor in intimate fellowship, by their leadership creating energy and constructive activity out of despair and decay. He wanted constant physical and mental activities and challenges so that all would participate together and grow in love of the leader and of the group, the propagation of a comradely striving by the individual for the group under its inspiring leadership together with healthy and challenging recreational activities, 'clubs and brigades and scout patrols'.[8] In these clean and active club fellowships the young would 'find that leadership and learn that comradeship which will give him an ideal and a spirit in which character may be built . . . new ideas of the right and wrong things to do, fresh examples to be admired and imitated, a new and healthier outlet for noise, excitement and energy. The gang becomes a team, the gambler a sportsman, the bully may form the devoted leader of a group. The process does not consist in pounding out the bad in a boy by preaching or by punishment. Rather is the good in him so developed as to master or transform what will otherwise be bad': for the adolescent the availability or lack of such an experience would probably determine whether he or she became 'a liability' or 'an asset', 'a criminal or a citizen'.[9]

Paterson emphasised character and spirit as able to rise above criminogenic social conditions and he urged the creation of human relationships in which spirit, mind and body would thrive so that the individual's free will might determine a clean and honest life thereafter. First and foremost, like T.H. Green, he lodged his aspirations in a Christian religious framework insisting that his project was intended to allow conditions for spiritual and moral development among rich and poor alike rather than social reconstruction in its own right. Nevertheless, like many new liberals, he believed that, without the vibrant, energetic, compassionate and active engagement of rich with poor, state socialism was likely to result. His objective was not therefore to convert borstals to public schools, rather to extrapolate the esprit de corps, group influence for good and stimulation of the individual to effort which he had experienced in public school, university, boys' clubs and army and to apply these to borstal boys on the basis of his Christian notion that good exists in all.[10]

Paterson came to believe that the settlements had become dry and distant from the poor who lived around them.[11] He wished to rekindle the intensity and intimacy of T.H. Green's vision in a milieu of pure minded sacrifice and example such as existed in the best sort of school or boy scouts' troop. He was sure that morality was absorbed from the group and so, in place of street gang devoted to plunder, criminogenic neighbourhood and apathetic spiritless family, Paterson aimed to set up a dynamic and bracing environment of effort, enthusiasm, achievement and challenge so that individuals would absorb these qualities and reach their full potential as children of God and able, as true men and women, to hand down their new found freedom to their children. Consequently to Paterson moral, physical and intellectual development was deeply effected for better or worse by corporate experience 'in club, brigade or bible class' for 'the spirit of a good club is against loafers: the hero worship of the younger boy leads him to emulate the athlete rather than dressy spindle-shanks who knows a thing or two' and the 'clean healthy boy who is constantly taking violent physical exercise can never brood over his temptations'.[12]

Paterson made a substantial contribution to the Labour Research Committee report, although it is not clear how much of the borstal section of it he wrote himself.[13] Although on the one hand well suited for his appointment to the Prison Commission, he was at the time closely involved with those organisations, like the Labour group, which were very critical of Ruggles-Brise. However, his appointment was seen as desirable, because the borstal system was itself under substantial attack. For example, the borstal recently set up at Portland Convict Prison, was the subject of public condemnation for its retention of a convict prison ethos. It seems likely that Home Secretary Edward Shortt realised that protest was swelling into demands for a royal commission into 'the abuses of the English prison system'[14] and felt that Paterson's appointment would forestall these demands. Certainly in critical circles the choice of Paterson as commissioner was greeted enthusiastically.[15]

Paterson never became chairman of the prison commission and died in 1947. He served under four chairmen during the inter war years, Maurice Waller (1922-7), Sir Alexander Maxwell (1927-32), Sir Harold Scott (1932-9) and lastly, after Scott was seconded for defence duties, C.D.C. Robinson who acted Chairman between 1939 and 1942. All contemporary accounts, whether eulogistic or hostile, describe Paterson as the major influence on the direction of the commission during the inter war years. So Lionel Fox, who was appointed Secretary to the Commission in the mid 1920s and became Chairman in 1942, called him 'the mainspring and the inspiration' of the commission.[16] Sir Harold Scott referred to Paterson as 'a decisive influence upon my life . . . one of the most remarkable men I have ever met'.[17] Gerold Clayton, son of the one time secretary of the commission and a prison governor who was critical of Paterson, described him as 'a strong and vital personality' influencing the commission towards his views.[18]

Between 1921 and 1939 the prison commissioners argued that there was in progress a steady mitigation of the severity of Ruggles-Brise's system and the implementation of new policies designed to reform and train prisoners and borstal trainees more effectively. As far as relaxation of severity was concerned the commission gave numerous instances. In 1923 convict separation was suspended[19] and in 1930 abolished—separation in local prisons was also abolished during 1931. In 1924 compulsory attendance at chapel services during week days and Sundays was suspended at most prisons.[20] The number of floggings for convict prison offences fell to nil in the mid 1920s.[21] In 1921 the broad arrows on prisoners' uniforms were removed and in 1922 the raised daises in chapels for surveying officers were removed, the close crop of convicts' heads also being abolished.[22] In March 1922 conversation was allowed in prison workshops and in 1924 the parti coloured uniform and heavy leg chains, which potential escapers must carry, were abolished.[23] In late 1921 it was agreed that prisoners might be transferred between prisons in civilian clothes and the old visiting boxes were abolished in favour of rooms with tables and chairs where spouses and relatives were allowed 'to embrace each other if they desire to do so'.[24]

In addition, wireless broadcasts were introduced into prisons and a remarkable increase in concerts, amateur dramatic performances, community singing and film shows occurred in the inter war period, to the astonishment of one newspaper which headlined 'Talkie Films For all Prisons—Education, Garbo and Glamour'.[25] Women's hair was no longer to be cut shorter than its length on admission.[26] At Maidstone convict prison coach parties of young convicts played away football matches and at the same prison a recreation centre with ping pong and bowls was set up.[27] In Parkhurst chess clubs played outside clubs and in other prisons concerts were staged by prisoners and prison jazz bands and orchestras set up together with mess rooms, where small groups of prisoners took meals, could talk and read newspapers.[28] Not all these blessings were unmixed, however, for the Dartmoor prisoners' band was 'ghastly . . . it was fantastically bad'![29] In addition physical conditions improved—cells were now centrally heated, whereas in Ruggles-Brise's time they used to be so cold in winter that prisoners would wear their clothes all night. Earnings were more widely introduced, canteens set up and smoking more generally allowed.

The Prison Commissioners also claimed that they were developing a radical new programme of intellectual, physical and moral reformation of prisoners. They particularly maintained that this applied to borstals but they insisted that progress in this direction was being made more generally in the prison system and they urged that they had updated Ruggles-Brise's methods to take into account modern approaches to physical, mental and moral improvement.

With regard to physical fitness, training was increased throughout the prisons and borstals. By 1924 all women under thirty were being put through programmes of weekly gymnastic exercises and at Aylesbury borstal in 1931 a full time instructress in physical culture was appointed.[30] In male prisons fully equipped gymnasia were set up and in 1930 the Commission was seriously worried by the number of accidents and fractures. Norwood East blamed the 'stupidity and lack of foresight shown by many of our cases'[31] rather than the equipment and for a time restricted gymnastics to the under 26 year olds and ruled that a qualified instructor must always be present. In addition sports events became common in prisons. So, although boxing matches were discouraged officially, Paterson covertly allowed them at Wormwood Scrubs and elsewhere[32] and at one prison the emphasis on sport had gone so far that the local village football team and the prison team were apparently inter changing members for fixtures, 'a practice which the commissioners with some regret felt bound to frown on when it came to our notice'.[33] At Maidstone convict prison an annual sports day was held at which the gymnastics 'would be an asset to the staff of a public school'.[34]

It was in the borstals, however, that the emphasis on physical fitness and development reached its apogee, for development of physical health and robust energy was the *sine qua non* of the Paterson ideal of moral and intellectual vitality and cooperative comradeship. Most aspects of Borstal Training had an element of physical training. The new borstals, opened in the inter war years at such places as Lowdham Grange near Nottingham, Usk, and North Sea Camp on the Wash, were all selected for their rural remoteness and the physical challenge of their environment. At Lowdham and North Sea Camp staff and trainees laboured together at reclamation and reconstruction of the environment and the two famous marches of borstal boys to found Lowdham in 1930 and North Sea Camp in 1935 exemplified well developed strong young men, transformed from slum bred loafers, marching in disciplined and cheerful fashion to establish new colonies for the spreading of the borstal gospel. In 1938 a third 'open' borstal was set up at Hollesley Bay in Suffolk and in these the emphasis was on staff and trainees living, exercising and working together as examples of physical fitness and strength confronting a harsh untamed wilderness. But, throughout all the borstals, athletics, games, swimming, summer camps in the wilds, team competition and constant physical activity were said to be characteristic. Paterson urged the value of all this with immense enthusiasm and himself arranged and refereed football matches with outside clubs such as Bermondsey boys' club.[35]

In borstals the promotion of drill was seen as essential to good co-ordination and physique. Ex sergeant majors were imported to teach this and enthused about its virtues to their charges. 'I love drill. Love it. Nothing pleases me more than a fine squad of well built smart men and nothing makes me more sad than a drooping doubled up youngster . . . I know what you're all thinking. "Silly ginger headed old sod" but wait, wait till you go to drill with your own houses. You'll say "Old McTavish is not so bad. What a bloody mess I'd look among my house if it hadn't been for him".'[36] Route marches and frequent inter house sports competitions also highlighted the physical training element of borstal.

The commissioners also claimed that they had constructed a new educational system for borstal trainees and prisoners by 1939. In late 1921 the Board of Education complained to Ruggles-Brise's successor that the standard of the work of schoolmaster and schoolmistress warders was unacceptably low and from then on certified teachers of basic literacy and numeracy were always appointed on the retirement of those officers, despite Home Office lamentation that better education merely gave 'a greater capacity for committing crime'.[37] Furthermore, at every prison an educational adviser was appointed from the local academic or educational community to advise the prison governor about provision of programmes of adult education and to recruit a cadre of voluntary prison teachers of such programmes for each prison. Indeed, there was a widening of the access granted by Ruggles-Brise to voluntary groups whose representatives were allowed into prisons in greater numbers than in Ruggles-Brise's time.

Educational expansion led to tension between the commission and the Home Office, which was plainly becoming uneasy about the entire policy in the 1920s. In 1923 H.B. Simpson wondered how many criminals 'taught raffia work in prison show any real desire to earn an honest living by it after their discharge'[38] and officials often refused to support commission claims for extra money to pay for the programme. H.B. Simpson especially considered these endeavours to be a waste of money and insisted that the only effective prison education was the example of staff 'in the way of industry, tidiness, cleanliness, self control and so on'.[39] Before long this tension had been picked up by members of parliament who began to press the Home Office towards greater support of the commissioners' claims on the Treasury. Simpson wearily reflected that 'there are other claims on the Exchequer which will have to be given precedence over the Prison Commissioners' proposals'.[40] However, the Home Office was also concerned at the type of organization being given access, for Ruggles-Brise had usually restricted access to religious or quasi religious bodies whose moral message was plain and unambiguously traditional. So there was great uncertainty about the admission of the People's League of Health which, between 1922 and 1925, ran courses in thirteen prisons on sexual hygiene, nutrition, alcohol use, the value of exercise and recreation and so forth. Home Office officials worried that such organizations were 'voluntary propaganda societies'[41] and noted that some governors had doubts about the 'desirability of discussing sex questions in the presence of others'.[42]

The limit of Home Office patience was reached when the Prison Commission began to use highly educated prisoners as teachers. Home Secretary Sir William Joynson-Hicks held office between late 1924 and mid 1929 and strongly objected to such use of prisoners like M.P. Horatio Bottomley sentenced in 1922 to seven years penal servitude for fraud. When Joynson-Hicks discovered that such prisoners were being used as teachers he prohibited the practice and the commissioners responded by arguing that such use emphasised to these prisoners their responsibility as citizens, pointing out that the introduction of leadership functions for certain prisoners was at the heart of their policy. However, Joynson-Hicks would have none of it and the commissioners bided their time until 1931 when they persuaded Labour Home Secretary, John Clynes, to agree to the practice, telling him stories about illiterate gipsies taught to read and write at Wakefield in the old days before prohibition. Clynes did however insist that classes were to be limited in numbers and notorious criminals were not to run them.[43] More generally the Home Office was sceptical about the educational initiatives between 1920 and 1930 and in 1927 quietly arranged with the Board of Education to kill off a private member's bill requiring the local education authority to run schemes in all prisons within their area.[44]

The rapid rise of the influence of male prison visitors during the inter war years enhanced the importance given to education. Following the growth of Ruggles-Brise's Lady Visitors a National Association of Prison Visitors was set up for men in 1924. These were to get to know male prisoners and converse at length with them so as to alter outlook by emphasis on obligation and selflessness, but they would also be sympathetic and kindly so as to win the affections of the prisoners and thus more deeply influence them. By 1939, with Prison Commission support, there were 1200 of these and they tended to justify various new schemes as educational in order for them to be accepted. They therefore collaborated with the local education advisers and voluntary lecturers to bring outside actors and performers into prison, to hold poetry and play reading sessions and to conduct debates among prisoners. So, in 1926, prisoners at Wormwood Scrubs rehearsed the play 'An Episode In The Trojan War'. When the Home Office got to hear of this they prohibited actual production although they allowed play readings: undeterred, a prison visitor brought in his musically skilled mother to start up a prison orchestra.[45] Indeed, Prison Visitors insisted that the discussions which followed play readings about, say, the morality of Cassius in 'Julius Caesar', were important to reformation of attitude.

In the adult prisons there was a remarkable expansion of education and by 1937 Paterson presided over a Prisoners' Education Committee to coordinate hundreds of courses being offered by voluntary groups and individuals, frequently financially supported by charitable bodies like the Carnegie Trust.[46] Plainly, as will be seen later, this project brought with it many conflicts and problems, yet the Commission argued that a remarkable change had occurred for the better. So, hire of films for educational purposes was funded by voluntary groups and later by the Exchequer and plays were performed by outside bodies such as the Cotswold Players at Gloucester: the hearty National Anthem which followed the production was duly noted in the press.[47]

Chaplains continued to play a part in education but increasingly were overshadowed by new figures such as educational advisers or the energetic voluntary workers. Indeed, the information given to prisoners became much more general than in the Ruggles-Brise era when it had been controlled by chaplains. The provision of news to prisoners illustrates this, for during the Great War and afterwards, news had been given to prisoners by chaplains from pulpits following services, a practice which some of them objected to, arguing that such items as football results distracted from the solemn act of worship. In 1932 Paterson suggested a weekly news sheet and the first of these was put out in selected prisons in 1933. From the first these included material about political developments and national achievements as well as sports results and tended towards a somewhat rosy, optimistic view of world progress. In 1935 the news sheets were sent to all prisoners under the title 'Weekly News Sheet' and the first number of the new general edition included such items as the building of the Mersey Tunnel, a new Cunard liner, heroic attempts to conquer Everest, as well as cricket, football, boxing, horse racing and motor cycling results. In addition readers were asked to ponder on certain questions. Should Britain remain in the League of Nations? Should nations combine to use force against an aggressor? Should the private sale and manufacture of arms be prohibited?[48]

This invitation to the prisoner to participate as citizen, weighing up the issues of the time, was also reflected in the debating movement which had begun under Ruggles-Brise and became widespread thereafter. So, it became common for prisoners to engage in organised debates with each other, led by staff, about such things as the sanctity of marriage or the ethics of citizenship. They must decide whether or not this house regretted 'the passing of the good old days' or whether the house believed the discovery of wireless to have been more important than that of printing, or, if Hitler, Mussolini, Churchill and Ford were together in an overladen balloon above the Sahara Desert, which of these should be thrown overboard to prevent the balloon from grounding.[49] Emotions ran high at these. At one debate about whether a woman's place was in the home, a participant leapt to his feet and roared at the supporter of the motion, 'rats, you old fool—you ought to be at home an' all but you ain't there, so what yer arguing for?'[50]

In the borstal system, which by 1939 included one female and nine male institutions[51] and whose population never fell below 1,700 youths and 105 girls between 1934 and 1936,[52] the emphasis on education was more marked still. From the outset Waller was determined to reform borstal education, which he considered had deteriorated and he emphasised the importance of a new type of certificated teacher, the borstal tutor, who had begun to be appointed in Ruggles-Brise's last years and on whom he and Paterson laid an immense responsibility. 'The chief part of their work is, and will continue to be, actual teaching but beyond this, as you may remember, the point is to get men with a touch of the missionary spirit, athletic and manly, who will exercise influence over the borstal inmates and take part in the games, if possible, on Saturday afternoon'.[53] These tutors, who in Ruggles-Brise's time were called by Colonel Rich and others 'wing commanders', were placed in charge of set groups of trainees now called 'Houses' as in public schools and were required to relate intimately to every trainee. Under the influence of these tutors, who were increased in number and became the housemasters and assistant housemasters of the inter war borstal system, teaching methods and curricula were reformed to make classes more appealing, to increase subjects taught and to allow for greater individual assessment of a trainee's educational requirements and capacities. For example, the teaching of history was changed and attempts were made 'to teach history backwards and it has been found possible to interest a rough lad and to satisfy his natural curiosity by tracing his present day experiences to their historical causes. This will be found more interesting and useful than beginning with Stone Henge'.[54] At Feltham the two tutors, Paterson Owens and James Brown, entirely redesigned the curriculum and system of allocation of each trainee to a class so as to allow more differentiation and meeting of educational need.[55] In general, the tutors were seen as vital to the entire borstal system—moral examples, sports organisers, intimate friends, wise counsellors, expert educators.[56]

In addition the tutors as housemasters were expected to plan the occupational and vocational training best suited to each trainee and this was increasingly seen as a function which required the aid of social science. In the mid 1930s housemasters were sent for training in up to date methods of career guidance and planning at the National Institute of Industrial Psychology so that the trainees might be systematically tested and assessed and appropriately occupationally trained in accordance with their capacities and aspirations.[57]

Above all borstal was held to exemplify the new ethos of cooperation, mutual responsibility and zealous group membership which was the reformatory aspiration of the commissioners. This period was the zenith of the Paterson ethos in borstals with the House as the basic unit often named, as at Portland, after British heroes, and its housemaster, assistant housemaster, colours, esprit de corps, monitors, sports teams, dining hall and traditions. Plainly, under Paterson's influence, this vision of social rehabilitation dominated the system and the prison commissioners reported enthusiastically about it to the Home Office. 'The house system solves many problems of training by substituting corporate for individual effort and house rivalry for personal rivalry. Public spirit is better developed through loyalty to the house with its obvious rivals than through loyalty to the Institution, a larger body with no competition in evidence. The House master is the guiding spirit of the house'.[58] In such a system jobs for borstal trainees proliferated, 'secretaries to house clubs, lads in charge of other lads, of books, of boots, of clothes, of football lists'.[59] Furthermore, the presence of matrons in male borstals was eulogised as having a refining effect: at Portland 'public opinion is intensely hostile to any indecorous reference or loose illusion and the matron's room is besieged at all hours by lads who . . . quite unconsciously seek a respite from the crudities of purely male intercourse'.[60]

The transformation was believed to be most strikingly revealed at the summer camps to which large numbers of borstal boys would go to live in tents, cook for themselves, march to local cinemas and churches and compete in long days of sports. Colonel Rich had begun this experiment but soon reports were flowing in of 'glorious weather', 'smiling faces' and congratulations about exemplary behaviour from local communities: funded by donations raised by public appeal, mornings were devoted to useful work in the locality, afternoons to games, swimming, fishing, rambles and explorations.[61] Borstal girls went to a hostel at Littlehampton whilst the male trainees camped and, although there was usually some absconding, these camps were seen as of great importance in building the corporate loyal and vital character. So, at Hawkeshill camp in 1923 among the Feltham boys 'a very striking incident took place; the prefects themselves, without any hint, paid their respects (to the Dover Patrol war memorial) by getting their sections together and giving Eyes Right as they passed'.[62] The press were fed such information by the commissioners and enthusiastically reported it to the public.[63]

These were the great days of the borstal system to later generations, an era of sport, hard work, trust, corporate loyalty and devoted service, the working out of Paterson's dream by such figures as William Llewellin at Lowdham and North Sea Camp or Lilian Barker governor of Aylesbury. In report after report the commissioners emphasised that a dramatic reform of the borstal system was producing excellent results and events such as the Lowdham march made clear that, if put upon their honour, these trainees participated fully and eagerly in the ethos of camp fire and open air with its teachers, earnest and challenging Christian housemasters and emphasis on corporate loyalty and selflessness. Thus Llewellin camped in the same gruelling conditions as the boys at North Sea Camp where marsh land was being reclaimed from the sea. Climate was often very severe and housemasters, staff and trainees worked, ate and lived together in accordance with Paterson's model of borstals as places of Christian example and endeavour, the learning of the lessons of life, citizenship and religion through actual practice. More than just the new camp or open borstals, throughout all the borstals the commission emphasised reclamation—as Llewellin put, it at North Sea Camp land reclamation symbolised the reclamation of what would otherwise be human waste and the whole of the borstal system was effected to a greater or lesser degree by physical exercise, hard work, close engagement between staff (no longer uniformed) and trainees, educational programmes to improve powers of concentration and give more food for thought.[64]

So, in the mid 1930s borstal trainees were allowed home leaves in order for them to find work, to test their own reaction to freedom and to discover that the reality of life outside was often very different to the 'roseate dream' of it in borstal and governors proudly recalled that almost all returned on time. Oaths of allegiance were taken before admittance to North Sea Camp or Lowdham: 'because of the trust put in me I promise on my honour to do my best to keep up the good name of Lowdham Grange'.[65] Rover groups and girl guides were set up; groups of trainees were allowed to go from Lowdham into nearby Nottingham on Saturdays; others were allowed to attend evening classes at nearby training centres; hobbies, such as 'keeping rabbits, bees, pigeons and allotments', were encouraged; Gilbert and Sullivan societies were set up. But behind it all, as the governor of Lowdham remarked, the aim was for 'the standard of Christ . . . the religious motive is behind the place'.[66]

To a lesser extent the emphasis on responsibility, participation and training for citizenship was also evident in those adult prisons which, under

Paterson's influence, were increasingly designated as training prisons for specially selected longer sentenced prisoners. In 1936 a two hundred acre site was acquired some sixteen miles from Wakefield and a hundred selected Wakefield prisoners sent to live at a camp set up there towards the end of their sentence. Here in huts which contained groups of ten prisoners, each with its kitchen and common room, they worked at clearing the site. As with Colonel Rich who had begun the borstal summer camps, Harold Scott, Chairman of the Commission, later recalled the acute anxiety the New Hall Camp experiment caused him, for an escape or a crime would have exposed him to public ridicule. He closely watched the experiment and noted that the prisoners were at first listless and apathetic but later became alert and cheerful. As some of the officers said to him, 'It's like putting a dead flower in water and watching it revive'.[67] The commissioners justified this on the grounds that only by giving responsibility to prisoners could they actually learn to exercise it. As a prisoner was told by the Wakefield governor: 'I propose to send you out to the prison camp. If you want to play the fool, play it; I cannot stop you. But, if you do, you are a rotter. You merely spoil an experiment which is being carried out and put the clock back five years'.[68] Both Home Office and public opinion supported this project although the conservative magazine, *John Bull*, warned the Commission that honest labourers must not be denied work as a result of prisoners doing the reclaiming of land at the camp.[69]

There were other projects which were clearly influenced by the work of the American prison reformer, Thomas Mott Osborne, who toured England in 1922 to widespread plaudits from the press.[70] At Nottingham and Wakefield training prisons, after three months, prisoners were placed in groups of nine ('a crew') under the leadership of one of their number ('a stroke') and allowed extra earnings to buy luxuries, encouraged to run debating societies and eat in their own mess.[71] At other prisons 'Honour Parties' were given a much greater degree of freedom at work. At Wormwood Scrubs in 1925 a first offender scheme was begun whereby unsupervised association was allowed in the evenings and a group mess allowed for each group. In the mess 'one man is the head of the table and uses his influence to promote decency in manners and conversation'[72] and was assisted by a deputy leader of the group. In Nottingham prison Helena Dowson, a magistrate influenced by Osborne, persuaded Waller to allow a 'League of Honour' in the early 1920s. This was an association consisting of herself, the governor, chaplain and fourteen stars and was run by the prisoners themselves, who chose a committee and association officers, and were given unsupervised recreation so that they could organise their own activities. As at Lowdham and North Sea Camp an oath was administered to 'adhere to the rules and regulations of the Prison and League and I do further give my word of honour to assist the governor and officers by doing all that may be required of me'.[73] At Wakefield all prisoners were assigned to one of three groups, searching was abolished and each group expected to take an active part in policing the behaviour of individual members.[74] At Winchester the Honour Party laid out prison gardens assisted by the National Gardens Guild which maintained a section devoted to advising prisoners about horticulture.[75]

Even before the appointment of a departmental committee to report on the management of persistent offenders by Labour Home Secretary J.R. Clynes in April 1931,[76] the commissioners had been contemplating designating some prisons as training institutions. However, the report of this committee gave added emphasis to the idea and indeed it heard evidence from Paterson, Hamblin Smith and governor of Aylesbury borstal, Lilian Barker, about the potential of the new ethos to reform such prisoners. So, the committee recommended that a new sentence of corrective detention should be created, 'reformative . . . remedial . . . rather than penal',[77] to be concentrated on younger persistent offenders in their twenties before they deteriorated into habitual old lags: for the latter a new long incapacitating prolonged detention was to be created to replace the Ruggles-Brisian hybrid sentence of penal servitude and preventive detention. The committee backed the idea of 'labour camps' and 'minimum security structures' as well as use of psychological treatment for younger persistent offenders and urged Lowdham as a model for the management of these.[78]

This emphasis on exporting the borstal method to a selected number of adult prisons and the idea of specialist training prisons was further emphasised two years later by another report from a committee whose members included Harold Scott and Margery Fry[79] and which praised the recent introduction of earnings schemes, as at Wakefield where the Prison Commission had gone into partnership with the Howard League. The League had donated £250 so that selected prisoners should be paid according to the industrial output of the small group to which each was allocated and the earnings could be spent on tobacco or taken out of the prison on release.[80] Subsequently earnings were introduced at Nottingham and Chelmsford.

Given the public support of these two committees the idea of the specialist training prison came to the centre of policy during the 1930s and therefore a new kind of institution was created alongside the convict prison and the local short sentence gaol. Thus prisoners who were serving a medium term sentence and who were selected for such training no longer served this locally but were moved out of their region to the training prisons such as those at Wakefield, Nottingham (up to 1930), Wormwood Scrubs (for adult stars) and Chelmsford (for younger convicts of recidivist tendencies). Furthermore, there was also a tendency to concentrate women in particular prisons such as Holloway, Manchester and Exeter and this also reinforced a specialist training emphasis.

During the 1930s, therefore, there was an attempt to reform industrial training, particularly at the training prisons, and new workshops and machinery were introduced under the supervision of a new Director of Industries assisted by three new industrial managers at headquarters. In the training prisons, in addition, the emphasis was, as has been described, to be particularly on the cultivation of responsibility and corporate loyalty together with improved conditions, luxuries and earnings.

Although the Prison Commissioners emphasised that 80 per cent of convicted prisoners were serving sentences of less than three months and therefore not deemed likely to be influenced by reformatory measures, they made widespread claims for the success of all the new initiatives in borstals and training prisons. They urged that around 60 per cent of borstal trainees were not reconvicted[81] and that the results of the new specialist training prisons were highly encouraging. In addition, they made clear that severity had greatly relaxed in all prisons and even dared to tell the public that 'prisoners are allowed and encouraged to laugh'.[82] So, it was believed that many prisoners no longer viewed the prisons and borstals with loathing but rather with warmth. Thus ex Roedean housemistress Miss Mellanby, governor of Aylesbury before the second world war, recalled the lonely girl who was faced with a long Easter break from work and made her way back to Aylesbury because she could think of nowhere else where she would be welcome.[83] Colonel Turner, governor of Wakefield, reported about ex-prisoners who would come to see him to talk about the old days. 'We talk about old times at school, old times at the University, old times in the regiment . . . but old times in prison! I came to the conclusion that . . . a man could look back with appreciation and with gratitude upon 12 months spent in Wakefield gaol'.[84]

The driving force behind all this was Paterson's vision and during the 1920s and 1930s he suggested various schemes for the improvement of the penal system—weekend custody, psychological regimes, cottage homes to replace women's prisons, camps for community service and so forth.[85] These were not then implemented but at the centre of all his ideas remained consistently the faith in corporate loyalty, earnest and intimate relationship between prisoners and staff, physical and mental exertion and activity within a framework of Christian challenge and love. It was in his view the power of Christian leadership and charisma which was the dynamo which drove the group to energise its members to reformation and a group 'that is not in the direct charge of a personality will never realise its existence as an entity or have any corporate life and spirit'.[86] To bring this to bear, risks should be taken and it was not work for the weak or the milk sop. So, in 1925, during a visit to Burma, he descended upon the local gaol and marched a band of young Burmese dacoits to found a camp in the jungle: the betting against his returning alive was 10 to 1 in the Rangoon clubs.[87]

Such in outline was the account which the Prison Commission gave of itself during the inter war years, arguing that there had been a far reaching reduction of the severity of penal conditions and the mounting of an enhanced reformatory project. It is now necessary to analyse further the truth of these claims to assess how far these policies affected the actual treatment of prisoners by staff but initially to examine some of the difficulties and conflicts which attended their implementation.

## NOTES

1. S. Hobhouse, *Forty Years On and An Epilogue* (J. Clarke &Co. 1951): 177-8.
2. S. Hobhouse and A.F. Brockway (eds) *English Prisons Today* (Longman, Green & Co. 1922).
3. M. Gordon, *Penal Discipline* (Routledge 1922): 88, 174.
4. Ibid: 238.
5. J.E. Thomas, *The English Prison Officer since 1850* (Routledge & Kegan Paul 1972): 252-3. Departmental Committee on The Probation of Offenders Act 1907, PP 1910, XLV: 46.
6. A. Paterson, *Across the Bridges or Life by the South London Riverside* (Arnold 1911).
7. S.K. Ruck (ed.) *Paterson On Prisons: Being The Collected Papers of Sir Alexander Paterson* (Muller 1951) 13.
8. Paterson, 'The Apprentice To Crime' *Police Journal*, 1928, 1: 141.
9. Ibid: 142. *The Magistrate*, Sept/Oct. 1933, 3 (XLVII): 721.
10. Paterson, *Across the Bridges*: 20. V. Bailey, *Deliquency and Citizenship: Reclaiming the Young Offender* (Clarendon Press 1987): 198.
11. Hobhouse, *Forty Years On*: 133.
12. Paterson, *Across the Bridges:* 116, 119.
13. A.F. Brockway, *Inside The Left: Thirty Years of Platform, Press, Prison and Parliament* (Allen & Unwin, 1942): 124. Bailey, *Delinquency and Citizenship:* 195-6.
14. ECRO Personalia Sir E. Ruggles-Brise, No. 1 of 3 ACC 5909 E. Ruggles-Brise to E. Shortt, 3 Aug. 1922; E. Shortt to E. Ruggles-Brise, 9 Aug. 1922.
15. Hobhouse and Brockway, *English Prisons*: 439.
16. L.W. Fox, *The English Prison and Borstal System* (RKP 1952): 67.
17. H. Scott, *Your Obedient Servant* (Deutsch 1959): 67.
18. G.F. Clayton, *The Wall Is Strong* (Long 1958): 21.
19. RCP & DCP yr end 31 March 1923, PP 1923, XII, pt. 2: 27.
20. RCP & DCP yr end 31 March 1924, PP 1924-5, XV: 20.
21. RCP & DCP yr end 31 March 1925, PP 1926, XV: 25.

22. Thomas, *Prison Officer*: 154. RCP & DCP for 1934, PP 1935-6, XIV: 10.
23. RCP & DCP for 1934, PP 1935-6, XIV: 10.
24. Various Relaxations, PRO HO 45-11033-428541, M.L. Waller to HO 9 Nov. 1921.
25. Entertainments in Prisons, PRO HO 45-16483-192637, Educational Films P.Com. 9/24, cut. *News Chronicle*, 28 Dec. 1937.
26. Female Prisoners' Haircuts, PRO P.Com 9/149.
27. Clayton, *The Wall is Strong*: 100-1, 103.
28. J. Phelan, *Jail Journey* (Secker & Warburg 1940): 335, 182. W. Holt, *I Was A Prisoner* (Miles 1935): 48. H.U. Triston, *Men in Cages* (The Book Club 1938): 153.
29. Phelan, *Jail Journey*: 182.
30. Introduction of Physical Training for Female Prisoners PRO HO 45-19647-201023.
31. Gymnasia 1930, PRO P.Com. 9/53. Norwood East to Chairman PC, 25 March 1930.
32. Boxing in Prisons 1934-5, PRO P Com 9/198, PC Minute, 11 June 1935.
33. Fox, *Prison and Borstal System*: 231.
34. Loughborough-Ball, *Trial and Error: The Fire Conspiracy and After* (Faber & Faber 1936): 154.
35. Gordon, *Borstalians* (Hopkinson 1932): 134.
36. Ibid: 121.
37. Education in Prisons 1921-49, PRO HO 45-24800-447129/7, H.B. Simpson HO Minute, 5 Nov. 1921.
38. Ibid. /16 H.B. Simpson HO Minute, 31 Dec. 1923.
39. Ibid. /24 HO Minute, 14 Nov. 1924.
40. Ibid. /19 HO Minute, 15 Feb. 1924.
41. Ibid. /33 HO Minute 17 June 1925.
42. Ibid. /33 Report on Lectures by the People's League of Health, no date.
43. Ibid. /25 M.L. Waller to HO, 4 Aug. 1925 /77 PC to HO 29 Nov. 1931, PRO P Com 9/134 Educated Prisoners Teaching Others 1930-31.
44. PRO HO 45-24800-447129 /53 Board of Education to HO, 8 March 1927.
45. J.A.F. Watson, *Meet the Prisoner* (Cape 1939): 135-40.
46. Ibid: 143-4.
47. PRO HO 45-24800-447129 /81 PC to HO, 11 Nov. 1937, PRO P Com 7/324 General Instructions on Lectures 1913-25, cut. *The Citizen*, 13 Feb. 1922.
48. PRO P Com 9/108 Weekly News Sheets 1932-5 PRO HO 45-17515-656577 Weekly News Sheets 1932-38 /1 L. Fox to HO, 28 Nov. 1932 /4 Weekly News Sheet, vol. 1 no. 1.
49. H.W. Wicks, *The Prisoner Speaks* (Jarrolds no date): 182-3.
50. Gordon, *Borstalians*: 43.
51. Borstal, Camp Hill, Feltham, Usk, Sherwood, Lowdham Grange, Portland, North Sea Camp, Hollesley Bay. Also for girls Aylesbury.
52. RCP & DCP for 1936, PP 1937-8, XIV: 16.
53. PRO P Com. 7/688, M. Waller to Legge, 5 Aug. 1921.
54. PRO P Com. 7/555, Notes of Borstal Education Conference 1924.
55. PRO P Com. 7/521, New Educational Scheme of Paterson Owens and James

Brown, April 1920.

56. Ibid. PRO P Com. 7/521 List of Tutors' Duties, no date.

57. PRO P Com. 9/21, Vocational Guidance 1935-9.

58. Introduction of Assistant Housemasters at Borstal 1923-4, PRO P Com. 7/689, PC to HO, 30 Nov. 1924.

59. RCP & DCP for 1934, PP 1935-6, XIV: 61.

60. RCP & DCP for 1929, PP 1930-1, XVI: 35.

61. Borstal Camps. PRO P Com. 7/544, Col. Rich to Home Sec. Shortt, 19 Sept. 1922.

62. PRO P Com. 7/544 Report on Borstal Camp—Feltham 1923.

63. Ibid. Numerous newscuttings.

64. Bailey, *Deliquency and Citizenship*: 237-8, 202-3.

65. Home Leave During Borstal Training 1933-7, PRO HO 45-17059-666054 /2 Governor Feltham to PC 29. April 934. /3 re Borstal /6 re Camp Hill. Visiting Justices' Association 1925-43 PRO HO 45—20084-482137 /20 Conference of Visiting Justices and Boards of Visitors, 24 Nov. 1936. Address Mr Cape, Governor of Lowdham Grange, W. Llewellin Governor North Sea Camp.

66. Ibid. /20 Mr Cape.

67. Scott, *Your Obedient Servant*: 89.

68. *Magistrate*, Nov./Dec. 1938, V (VI): 143-4.

69. Wakefield Prison—Outside Employment, New Hall Camp 1923-35, PRO HO 45-16456-160787, John Bull cut. 3 Sept. 1932.

70. R.W. Chamberlain, *There Is No Truce: A Life of Thomas Mott Osborne* (Routledge 1936): 399.

71. A. Crew, *London Prisons of Today and Yesterday* (Nicholson 1933) 198. RCP & DCP for 1930, PP 1931-2, XII: 53.

72. PRO HO 45 -24800-447129 /25 M.L. Waller to HO, 4 Aug. 1925.

73. *Magistrate*, April 1925, 1 (VII): 79-80.

74. *Magistrate*, Oct. 1929, 2 (XXIV): 343-5.

75. *Justice of the Peace*, 23 March 1929, XCIII: 182.

76. Report of the Departmental Committee on Persistent Offenders PP 1931-2, XII.

77. Ibid: 16.

78. Ibid: 66, 44-8.

79. Report of the Departmental Committee on the Employment of Prisoners Part 1 PP 1933-4, XV.

80. Prisoners' Earnings 1929-47, PRO HO 45-22974-542336 /1 PC to HO, 19 Aug. 1929.

81. RCP & DCP For 1935, PP 1936-7, XV: 25.

82. *Magistrate* Nov./Dec. 1938, V (VI): 140-2.

83. *Magistrate* Nov./Dec. 1938, V (VI): 136-8.

84. *Magistrate* Oct. 1929, 2 (XXIV): 345.

85. *Magistrate* Oct./Nov. 1931, 2 (XXXVI): 535.

86. Classification 1927-44, A Scheme for the Redistribution of Prisoners among the Prisons of England and Wales, A. Paterson Nov. 1925, PRO HO 45-19453-507631/1.

87. Ruck, *Paterson*: 13.

# Chapter Twelve

# Conflicts and Problems 1921–1939

There were of course those who refused to believe any of it. In particular there were members of parliament who had experienced imprisonment and were deeply distrustful of Prison Commissioners' rhetoric. So, there were criticisms from such figures as the 'Red Clydesiders', James Maxton of the Independent Labour Party and William Gallacher a Communist, and from Labour members of Parliament, conscientious objector Morgan Jones and veteran suffragist Frederick Pethick Lawrence, who had all experienced the prison system first hand. But there were other critical Labour members such as George Lansbury, Rhys Davies and James Lovat Fraser who questioned the reassuring reports of Home Secretaries and a favoured, albeit invariably unsuccessful, ploy was to move a reduction of the salary of the Home Secretary on account of his mismanagement of prisons. Some of these members were equally distrustful of the Labour governments of Ramsay MacDonald which held office between January and November 1924 and June 1929 and August 1931. Although Home Secretary J.R. Clynes abolished separation in local prisons and set up the Persistent Offenders Committee, in other respects he sounded much like his predecessors as he carefully explained to Honourable Members why it was unnecessary to have a female prison commissioner, the inevitability of long hours spent in cells and the undesirability of prisoners writing and producing their own news sheet as happened in Belgium.[1] Indeed, one convict later recalled that many prisoners expected great improvements when Labour came to power. In fact, he added, they concluded that things got worse.[2]

In Parliament, however, the majority of members supported the policies of the commissioners during the 1920s. Certainly there were controversies, such as the reprieve of Ronald True sentenced to death for an atrocious murder but reprieved after he was found insane in 1922, but these were incidents which did not undermine the general confidence. It seemed that, after the troubled years of suffragettes, conscientious objectors and investigation by the Labour Research Group, the prison system no longer held the attention of parliament which had heard enough about penal short comings and was confident that things were now progressing.

This confidence was rudely shattered on January 24, 1932 when a very serious riot occurred at Dartmoor during which convicts armed with hatchets, butchers' knives, pickaxes and iron bars took control of the prison and burned out the entire central block. At once, distrust of the Paterson approach, which had been growing amongst some right wingers, was voiced. It was argued that the new approach weakened confidence among officers that stern maintenance of discipline would be supported by the commission and that convicts were out of control. However, on the left criticism was also made that the riot resulted from harsh repressive treatment of the prisoners. As Maxton urged: 'you have to find the cause of that trouble not in the characters of individual prisoners but in something about the administration of that prison at the beginning'.[3] Suspicions were hardly allayed by the refusal of the government to publish the minutes of evidence of the enquiry by leading barrister Herbert Du Parcq assisted by Paterson.[4] The press continued to watch Dartmoor and other prisons closely and reported incidents elsewhere. Although Du Parcq made clear that he did not blame 'the more humane and reformative treatment' for causing the disorder,[5] there continued to be a more critical attitude to the Prison Commission and Paterson in particular thereafter in parliament. Harold Scott, chairman at this time, was very aware of the reaction against Paterson.[6] Home Secretary Sir John Gilmour, who presided over the Home Office between September 1932 and June 1935, found himself on the defensive. Thus he had to reassure members that newspaper reports about planned breakouts from Parkhurst were exaggerated and that gymnastics in prison did not increase the efficiency of cat burglars: indeed Harold Scott believed that the confidence of Gilmour in the liberal reforms of the commission came close to breaking as a result of these events, although he later recovered his enthusiasm.[7]

Before this the prison commissioners and Home Office had become well aware that they must carefully explain and justify their new policies to the public and they did so by a sustained and expertly organised exercise in propaganda. Throughout the inter war years this was so persistent that it cast into shadow the initiatives of Du Cane and Ruggles-Brise, both of whom had used the news media to good effect despite the fact that Du Cane had suffered at the hands of journalists at the end. Examples of this campaign litter the pages of contemporary newspapers and periodicals and it is clear that each commissioner was frequently before the public addressing a multitude of organizations, groups and guilds, supplying information to journalists and addressing the public on the radio. Journalists were given access to all kinds of information which would add to the credit of the commission. So, 'a special correspondent' for *The Times* eulogised borstal in the mid 1920s and glowing accounts of borstal summer camps in the popular press were based on information carefully fed to the journalists.[8] In addition ceremonial occasions were set up to attract maximum publicity. An example of this was the laying of the Lowdham Grange foundation stone in July 1930 which received wide national publicity.[9] Victor Bailey described the way in which the hostility of the press to the borstals in the early 1920s was turned around. Wemyss Grant Wilson, director of the Borstal Association, invited Sydney Moseley of the journal *John Bull*, one of the leading critics, to come to the borstals and examine them for himself: as a result of this gamble Moseley became a eulogist of the system and, in consequence, the general climate of press opinion improved.[10]

Scott, Paterson and Norwood East were expert also at using the professional press such as the *Magistrate, Justice of The Peace* and *Lancet* to propagate their own views, but they also began to use the radio and encouraged selected governors, such as Colonel Turner of Wakefield and Lilian Barker of Aylesbury, to provide material for press and radio.[11] Consequently both these officials, when later made up to inspector and assistant commissioner, proved formidable publicists with great experience of using the media.

In addition Home Secretaries, on occasion, gave great impetus to the oft repeated faith in knowledge, intimate engagement, improvement and progress. Home Secretary, Sir William Joynson-Hicks, identified himself with the general thrust of the commissioners's aspirations in the popular press, making appeals for money to pay for chapel organs and borstal camps. So, just after his elevation to the peerage, 'Jix' regaled readers of the *Saturday Evening Post* with accounts of visits to prisons where he met humane, vigilant and hard working staff and, in the main, sensible and thoughtful prisoners, although some burglars were dedicated to their craft and refused to take advantage of the help offered them.[12] J.R. Clynes assured the people that Dartmoor was far more reformative than 'the public ever imagined'.[13]

Behind the scenes, however, things were not as rosy. The Prison Commissioners and Home Office had become involved with an increased number of voluntary groups and associations, all with some interest in prisoners. Indeed, the voluntarist aspect of prisoner reformation was a marked feature of the inter war years and it was by no means certain that major projects would be supported by the state at all. At one time Joynson-Hicks made attempts to fund Lowdham Grange by charitable donations but this fell through when the philanthropist in question found other uses for his £100,000.[14] In fact many of the educational and rehabilitative functions funded by the state today were then carried out by private agencies and it has already been noted that the payment of prisoners at Wakefield was initially by voluntary contributions of the Howard League. Furthermore, in six of the larger prisons Church Army evangelists supplemented the work of the chaplains although this was in fact subsidised by the Treasury.[15]

The education and entertainment of prisoners by voluntary groups proved to be a fruitful source of conflict. In particular, local education groups were outspoken and determined critics if they felt that their work was being undermined. Complaints were made in Kent in 1925 when Joynson-Hicks put an end to prisoners being used to educate others[16] and two years later a dispute broke out regarding Parkhurst. There the previous governor, Colonel D'Aeth, had worked closely with the Newport Director of Education, H. Jervis, who informally and voluntarily assisted him in the establishment of numerous courses and lectures. D'Aeth's successor was less keen on these events and reduced the number of convicts allowed to attend, stopped 'ladies' being present and forbade convicts proposing votes of thanks and applauding.

Jervis at this point got in touch with the local Labour Party and complained and this was seized upon by the parliamentary party. George Lansbury made a number of serious allegations which the Home Office shrugged off—'his like wear the robe of the pharisee'—but soon the press were reporting disturbances at Parkhurst: 'they sang the Marseillaise ... they sang Sailors Beware'. Jervis wrote a number of 'very crabby letters' to the new governor and stopped supplying public library books to the prison. By now the commission and the Home Office were convinced that they had to do with a militant socialist who had manipulated Colonel D'Aeth and insisted in public that education at Parkhurst was unaffected with lectures on 'the progress of aviation, the history of the British Empire', choral singing, prisoners'' bands and so forth. Criticism was not however stilled and in June 1926 socialists in parliament were still baying for blood. Wearily the commission approached Southampton University for educational help but the academics there were unwilling to venture over the water into 'other people's preserves'.[17]

Another voluntary group which was in frequent conflict with the commission and the Home Office was the trade union movement. Trades unions opposed any expansion of prison labour on the ground that this deprived men of work. Indeed, almost every initiative to expand the work was at once met with protest from the union concerned—a response which contrasted with the united demands of Labour members of parliament for reformed industrial conditions in prisons. Furthermore, manufacturers also watched prison industries intently lest such work undercut their business. The fact that prison made goods were only sold to the state did not alleviate their anxiety, because this nevertheless was the shrinking of a potential market by the manufacture and purchase of subsidised goods and privileged competition. In the years of the great depression of the 1930s complaint was frequent. British manufacturers sent delegations to the commission; building and construction workers' unions objected to borstal boys building Lowdham Grange; electricians' associations were furious that convicts had themselves done electrical installations at Chelmsford.[18] Indeed, even before the very bad times of the depression, trades unions had resented prisoners painting at Camp Hill and Parkhurst, convicts 'living in the lap of luxury doing work by which we could support our wives and families . . . it is the unemployed who get the punishment if you use convicts for such labour'.[19] This made it harder for the commission to implement their policy of allowing selected prisoners to work in parties outside prisons in high local visibility. However, complaints could be more poignant—for example that basket makers in prisons made it harder for work to be found for the blind.[20]

As in Ruggles-Brise's day religion was the cause of much bickering. The issue of non-conformist ministry to prisoners had largely been settled in England by the end of Ruggles-Brise's period. However, in Wales the situation was more difficult. During the inter war years there were long exchanges between the Home Office and the Welsh Free Churches which claimed that Welsh disestablishment gave their churches an equal right to the Welsh Episcopal Church to have a candidate selected for the Cardiff prison chaplaincy. The complexity of Welsh religious concerns left Home Office officials somewhat baffled and they consulted extensively about this. Previous legislation unhelpfully referred only to 'the established Church of England' which no longer existed in Wales. Delegations and letters from councils of Welsh evangelical churches continued to arrive at Joynson-Hicks' office but the matter was not resolved. At length, the Home Office decided that enough was enough and told the Free Churches that it construed a 'clergyman of the Established Church' to mean the Episcopal Church of Wales and nobody else.[21]

The deliverance of the commission and the Home Office from religious controversy was not, however, entirely at hand for Christian Science had made its appearance as a reforming agent in American and Australian prisons. It was not long before puzzled civil servants began to be subjected to pressure to allow Christian Scientists into English prisons. In 1928 a row broke out because some chaplains had prohibited Christian Science literature in prisons and Christian Scientists lobbied the Conservative M.P. Victor Cazalet who mounted a campaign in parliament to persuade Joynson-Hicks to allow books and the Christian Science Monitor into prisons. Here Cazalet had little luck, for Joynson-Hicks was an old warrior in religious battles, President of the National Church League and at this time fiercely resisting the revision of the Prayer Book amidst the storm of controversy aroused by that issue. With Christian Scientists he would have no truck and he sent Cazalet packing.[22] Later, after Joynson-Hicks' time, Christian Scientists did get into prisons.

The provision of concerts and lectures also caused difficulties. Since Ruggles-Brise's retirement increased numbers of singers, musicians, lecturers and players had been allowed entry to prisons despite the general disapproval of the Home Office. Both commissioners and Home Office were also uncertain about the introduction of wireless and were somewhat alarmed when the Daily News suddenly offered to provide wirelesses for prisons in 1926. Joynson-Hicks pondered over this and at length agreed to accept two for Borstal and Aylesbury. However, there was much worry about control of the output from these. If, for example, a broadcaster suddenly began to make unsuitable remarks over the air waves, how could the supervising officer anticipate this? Was there not, in addition, a loss of dignity if officers had to rush across the room to switch off the set in time to stop prisoners hearing the remainder of such offending remarks?[23]

It was, however, the concerts which caused most trouble and in 1927 the Home Office nearly put a stop to them altogether. Two years earlier a disgraceful brawl had occurred in Maidstone chapel when the chaplain had rebuked an entertainer for singing inappropriate ditties and this had led the commission to make a ruling that 'no comic songs' were to be allowed and that 'there are also other matters of good taste and discretion, such as the appearance of ladies in full evening dress', which must be considered by governors on the spot.[24] The ideal was 'a sentimental ballad, sweetly sung, or a familiar selection of instrumental music' to send 'imaginations rushing through happy channels'.[25]

In May 1927 a concert party arrived at Maidstone and all apparently went smoothly. 'When Miss Hebe Simpson sang Dvorak's "Songs My Mother Taught Me", accompanying herself on the violin, I saw tears running down one young face. "Rose In The Bud" and "I Love The Moon" were cheered again and again but the convicts knew too how to appreciate "The Lass With The Delicate Air" and a serenade by Schubert, "Where My Caravan Has Rested", which Miss Nina Crispin gave ... when it came to "Abide With Me" and "All Hail The Power Of Jesu's Name" every voice was lifted'.[26]

However things were not well. In the first place, the concert group in question had, unknown to Maidstone's governor, been banned from the London prisons for 'singing an unsuitable song at Brixton'.[27] Now they committed an unforgivable sin for, in the customary eulogistic report given by the concert party to the press, their leader mentioned that Horatio Bottomley and other notorious criminals had attended and been moved and complaints arrived at the Home Office about the suffering caused by such publicity to the families of the convicts. Joynson-Hicks was outraged and at once wrote to Waller: 'if this sort of thing is repeated I will stop all concerts. It is monstrous'.[28] Thereafter, the media showed more caution and in 1936 anxious enquiries were made as to whether a photograph of the Dickensian Players leaving Holloway, after a performance of David Copperfield, might be published.[29]

The prison commission was in the midst of groups with different interests to serve or axes to grind and a great deal of commissioners' time was taken up coordinating and negotiating with philanthropists and voluntary groups and discussing projects with these. For example, philanthropists such as Hector Sassoon gave large sums of money to be used for particular charitable purposes and Paterson was greatly interested in the use and distribution of these. Indeed he searched out contacts with well known philanthropists and in 1927 William Morris was persuaded to give £10,000 to enable parents and relatives to visit borstal trainees.[30]

There were often disputes over philanthropic involvement with prisoners. Although the history of the embattled Prisoner Aid Societies is to be the subject of the final chapter of this work, both prison visitors and prisoner aid personnel serve to illustrate this here. As explained the commission saw prison visitors as a major part of their reformatory work and lauded the 'quasi motherly' visitors to young prisoners at Wandsworth who showed them 'photographs and pictures portraying familiar objects—places and various phases of life (family life—sea scenes—scout pictures—children—horses—factory life). I find that after the boy has glanced at them he feels prompted to give particulars of his own life and habits'.[31] The commissioners were determined to maintain the purity of these reformatory agents and so they excluded undesirables, such as conscientious objectors,[32] from prison visiting and maintained a close paternal interest in the new Male Visitors Association set up in 1924.

There was, however, deep seated distrust between the established Discharged Prisoner Aid Societies and these visitors and in the early 1920s the large and influential Surrey and South London Aid Society refused to accept them as automatic members of their society, arguing that prison visitors were uncooperative and unreliable. The aid society in question resented the favouritism shown to the visitors by the commission and, when pressed to accept visitors in their ranks, warned the commission that they would pull out of Wandsworth altogether if forced to take them.[33] On occasion things were little better between the prison visitors themselves and in 1928 the women visitors turned on one of their number, who had informed Holloway prisoners that they 'should not object to being spoken to by black men and that they should not mind marrying coloured men' going on to speak about 'the decay of England, Home Rule for India . . . Irish politics . . . the pictures in the National Gallery and art treasures should be sold for the people': this was 'bolshevism' of the worst kind and the visitor had to go.[34] What was needed was 'classes on infant welfare, mothercraft and first aid'.[35]

The commissioners developed a way of managing all the various interest groups during the late Ruggles-Brise era. This involved calling each group to its own annual conference at the Home Office where the members would listen to speeches and instructions from senior politicians and penal experts, discussions would be held and resolutions passed. So, every year there occurred separate meetings with prison governors, prison chaplains and prison doctors and during the inter war years this method of instruction and consultation was extended to discharged prisoner aid societies, visiting justices and prison visitors who duly each sent representatives to their separate annual conferences. At these events they would be welcomed by the Home Secretary, who invariably told them that, without their work, the prisons would be unable to work successfully and they would then be addressed at great length by the chairman of the commission and commissioners such as Paterson as well as by a number of experts such as Llewellin, Barker or Turner. Clearly on one level this was an effective way of communicating information but it was also an attempt to manage such groups and if possible ward off or dilute the criticism implicit in the resolutions which usually followed. Certainly the speech making on these occasions was somewhat awe inspiring and there seems to have been a general attitude of genial condescension on the part of the Home Office and prison commission officials. On occasion, however, these meetings could deteriorate into bitter exchanges and this is well illustrated by the meetings of the visiting justices.

It will be recalled that visiting justices were appointed to award punishment for prison offences and to be a local watchdog of prisons. During Du Cane's time they had been largely ignored by the commission and, although Ruggles-Brise had taken them more into his confidence, in general visiting justices were not regarded as major figures in the new policies of the commission in the early 1920s.

Now the fact was that almost all visiting justices were members of the local discharged prisoner aid societies and under Ruggles-Brise resentment had built up in regard to the way the commission had handled these societies. In addition there were memories of the Home Office handling of Arthur Andrews, chairman of the local advisory committee at Camp Hill and chairman of the Visiting Board at Parkhurst. Between 1916 and 1921 faction fighting had occurred in the London aid societies (to be discussed later) and Ruggles-Brise was widely seen as implicated in a prolonged period of dispute between these. So, when the visiting justices with their colleague visitors for the convict prisons assembled on June 11th, 1925 to discuss with the Home

Office and prison commission whether to set up an annual conference, there was a background of distrust. Furthermore, since 1919 women had been allowed to become magistrates and one of these, Miss E. Kelly who visited Portsmouth and Winchester, was a determined, knowledgeable and intelligent leading critic of state policy.

At the first exploratory meeting in June 1925 the government side launched into a long eulogistic preamble about the forthcoming International Penitentiary Congress in London and ended this with a request that justices contribute money to the reception and entertainment of the foreign dignitaries. This was greeted by an uproar with some refusing 'to entertain somebody that we don't know and may dislike'[36] and others demanding to know why time was spent on such a tarradiddle rather than on discussion as to whether an annual conference should be held.

Thereafter the Home Office and commission wheeled out their heaviest guns for each conference and visiting justices were subjected to long analyses of progress and success by Home Secretary, chairman, Paterson, Barker and so forth. This tactic was not particularly successful for the Conference, led by Miss Kelly and Arthur Andrews, showed itself independent and critical and in 1930 successfully demanded the appointment of the persistent offenders' committee of J.R. Clynes, thereafter singlemindedly attacking the failure of the government to act on its recommendations. Overall, between 1925 and 1935 the view taken was that the Home Office and prison commission were slow to act and half hearted in their adoption of a full blooded reformatory approach resonant to experiments in America and elsewhere.

The problem was also in part the fact in the 1920s and 30s an influential group of magistrates, such as William Clarke Hall, Margery Fry, John Watson and Basil Henriques, were self confident and high principled radical thinkers who were not to be put off by managed conferences, sheaves of memoranda or condescending explanations about the criminal justice system. In 1921 the Howard League and a group of magistrates had formed the Magistrates Association and through its journal this continuously urged better labour facilities, more reformatory training, improved psychological treatment, application of foreign methods and increased borstals. Obviously large numbers of magistrates did not choose to join this body and strongly disagreed with it, but nevertheless the Association was a vehicle for a highly articulate and knowledgeable group of reformers who were determined that there should be major changes.

The 1935 annual conference of visiting justices closely followed in time the publication of yet another government report about prisoners aid societies. This report, however, outdid in its swingeing attack anything in the past and on 26th November, 1935 76 visiting justices confronted the

Home Secretary, chairman Harold Scott, Norwood East, Lilian Barker, Paterson and other leading governors and officials in an atmosphere of open hostility. As soon as Home Secretary, Sir John Simon, concluded his welcoming remarks a furious exchange began. Visiting justices lambasted the Home Office and commission for insulting and demeaning their aid societies and for their slowness to reform their own institutions. Paterson shouted back that their sentencing practices were outmoded and that, difficult as borstal boys were to train, magistrates were more so.[37] After this the visiting justices intensified their demands for the implementation of the Persistent Offenders' Committee report and were at last satisfied when Sir Samuel Hoare took up this matter between 1937 and 1939.

Bloodied but unbowed by the controversies and conflicts which had increasingly occurred in the late 1920s and 30s the prison commission remained committed to its programme of relaxation and training. Some of the walls of prejudice were lowered, if not levelled, and women gained a somewhat stronger presence during these years despite Home Office grumbling about 'feminism' and 'extravagance'.[38] At Aylesbury borstal, following intense pressure from women's organisations, two female governors had been appointed before, in 1923, Lilian Barker was persuaded by Paterson to apply to succeed these. Again, following twelve years in which Barker transformed the regime there and following lengthy discussions between Harold Scott and Sir John Gilmour as well as forceful deputations from Nancy Astor and the National Council of Women to the Home Office, in 1935 Barker was promoted to Assistant Commissioner and Inspector.[39] With Holloway it was a longer struggle, for the commissioners insisted that there were no female candidates with sufficient experience of psychological treatment, staff management, forensic cross examination, and that senior women staff there possessed insufficient 'medical knowledge . . . skill. tact and personality'[40] to compete with the men for the post of governor. In 1935 Mary Size the deputy governor was thus passed over in favour of the male medical officer of Maidstone.[41] Although the Women's Freedom League harried the commission over this,[42] it was not until July 1945 that the first female governor of Holloway was appointed. To the mind of this writer the phrase Catch 22 occurred frequently when reading the records on this aspect: women would be appointed, they were assured, if they had the appropriate experience, yet the system frequently operated to prevent them from gaining that experience.

In 1939 the prison commission ruled the lives of a daily average of some 11,000 men and women confined in the ten borstals, twenty six local and training prisons, four convict prisons at Chelmsford, Maidstone, Dartmoor and Parkhurst and the Preventive Detention prison at Portsmouth. Between 1934 and 1936 there were around 120 preventive detainees, 2,000 borstal trainees serving an average two years before license and 1,700 convicts.[43] The proportion of women to men serving actual sentences of imprisonment had fallen to one in thirteen[44] and at the outbreak of war the system shrunk still further, for nearly six thousand were immediately sent home and Wormwood Scrubs, Pentonville and Brixton emptied of criminal prisoners. However, it is now time to turn again to the prisons themselves to discover, amidst all the rhetoric and controversy, what was the effect of these projects upon the prisoners themselves.

NOTES

1. Parl. Deb. Fifth Series vol. 231 col. 317 vol.235 col. 1886 vol. 254 col. 2246.
2. W. Macartney, *Walls Have Mouths: A Record of Ten Years Penal Servitude* (Gollancz 1936): 160-61.
3. Parl. Deb. Fifth Series vol. 263 col. 1170.
4. Report by Mr Du Parcq on the Circumstances Connected with the Recent Disorder at Dartmoor Convict Prison PP 1931-2, VII.
5. Ibid: 32.
6. H. Scott, *Your Obedient Servant* (Deutsch 1959): 72-3.
7. Parl. Deb. Fifth Series vol. 280 cols. 24-5 vol 289. col. 152. J.E. Thomas, *The English Prison Officer since 1850* (Routledge & Kegan Paul 1972): 161-2.
8. *The Times* 4 Aug. 1925: 11 col. f to 12 col. a; 5 Aug. 1925: 7 col. g; 6 Aug. 1925: 8 col. f. PRO P Com. 7/544 cut. *Daily Mail*, 4 June 1923; *Daily Telegraph* 2 June 1923; *Manchester Guardian*, 2 June 1923.
9. Lowdham Grange Borstal 1927-30, PRO P Com. 9/55.
10. V. Bailey, *Delinquency and Citizenship: Reclaiming the Young Offender* (Clarendon Press 1987): 215.
11. For radio see Colonel G.D. Turner's remarks. *Magistrate*, Oct. 1929, XXIV: 345.
12. *Saturday Evening Post*, 14 Dec. 1929: 140.
13. *The Times,* 13 April 1931: 9 col. c.
14. Parl. Deb Fifth Series, vol. 225 cols. 523-4.
15. Pay and Conditions of Church Army Officers in Prisons 1913-30. PRO HO 45-17881-246233/7 HO to Treasury, 13 July 1927.
16. PRO HO 45-24800-447129/27 Director Kent Education Cttee. to M.L. Waller 13 April 1925.
17. Parkhurst Prison PRO HO 45-13776-49822. Cut. *Daily Express* 29 Nov. 1926, 30 Nov. 1926 HO Minutes, 21 Oct. 1926, 14 July 1927, 18 July 1927, 23 Nov. 1927, 24 Nov. 1927 Cut. *Isle of Wight Press*, 2 June 1928.
18. Labour in Prisons 1906-1934, PRO HO 45-15528-143172, HO memos. 31 and 24 Oct. 1933.
19. Use of Prison Labour Outside 1922-49, PRO HO 45-24815-453142/13, Newport House and Ship Painters and Decorators to Home Sec., 18 March 1924.

20. Ibid. /40 J.S. Dodd to HO, 10 Oct.1938.

21. Prison Chaplains in Wales 1923-35, PRO HO 45-16197-445669/4, /5, /8./9, /11, Home Sec. to National Council of Evangelical Free Churches, 4 April 1935.

22. Prison Libraries 1928-1943, PRO HO 45-19210-288578/10. V. Cazalet to W. Joynson-Hicks 18 Feb. 1929, 30 July 1929. /8 W. Joynson-Hicks to V. Cazalet no day. Sept. 1928 /9 V. Cazalet to W. Joynson-Hicks, 3. Dec. 928.

23. Entertainments in Prisons 1910-1936, PRO HO 45-16483-192637, PC to Home Sec. 23 March 1926.

24. General Instructions on Lectures 1913-25, PRO P Com. 7/ 324, PC Circular 11 Dec. 1925.

25. Ibid. cut. *Hull Daily News*, 8 June 1922.

26. PRO HO 45-16483-192637, Cut. *Daily Chronicle*, 9 May 1927.

27. Ibid. M.L. Waller to W. Joynson-Hicks, 14 May 1927.

28. Ibid. W. Joynson-Hicks to M.L. Waller, 13May 1927. A.S. Lawrence, 12 May 1927.

29. Ibid. Fox Photos Ltd. to HO, 11 Oct. 1936.

30. Sassoon Bequest. PRO P Com. 7/411, PRO P Com. 7/410. A.B. Urmston to Mr Ruck 7 April 1927 P.Com 7/570.

31. Lady Visitors at Wandsworth 1924-27, PRO P Com. 7/176. M. Samuel Report, no date (mid 1925).

32. PRO P Com. 7/177. PC Circular, 13 Feb. 1923.

33. Prison Visiting in Relation to Discharged Prisoners Aid Societies 1922-3, PRO P Com. 7/400. W. Negus to PC, 11 Jan. 1923.

34. National Association of Prison Visitors to Women PRO P Com. 9/31 'Teaching In Holloway Prison', 27 Nov. 1928.

35. Ibid.

36. Visiting Justices' Association PRO HO 45-20084-482137/2. Meeting of cttee. 11 June 1925.

37. Ibid. Report of Conference, 26 Nov. 1935.

38. Appointment of Women as Prison Governors and Prison Commissioners PRO HO 45-16184-424021. HO Minute, 28 April 1926.

39. E. Gore, *The Better Fight: The Story of Dame Lilian Barker* (Bles 1965): 117-20, 207-8. PRO HO 45-16184-424021, Deputation of the National Council of Women to Home Secretary Gilmour, 5 Dec. 1934.

40. Appointment of a Woman Governor at Holloway, PRO HO 45-19752-684153 /1 PC to HO, 2 July 1935.

41. Ibid. /5, /6.

42. Female Governors and Medical Officers 1913-38, PRO HO 45-24643-234940 /5, /8, /9.

43. RCP & DCP for 1936, PP 1937-8, XIV: 16.

44. Ibid.

# Chapter Thirteen

# Prisons and Prisoners 1921–1939

The staff of the prisons watched the rise of the new ethos with intense interest and from 1921 onwards superior grades increasingly found that they were attending meetings and consultations at the headquarters of the commission, returning to their prisons to announce to officers and prisoners that the institution was henceforth to be seen as a 'school of constructive citizenship'.[1] Some, as indicated, were clearly strong advocates of the new policy and close associates of Alexander Paterson. Reference has already been made to Lilian Barker who, on the women's side, exemplified Paterson's project. On arrival at Aylesbury she was convinced that its regime for borstal girls was repressive with rates of solitary confinement and strait jacketing unacceptably high. Her two female predecessor governors had in her view been rigid disciplinarians and the borstal girls particularly were angry and resentful when Barker arrived, with smash ups of cells frequent and the institution characterised by collective hatred of the staff.

There is no question but that Barker brought a formidable and charismatic personality to bear on Aylesbury in which were combined blunt fearless challenge of attitude and behaviour of both staff and inmates and tenderness, sensitivity and enthusiasm. Aylesbury therefore became a place of creative hobbies, open air activity in the grounds and the farm attached to the institution in place of frequent punishments, institutional routine and mechanical obedience. Barker shared Paterson's faith in the value of constant activity and the absorption of morality from staff and the group, also sharing his belief that human energy, if not used up in exhausting activity, would either lead to immoral conduct or be caged up to result in brooding preoccupied self-absorption. As she explained to magistrates in 1929: 'I can tell you my girls are absolutely untireable. All their violence and all the things that cause so much trouble are owing to their being oversexed. It has to be got out of them somehow'.[2]

Initially Barker experimented with a much freer regime in accordance with the wishes of the prison commission. However, she found that this did not lead to enthusiastic cooperation but seemed to heighten the defiance and outbursts of the girls. She therefore created a disciplined framework within which would occur intimate engagement between staff and girls, dominated by her own energy and obvious love of and commitment to them. So, constant activity, stern confrontation with sulkiness, the winning of participation in an outward looking community were placed at the heart of the Aylesbury endeavour. Victor Bailey was sceptical of the changes which were said to have occurred in the morale there as the regime was transformed to picnics, group discussions about Christianity, rambles, blackberrying, annual holidays at Littlehampton, fancy dress, netball and so forth. However, some ex-trainees spoke with great warmth of Lilian Barker. As one said, 'we started as prisoners living in a prison and we ended as citizens living in a community. Miss Barker gave us responsibility and made us feel we had something to contribute; even expected us to make our own decisions . . . "don't be like cats" she would say "who hug the fire and are devoid of faithfulness, but be like terriers, wag your tails, and get up and around".'[3]

There was, however, much anxiety about the new ethos of activity, responsibility and trust elsewhere in the system. Waller and Paterson inherited a staff of prison officers emerging from the disputes of 1919 and of ex-military gentlemanly governors who were usually devotees of Ruggles-Brise. Many officers clearly felt that discipline was suffering at the hands of the commissioners and that prisoners were now 'humoured and coddled and made heroes of'.[4] Furthermore, many officers were deeply antagonistic to the introduction of new personnel, such as borstal housemasters, feeling that these derogated their status by further hiving off the reformatory task into the hands of non uniformed specialists. Thirdly prison officers were apprehensive about the increase of freedoms within prisons for such things as provision of razor blades increased danger—indeed two days before the Dartmoor riot an officer was very severely injured by a razor attack. Lastly, officers often felt that their work was poorly paid, difficult, severely regulated and taxing and resented the continuous harping on care and rehabilitation of offenders whilst the commission appeared to many of them to trouble little about their welfare.

Many of the governors were also critical. Gerold Clayton noted a feeling that the commission had become mawkish and sentimental after Ruggles-Brise had gone and that Paterson was a naive and unsuitable appointment. He reported that his superior had rung the commission to report an escape and that Paterson had replied 'dear, dear, What a pity' adding that at a Pentonville reception Paterson had caused deep offence by ignoring the governor grades and spending the entire evening in deep discussion with the staff representatives of the Prison Officers' Representative Board.[5] Others learned to take advantage of the ethos to diminish blame attached to them.

Major Blake, for example, released a prisoner on day parole without authority and the man absconded. Blake then rang the commission and conversed generally about the immense value of the new policies of trust and responsibility, adding casually that he had day paroled a man. The assistant commissioner in question at once said 'splendid, doesn't that prove that we can trust them'? at which Blake mentioned the absconding—he was gently rapped over the knuckles for this rather than formally reprimanded.[6]

All staff, whether hostile or favourable to the new ethos, were agreed that by 1939 the prisons were less severe than in Ruggles-Brise's time. Most argued that the system, particularly the borstals and training prisons and the Howard House (a borstal type regime for convicts under 21 at Maidstone convict prison), was more firmly grounded on a reformatory and training ideal. Although some of them claimed that the programmes did not actually succeed,[7] there was a general agreement that the reformatory endeavour was made as the commissioners claimed with trainees and prisoners serving longer sentences. It was of course never claimed that those serving sentences of under six months could be reformed by a prison programme and at no time did the commission claim that more than a minority of local prisoners, around one sixth, were involved in all the education, instruction, concerts, music, clubs and so forth discussed earlier.

Accounts by prisoners of their experience during this period are compelling and vivid. They are also unusually convincing and the reader is at times swept away by the colourful detail and eloquent intensity of two writers, in particular, Jim Phelan and Wilfred Macartney. Before embarking upon a discussion of the general prisoners' view of the prisons it is necessary to discuss these two writers. Phelan was reprieved from execution in the early 1920s for a murder carried out in connection with a post office raid when he was 28 years old. He was a Dublin Irishman with connections in the Irish Republican Army and was on the fringes of that organisation in Liverpool when sentenced.[8] After release from prison he wrote many novels and autobiographical accounts. Whilst he was serving his life sentence, he came to know Wilfred Macartney, who was convicted of being a Soviet agent in January 1928, and sentenced to ten years. None disputed that Macartney was a Communist but many argued that the case against him had been exaggerated by the state.[9]

Both Phelan and Macartney were therefore ideologically opposed to the British state, the former on nationalist, the latter on Marxist Leninist grounds. Secondly, they were serving long sentences and therefore were able to observe the system over many years. Both these facts need to be remembered when reading their work, for they argued a particular thesis about the English convict prisons[10] which certainly casts a different light upon them from that to be found in official publications and reports.

The essential of the thesis was that there was an unalterable and inevitable hostility between the captor and the captive which made genuine trust and mutual respect between the collective body of convicts and of staff impossible, because the two groups had irreconcilable opposite objectives. The prisoners wanted their freedom and saw themselves as caught in a carceral tyrannical bureaucracy whilst the staff aimed at their continued imprisonment. Based on this notion of irreconcilable objectives Phelan propounded the conclusion that prison society at its very core was nothing more than an exercise in manipulation in which staff strove to maintain mastery and prisoners schemed to gain advantage. This did not mean that individual prisoners and staff members did not on occasion form respect for one another and both writers instanced this on numerous occasions. What it did mean was that there was a social dynamic of irreconcilable aims, contradictions and manoeuvres at the heart of the institutional system, regardless of behaviour of certain individuals.

There was more than material advantage to be won, for Phelan particularly argued that the survival of human personality was at stake, that human feeling and mind were in jeopardy of permanent destruction by one of two processes. The process of challenge and defiance would lead to suppression by continuous and escalating punishment so that ultimately, with its limitless opportunities for punishing, the prison must break the convict. But a more insidious danger was mere compliance which would lead to the enslavement of body and mind, the blanking out of original thought, sensitivity to others, awareness of personal vitality until the prisoner became a dulled, robotic, shambling, empty husk—'an old blank eyed lifer mumbling in fantasy'[11] or the convict 'squeezed into mummification'.[12] The consequence of surrender was thus the death of all that gave meaning to life—'apathy, quietude, languor, laziness and silence with a desire to be left alone—these things mark the man who has gone dead'.[13]

Convicts, therefore, gained life from avoiding open defiance and wearing a mask of obedience, but in effect engaging in unremitting deception and manipulation. In this they were extraordinarily inventive. They made tiny illicit stoves to brew up purloined tea in their cells; they constructed cigarette lighting equipment out of stones, scissors and handkerchiefs.[14] They were precise in their calculation of how far they could defy staff without incurring penalty and indeed 'balmies', those diagnosed insane, were adept at humiliating and demeaning officers, knowing that they enjoyed relative immunity from punishment. Furthermore there existed a rich and intense underlife in prisons hidden from staff and commissioners, flourishing to glorify defiance and crime with intricate mechanisms to satisfy appetites for sex, nicotine, food or whatever.

The officers appeared in a new light compared to the description of them as vigilant, dutiful and loyal agents of the service in commission reports. At Dartmoor Phelan argued that the convict prison was run, not by governors or commissioners, but by dynasties of Princetown families who had born sons to be officers and daughters to wive them and breed yet more sons for the system. The prison was therefore run according to time honoured unwritten customs of a prison officers' culture, handed down in Princetown from generation to generation against which the circulars of the commissioners prevailed not—'strange book—larnin' bits, on brinted babers from Lunnon or zum o' they parts. Don't madder though . . . Noa, doan't hold with they new ideas . . . Tooth powder, ses ee. Tooth powder for he. I lyike fetchen tooth powders for them uns. Ho. Ho.'[15]

The 'jail', however, was a 'machine' which could be worked to advantage not by those 'mugs' who whinged and claimed their rights or by those who engaged it in open combat but by those who were wise and experienced enough to understand the workings of the 'jail mind' of their custodians, to know the mentality which lurked behind all the lofty claims about penal progress and prisoners' reform which were, in gaol slang, 'Madame De Luce' (lying propaganda). In short the staff were levers to be pulled at will.

Phelan illustrated the pulling of the levers thus. He wished to be transferred from Dartmoor to Parkhurst but knew that the surest way to prevent this was to ask for such a transfer, for this would lead staff to suspect a hidden motive. So, he set in motion a series of events which would logically draw the officials into making the necessary decision. He engineered a slow but perceptible build up of health problems but he prevented the suspicion of malingering by playing the heroic figure to the doctor, insisting that he be allowed to return to work and attracting the attention of staff by working exceedingly hard. He then enlisted his genuine asthma and collapsed through over work. Again he refused hospital care and demanded to be allowed back to work. By now the doctors and officers were convinced of his genuineness because he made no claim for amelioration, yet they were disturbed by the strange insistence on return to work and ferocious industry. For a physically sick convict who was mentally suspect there was only one place in England—Parkhurst—and there Phelan duly arrived.[16]

Collective action was also part of survival and at Parkhurst the prisoners determined to obtain the privilege of conversation which had been promised by the commission yet not implemented by the governor. But they knew that they must avoid any insult or sarcasm which would lead to their punishment. So 'it is a matter of record . . . that men stood up at the windows and shouted. Not "To Hell with Colonel Hales", not "Burn the Jail", not "Kill the Warders" but "Ship Ahoy. Hello. Ship Ahoy" . . . all the desperate "leaders" of the Parkhurst riots of which the reader doubtless read—stood up at their windows and called defiantly "Ship Ahoy. Hello. Ship Ahoy".[17] It was thus not a matter of mutual goals, trust and care but of levers and exploitation and this grim picture of conflict and manoeuvre was substantially the same as that of Wilfred Macartney whose book in fact predated Phelan's by four years. He described an underlife in which the currency of tobacco could buy a maimed enemy or a fellow convict's sexual favours[18] and the overall attitude to convicts by officers was that they were 'another biological species'.[19]

There was plainly a core of truth in this thesis and indeed books about prison 'subculture' have proliferated in modern Britain written by criminologists, penal theorists and prisoners. However, as far as prisons in the inter war years are concerned, the bulk of prisoners' writings make it clear firstly that there were substantial relaxations of severity for prisoners serving over six months in local prisons and for convicts and that the relationships between such inmates and the staff were often more intimate than Phelan's and Macartney's thesis gave readers to believe. So, one prisoner reflected that immense improvement of conditions had occurred in his time and doubted if 'more grateful prisoners will ever pass through the gate than the more intelligent ones of my generation'[20] and all, Macartney and Phelan included, recorded in detail the concerts, debates, clubs, musical associations and so forth in great detail and gave due credit for these. Indeed Phelan believed that the thriving chess club at Parkhurst had a genuine 'esprit de corps'[21] and Macartney believed that this was 'one of the most important developments in English penology during the last twenty years' and gave long accounts of musical appreciation societies with gramophones and jazz, operatic and popular records.[22] Indeed it was recorded that at Parkhurst Clayton even allowed the convicts to construct and type their own news letters.[23] Almost all were positive about these ameliorations although admittedly some were sceptical: as one wrote, 'Hooray for nothing . . . it is announced that from now on we may have jig saw puzzles sent into us by our friends'.[24]

There were also detailed and moving accounts of prison staff who were popular with prisoners. The convicts gave a farewell to 'Jumbo' at Parkhurst who made a speech to them just before leaving for another prison: 'it is very good of you fellows to give me such a send off as this. I'm very sorry to be leaving Parkhurst. I had two very happy years here and I want to say that I've found you fellows a jolly fine set of sports'.[25] Others reflected upon the kindness of individual staff: ' "keep your hearts up . . . they've given you a big packet, but prison won't hurt you if you keep your heart up". So may angels visit us'.[26] Indeed many prisoners had nothing but good to say of numerous staff and Macartney spoke of chaplains and medical officers who would 'buck the system' on behalf of prisoners and of uniformed staff 'with a heart of gold and a nature as sweet and open as a pleasant child'[27] and others who were 'humane and decent'.[28] Phelan described the Dartmoor chaplain thus: 'day after day he dispensed injustice, always to the advantage of the convict . . . every single thing he could do to favour the helpless men of the Moor he did'.[29] James Leigh saw chaplains as 'honest and hard-working servants of their master' and added of the officers, 'throughout my long years within the walls I do not recall one deliberate act of dishonesty or unkindness to myself: among the present staff I should be troubled to find one who has not gone out of his way to do me some uncovenanted act of kindness. Should I ever in happier days meet one of them again he will, I know, offer me the ready handshake of a friend'.[30]

Prisoners' literature corroborates the commissioners' argument that since 1921 conditions had relaxed and it also points to many highly respected staff within the system. Plainly Phelan and Macartney correctly pointed to an element of basically irreconcilable interest and manipulation in the system, but equally there was a closer and more respectful and genuine relationship between many prisoners and staff than their thesis implied: indeed they themselves bore witness to this and it is beyond dispute that severity was markedly relaxed in English prisons in the inter war years.

The commissioners argued that for longer sentenced prisoners more effective reformatory programmes were set up between 1921 and 1939 in convict and local prisons. The validity of that view is almost universally challenged by prisoners, who acknowledged the existence of schemes of physical improvement, mental and spiritual instruction and new opportunities for improvement and responsibility, yet almost all urged that the most notable effect of the prison system overall was not improvement but rather emotional and spiritual deprivation.

By some this was frankly and vividly linked to sexual deprivation and Macartney told his readers about this. 'When I went to prison the idea of becoming even temporarily homosexual never entered my head. There are many homosexuals in gaol and for at least four years I took no interest in them. The first knowledge that the mind was being perverted by the unnatural existence of gaol came to me through my dreams. The imagery began to change. This persistent sharply accentuated image of womanhood became clouded after about three and a half years. Even when awake I began to find that fantastic images were pushing the original normal image out of the way. Gradually a homosexual shadow obscured the normal picture and I began to have definitely homosexual dreams. I do not propose to enlarge further upon my own sex life, but I shall assert that within my observation the beneficial effects of such contacts upon the mental and physical health were undeniable and my experience was that of the average man'.[31] Phelan, indeed, believed that the deepest purpose of the system was to castrate aggressive, potent, male convicts but many took it as read that homosexual experience was endemic within the prison system and some described extraordinary sexual inventiveness as well as careful planning of opportunities for homosexual expression. In Parkhurst there were apparently forty places in the prison where sex was known to occur.[32] Sexual yearning and discussion about sex was a constant feature of prison and borstal life—sex offenders, however, were regarded with the deepest distrust, being 'filthy swine . . . sycophants, liars, informers and frequently petty thieves and yet they nearly always got the red collar in gaol'.[33]

In most of the literature writers insisted that a general personal deterioration was occurring among men and women enduring a system which retained long hours of evening and nocturnal separate isolation, strict discipline and close regulation of normal human functions such as conversation or excretion. Stuart Wood served sentences from 1901 onwards and was an advocate of the new reforms, arguing that prisons were far easier than in his youth and that prisoners must throw themselves 'heart and soul into the reform movement because that movement had to be developed by us or not at all . . . the underlying idea of reform was that of self government . . . we suggested ideas and the authorities either sanctioned or modified them, but the actual working of them was our job'.[34] Despite this, however, he described a remorseless process of moral and spiritual deterioration. To him the deepest effect was the erosion of the human spirit, the reinforcement of introverted selfishness, apathy, morbid resentment, brooding, solitary withdrawal from human contact by prisoners who were convinced of their own unique badness and destructiveness. During his early years in prison from 1901 onwards he encountered a good many harsh and condemning prison chaplains[35] and at times drew the wrath of chaplains by his arguments. 'You are an atheist. You are one of those clever people who can do without religion. Yes, you vapour about science and philosophy but they haven't saved you from all this. You make me sick'.[36] Later, during the inter war years, Wood was clear that there were many excellent and persistent chaplains and visiting ministers and that these were often deeply engaged with prisoners, yet he believed that it was the tendency of the institutional system to exacerbate the self-contempt created by early family neglect or abuse. Thus the prison system by its very existence loaded prisoners with further self-condemnation and he freely acknowledged that by his arrogant contempt of chaplains and others who tried to engage him he made the process of self-denigration worse. Another, who served twelve months in 1936, had no doubt that, despite kindly officers, plenty of classes, play readings, Christmas pantomimes, 'skits on some of the officers', theatrical performances and so forth prison diminished or deadened 'all spiritual, mental and intellectual faculties'.[37]

In almost all the literature is poignantly expressed the guilt and shame of many and the daily monotony of cell, workshop and regulation. So, one mused over 'a young man who had killed the wife he loved' and who exclaimed 'what is the sense of heaven or hell?: she's too far away and I can't reach her'. It seemed to me that in the intensity of his suffering there echoed a sound from the eternal places'.[38] In this environment the bodily senses became more acute because starved by deprivation—intense sexual yearning, the smell of hay from outside, the sound of officers padding the corridors by night, the jangle of keys. So, one recalled the 'excruciating pleasure of a violin concert'[39] and others recalled the devotion of convicts to officers' children, 'rays of pure light in the land of the Damned . . . makes yer believe there must be a Gawd a—knockin' around somewhere, don't it, ter see 'em like that'.[40]

Prisoners drew what comfort they could and showed deep devotion to pet sparrows, mice and rats which many kept in their cells with the connivance of the authorities.[41] One officer recalled 'a convict who taught a mouse to sit on its hind legs and hold a splinter of wood in its fore paws, much like a soldier on guard'[42] and great interest was taken in prison governors' dogs which roamed at will. So, Bonzo at Dartmoor was 'a favourite with the old lags . . . a useful mediator between many a morose prisoner and those who wished to help him'[43] and deeply felt grief was expressed when these died.[44] Some pets could be put to good use and one convict trained a jackdaw to collect cigarette ends for him.[45] Others were devoted bird watchers and manufactured telescopes out of lavatory paper and glass stuck together with porridge.[46] At Christmas in some prisons the carefully coordinated kidnap of the prison cat was carried out so that the sparrows could enjoy a special feast of bread crumbs in peace.[47] In fact in 1930 the commission regulated the keeping of mice, because they caused disputes between convicts and thereafter only certain grades were allowed them in their cells and transfer of mice within the system was forbidden.[48]

In the borstals, as the prisons, the regime was strange to new arrivals who must learn quickly a great quantity of information in order to cope with the regime. The trainees were distributed from the allocation centre, at first at Wandsworth and later Wormwood Scrubs, and sent off with much fatherly encouragement. 'Ye have a great opportunity and many of you lads here won't know yourselves in a few weeks you'll be that fit and healthy . . . Good bye and Good luck. That's what red headed Murphy's wishing ye'.[49] In the borstals there was often acute loneliness and sense of loss of family and of dignity: 'Oh God, there are . . . times when our hearts are breaking and we yearn for the sight of a brother or sister and the good night blessing of mother and dad'.[50] At other times trainees would sit sobbing unrestrainedly over lost families and memories of happier times: 'My people don't write and I'm alone—I didn't see it until this afternoon. I've imagined that I was treated badly by my people . . . tonight I'd beg them to forgive me'.[51] And often they were treated as outcasts by their communities when they returned. As an Aylesbury girl wrote, 'I cry myself to sleep with my baby snuggled near to me utterly miserable and I wonder when will it all end' whilst others recalled the very severe penal labour inflicted for defiance of borstal rules, trainees working with huge wheelbarrows, picks and shovels moving tons of rock in the quarries of Portland.[52]

The social structure in borstals was only partly visible to staff and commissioners. As in prisons sex offenders were loathed and trainees who appeared effeminate were tormented and called 'she' and 'Nancy'.[53] Yet homosexuality widely occurred in the borstals[54] and in the underlife of trainees glorification of criminal and sexual exploits was widespread at dead of night.[55] Furthermore, although the open borstals at North Sea Camp, Lowdham and Hollesley Bay were the jewels in the borstal crown the experience elsewhere was less encouraging. In 1922 William Clarke Hall had made swingeing criticisms that Portland Borstal retained all the severities of its convict prison tradition and it remained the fact that Portland took those who were 'a tough proposition', whilst Feltham took 'the medical and temperamental type'.[56] Overall, however, despite Horatio Bottomley's allegation that staff were afraid that they would be reprimanded if they firmly checked borstal boys' behaviour and were therefore weak with them and other complaints that monitors were only effective when staff were present, there is little doubt that the borstals came closer to the reformatory programme preached by the commission. So, for example, a pre-release discharge home was set up at Camp Hill and earnings schemes extended to all borstals in early 1934 and some at least of the borstal boys sincerely valued Paterson's commitment to them: 'pop'lar mate? 'E is an' all. 'E deserves it too . . . 'e joined the army as a private . . . Yuss, went with the Bermondsey boys 'e did. I come from Bermondsey meself . . . No captain's peaked cap for me 'e said. Yuss that's wot 'e said. Goin' as a private 'e said—that's why 'e's pop'lar'.[57]

Although there were horrors such as the death of Reginald Russell at Bedford in 1926 through a neglectful medical officer or the systematic beating of two escapees by Wandsworth Officers,[58] the literature of prisoners does not suggest institutionalised brutality or torture such as was alleged in Du Cane's time, and it widely corroborates the commissioners' claims about relaxation. However, prisoners also were clear that prisons were ineffective agencies of reformation, failing even to discriminate between those who genuinely wanted to reform and those who did not and that the atmosphere overall was oppressive, regulatory and crushing. Prisoners were, however, perfectly willing to attest to the value of the reforms in ameliorating their conditions, although they were critical of 'execrable performers' and charitable condescension by 'stolid, middle aged songsters' preferring 'cheery mummers' like Wee Georgie Wood.[59] They were nonetheless unanimous that, apart from the borstals, the prison system was not a system which pursued individualised reformatory programmes.

This is not to denigrate the liberal reformers of the inter war years or to reduce the importance of the great relaxation which occurred. However, the conclusion is inescapable that the effect of the policy was one of amelioration rather than reformation and this was undoubtedly realised by the great majority of governors. Indeed, all the education, libraries, concerts, bands, play readings and so forth were not viewed by practical governors as reformatory instruments but were to make life more tolerable. This was summed up by Major Munn, governor at Lewes preventive detention prison in 1932. There the detainees were 'embittered, suspicious of each other and of authority, egotistical and utterly selfish. On the other hand they are disciplined and can understand an order and will always obey so long as the trumpet does not give an uncertain sound, provided that the order is reasonable and that they are treated with even handed justice. They are easily led but become mulish and even dangerous if they are driven or if they think that their rights are not being respected'. To government of these Munn brought three cardinal rules—to make them laugh, to appeal to their sense of honour and to rule firmly and fairly. He clearly had a fondness and respect for his detainees and believed that 'in most of them the good outweighs the bad'. It had become clear to Munn that almost all preventive detainees resented preventive detention as 'an unjust second sentence' and that 'the unfortunate and the mentally or physically afflicted' made up a large proportion of them (which was precisely what Churchill had feared and what Herbert Gladstone had blandly promised would not be the case). So, he sought to engage with them: 'By cheering the men at football, leading them at cricket, playing shove ha'penny with them, taking part in their concerts and treating them as if they were in my company in the Army, I have, I think obtained their friendship, thus breaking down the barrier which has always existed between them and authority'.[60] The best governors of the inter war years aimed at no more than this in an attempt to reduce the moral decline which attended imprisonment and to make conditions more bearable for both staff and inmates.

It was not public attitudes or resistance among Home Office officials or parliament or press which undermined the projects of Paterson and his colleagues but a number of inherent weaknesses in their scheme of prisoner reformation. In the first place, the majority of prisons had been erected by those who believed in the separate system some hundred years earlier and these institutions with their radiating tiered corridors of cells were irresistible inducements to ponderous regulation and unmistakable domination, contrary to the notion of freer conditions and responsibility. Towards the end of the 1930s the commission seemed to recognise this and began busily to plan for the abandonment of such places as Pentonville or Reading, the expansion of rural camps for men and women where challenging activity and energetic out door life would develop moral strength, physical robustness, striving and comradeship. So, Paterson and the new Home Secretary, Sir Samuel Hoare, told magistrates in 1938 that the Victorian institutions were to be steadily replaced by new camps and prisons and Harold Scott was horrified by the conditions in the old gaols and the survival of the 'futile and soul destroying methods of the past'.[61] Yet the expense of such a programme would have been great and the plans were shelved when war broke out in September of 1939,

There was, however, another problem with the Paterson ideal in that it required staff with superhuman qualities and the variety of skills and strengths shown by such as Lilian Barker or William Llewellin was immense. Paterson himself underestimated this problem and refused to consider that borstal housemasters, for example, should be motivated by any other consideration than love of the job. Indeed, he went out of his way to impose additional burdens on those who asked to be taken on, insisting that one young man sail before the mast for two years before accepting him as a housemaster at North Sea Camp.[62] Jim Phelan saw clearly this problem in the vision as well as its potential for encouraging longer sentences if courts began to sentence on the basis of reformation. So, he deemed it absurd to expect that a prison officer, working long hours under strict discipline on three pounds a week, would be 'a father, schoolmaster, psychologist, philosopher, evangelist, logician, technical instructor and past master in tact'.[63] The best type of staff from his point of view were not idealists who dreamed dreams but ex military officers who had known war, for they knew the reality of men's attitude and conduct, understood the 'brutality, cruelty, maiming and murder and the lust for power over another's body', the difference between 'pretty phrases' and reality.[64] This explains why so many deeply respected Clayton, who made no grandiose claims and advanced no abstract theories, yet always treated men with respect and dignity, never taken in by them and able to sense when feuds were brewing up to violence and able to take effective avoiding action.[65] In such as Clayton prisoners placed confidence and, indeed, Phelan considered suicide when Clayton was transferred, for he feared that the new governor would not give him credit for his efforts in the forthcoming report which would determine whether he was released.[66]

Much more than prison commissioners prisoners knew and accepted that staff varied immensely and they categorised them painstakingly. So, there was a spectrum of possible types, 'a bleed'n gent, bleed'n good, thumbs up, all right, not bad, a bit crooked, wicked, a bastard, a bitches' bastard and bleed'n murder'.[67] Interpretation of rules varied from one to the other and this was again an inevitable problem in Paterson's ideal. 'Jumbo' would allow Macartney fifty texts on Communist theory, but his replacement would withdraw them[68] and even the best of staff were at times baffled by situations calling for huge tact: so, as Phelan lay under sentence of death, the officer was deeply distressed, because he had mentioned fruit in his garden which would not mature until after the execution and others must convey dignity and depth of feeling to their ever watchful audience at such events as funerals of convicts, where 'the only mourner to walk behind the hearse is the jailer in charge of searching'.[69] Distrust and suspicion was never far away and at times was justified by the behaviour on both sides. Phelan bitterly recalled that a prison educator showed his essay, which lampooned the Conservative party, to the staff at Maidstone and that he was then sent as an anarchist to Dartmoor:[70] although many related that prison visitors were of great importance to them, there was always a fear, at times justified, that these were spies for the system.[71]

What there was therefore was an increase in mercy to those who were at the disposal of the state and an attempt to deal with them with greater dignity and concern. Perhaps this is illustrated by the governor of Maidstone doing something which was unheard of in Du Cane's time—releasing a convict unescorted to attend his child's funeral. The procedure was entirely illegal, although lauded by the press, and when they came to investigate it the Home Office discovered an extraordinary set of precedents allowed secretly without consultation by the deeply conservative civil servant H.B. Simpson. In the early 1920s Simpson had allowed a string of requests, without the shadow of a legal justification, merely signing the order in the secrecy of his office. As one official noted just after his retirement, 'it is now possible to say more bluntly that Mr Simpson, who dealt with all applications, if he was here, granted freely, but in his absence it is believed that no one else ever granted applications at all'.[72] This example illustrates two aspects of prison discipline in the inter war years—that what actually happened depended upon the personality of officials as much as state policy, and that old style conservatives like Simpson or Blake were just as compassionate in their way as the new style Paterson appointments such as Barker or Llewellin.

Paterson himself knew that long sentences caused deterioration and it was partly on that ground that he supported capital punishment, feeling 'that on the whole it was better to put an end to the physical life and leave the man's spiritual being untouched, rather than leave him to continue his physical life for twenty years or more and to allow the deterioration which

I think must come in prison conditions'.[73] He believed, however, that the application of his ideas to less long term prisoners would lead to their reform by unleashing their energy and sense of responsibility. As has been seen implementation of the vision was an exceedingly problematic project.

The groups and fellowships which were formed under the new ethos often had difficult and turbulent lives. James Leigh recalled a Christian confession group formed in one prison, which became 'an orgy of . . . confession . . . as one neurotic competing with another told his story of horrifying thoughts and secret sexual activities' and which was stopped by the governor after a period.[74] At the same prison a fellowship was begun and elected its own members and committee, meeting weekly to 'achieve moral perfection' but the officers distrusted the ultra-enthusiastic prisoner secretary and it ceased to meet after the chaplain who supported it left.[75] Governors had to work hard to restore peace at the debates which at times deteriorated into slanging matches, after prisoners had devoted immense efforts to gathering and researching information to support their case during the weeks before the actual event.[76] The formation of the Parkhurst jazz band and its separation from the ordinary orchestra of the prison 'was a long and ticklish job'.[77] Yet these new things did lead to great enthusiasm amongst many prisoners as did the sports days and Christmas celebrations, camps and house spirit among borstal trainees. Nevertheless these, alongside sports days for Maidstone convicts and cricket matches between preventive detainees,[78] merely lightened a hard monotonous, grinding and uncreative waste of human energy. As an ex-convict faced with another stretch of penal servitude said to another in the cell below the court. 'It's bloody awful . . . I've bin out eight months an' I'm 'ere again . . . I know every hymn in the ancient and modern book, but I've got ter chant the blasted rhymes all over again . . . save all the strength you've got, you'll need it . . . don't make light of it 'cos it hurts'.[79]

## NOTES

1. S. Wood, *Shades of the Prison House: A Personal Memoir* (Williams & Norgate 1932): 315.
2. *The Magistrate*, April 1929, 2 (XXI): 290.
3. E. Gore, *The Better Fight: The Story of Dame Lilian Barker* (Bles 1965): 161-2. V. Bailey, *Deliquency and Citizenship: Reclaiming the Young Offender* (Clarendon Press 1987): 209-10.
4. J.E. Thomas, *The English Prison Officer since 1850* (Routledge & Kegan Paul 1972): 165.
5. G. Clayton, *The Wall is Strong* (Long 1958): 61, 66.
6. W. Blake, *Quod* (Hodder & Stoughton 1927): 229.

7. C. McCall, *They Always Come Back* (Methuen 1938).
8. J. Phelan, *The Name's Phelan* (Sidgwick & Jackson 1948).
9. W. Macartney, *Walls have Mouths: A Record of Ten Years Penal Servitude,* prologue by Compton Mackenzie (Gollancz 1936).
10. Macartney, *Walls have Mouths.* J. Phelan, *Jail Journey* (Secker & Warburg 1940).
11. Phelan, *Jail Journey*: 79.
12. Ibid: 28.
13. Ibid: 296.
14. Ibid: 61. W. Holt, *I Was A Prisoner* (Miles 1935).
15. Phelan, *Jail Journey*: 122.
16. Ibid: 188-9.
17. Ibid: 241.
18. Macartney, *Walls have Mouths*: 251.
19. Ibid: 111.
20. J. Leigh, *My Prison House* (Hutchinson & Co. 1941): 84.
21. Phelan, *Jail Journey*: 335.
22. Macartney, *Walls have Mouths*: 367, 368-71.
23. Ibid: 375.
24. F.W. Harland-Edgecumbe, *The Lord High Executioner: An Amazing Account of Prison Life in England and America* (Long 1934): 260.
25. Macartney, *Walls have Mouths*: 208.
26. Leigh, *My Prison House*: 92-3.
27. Macartney, *Walls have Mouths*: 104, 105-7, 110.
28. Ibid: 111.
29. Phelan, *Jail Journey*: 184.
30. Leigh, *My Prison House*: 202, 219.
31. Macartney, *Walls have Mouths*: 419-20.
32. Phelan, *Jail Journey*: 264, 291.
33. Macartney, *Walls have Mouths*: 320, 321.
34. Wood, *Shades of the Prison House*: 328.
35. S. Wood, *Glorious Liberty: Dartmoor to Calvary* (Hodder & Stoughton 1933): 67-8.
36. Ibid: 98.
37. H.W. Wicks, *The Prisoner Speaks* (Jarrolds no date): 129-30, 187.
38. Leigh, *My Prison House*: 58.
39. Holt, *I Was a Prisoner*: 60.
40. S. Scott, *The Human Side of Crook and Convict Life* (Hurst & Blackett 1924): 79-80.
41. S.A. Moseley, *The Convict of Today* (Palmer 1927): 101.
42. H.U. Triston, *Men In Cages* (The Book Club 1938): 57.
43. Moseley, *Convict of Today*: 57.
44. Clayton, *The Wall is Strong*: 113.
45. Phelan, *Jail Journey*: 33.
46. Ibid: 32.
47. Leigh, *My Prison House*: 197.

48. PRO P Com. 9/103 Pet Mice, PC to Governors of Parkhurst, Dartmoor and Camp Hill 11 Oct. 1930. For other examples of mice and rats as pets, see Boden, P.H. Ball, *Prison was my Parish* (W. Heinemann 1956): 89-90.
49. J.W. Gordon, *Borstalians* (Hopkinson 1932): 78.
50. Ibid: 136.
51. Ibid.
52. Ibid: 264. Bailey, *Deliquency*: 206.
53. Gordon, *Borstalians*: 103-5, 181.
54. Ibid: 106.
55. Ibid: 147.
56. Portland Conversion to a Borstal 1921-37, PRO HO 45-16953-415065 /18. W. Clarke Hall to Home Sec. 5 March 1922. *The Magistrate*, April/May 1937, 4 (LXXIII): 1143-4.
57. *Justice of the Peace*, 26 April 1924, LXXXVIII: 270-1 Review of H. Bottomley's *Prison Diary*. Bailey, *Deliquency*: 245, 247. Gordon, *Borstalians*: 191.
58. Death of Reginald Russell By Neglect, PRO HO 45-24869-494062. *The Times* 29 Dec. 1937: 17 col. c.
59. Leigh, *My Prison House*: 191-2.
60. Major Munn to PC on Preventive Detention, 13 Sept. 1932, PRO P Com. 9/157.
61. *The Magistrate,* Nov./Dec. 1938, V (VI): 140-2, 132-5. H. Scott, *Your Obedient Servant* (Deutsch 1959): 90.
62. Scott, *Your Obedient Servant*: 78.
63. Phelan, *Jail Journey:* 304.
64. Ibid: 305.
65. Macartney, *Walls have Mouths*: 153-5.
66. Phelan, *Jail Journey*: 359, 370-1.
67. Ibid: 95.
68. Macartney, *Walls have Mouths*: 225.
69. Phelan, *The Name's Phelan*: 286.
70. Phelan, *Jail Journey*: 71, 80, 83-4.
71. Harland-Edgecumbe, *Lord High Executioner*: 199.
72. Release of Prisoners to Attend Funerals 1925, PRO HO 45-24838-470256 /4 Note in light pencil, 27 Aug. 1925.
73. Select Committee on Capital Punishment, PP 1930-31, VI, Minutes of Evidence: 490.
74. Leigh, *My Prison House*: 202.
75. Ibid: 204-5.
76. Wood, *Shades of the Prison House*: 326, 327.
77. Macartney, *Walls have Mouths*: 357.
78. Scott, *Your Obedient Servant*: 90, 91.
79. Gordon, *Borstalians*: 53.

## Chapter Fourteen

# The Aid Societies 1895–1939

The working of prisoners' aid societies was contentious throughout the Ruggles-Brise era and the inter war years. There was one major cause of this, the suspicion on the part of the aid societies that the central state was seeking to undermine substantially their independence. In that suspicion the societies were entirely correct.

There were four kinds of aid society during the period under discussion. Firstly, there was the Borstal Association formed in 1904 out of a group of male prison visitors to London juvenile adult prisoners, which had been set up three years earlier. The director of this was Wemyss Grant Wilson and, after 1908, the association held statutory responsibility for administering the license of each borstal trainee released. It was partly subsidised by the Treasury and partly by voluntary contribution.

Secondly, there was the Central Association for the assistance of convicts and preventive detainees. The proposal to set this up was announced in July 1910 by Churchill and Ruggles-Brise and its director was also Wemyss Grant Wilson. It shared the same office with the Borstal Association. The function of the Central Association was to assist convicts who were all subject to police supervision under conditions of their license. This police supervision had prevailed since the mid Victorian era and thus, as far as convicts sentenced to penal servitude alone were concerned, the Central Association had no legal powers of control or supervision. With preventive detainees, however, there was no police supervision and the Central Association had statutory power to enforce supervision of these. The Borstal and Central Associations worked at an office in the Strand, London and it was as assistant director of the Central Association that Paterson was originally recruited by Ruggles-Brise. The Central Association was entirely state subsidised and tried to attract convicts from penal servitude by offering greater grants than given to those refusing its assistance.

Thirdly, there were some aid societies set up by charitable bodies or individuals such as the Salvation Army, the Jewish religious bodies, Free

Churches, Methodists, the Catholic Church or the St. Giles Christian Mission set up by William Wheatley in London in the nineteenth century. These tended to aid prisoners of their own particular faith or leaning but there was often a hidden objective of proselytisation for the particular faith or for a particular stance such as temperance or salvationism. These charitable religious bodies were at times in competition with each other to gain beneficiaries and had a restricted role within the prisons. Du Cane tended to keep them out and they therefore set up missions opposite a number of prisons, offering breakfasts to released prisoners to attract them. Such societies were maintained by private subscription.

Lastly at each local prison there was a discharged prisoners' aid society. At the very end of the nineteenth century membership of these followed a pattern. In almost all the governor and chaplain were ex officio members of the society and its committee although, in a few prisons, this was not the case. In addition the visiting justices always played a very important role in these societies, clinging tenaciously to them as one of the few survivals of their influence in prisons before 1877. Thus the local prisoner aid society may be seen as a body of visiting magistrates, governor and chaplain: indeed by 1900 in around half the chaplains were the honorary secretaries. The operation of these societies involved annual general meetings, committee and sub committee appointment and election of officers and the committee (or a sub committee thereof) would meet weekly or monthly to hear applications and award grants. In order to receive treasury grant the society had to be certified by the Home Office but private subscription also played a large part in financing them. Lastly, by 1897 around forty of the total of fifty six societies employed 'agents' to aid, advise and influence ex prisoners living locally and to advise the committee about applicant prisoners' claims for help. Where ex prisoners lived further away from the prison or where there was no 'agent', societies made use of volunteers or helpers paid on a case by case basis—local clergy, policemen, police court missionaries and so forth.

Two theories underpinned the system of prisoners' and borstal trainees' aid. Firstly all agreed on the importance of 'patronage' or shepherding of those who had already shown by their offences that they were constitutionally at risk of offending under the stress of environmental circumstance. Firm but sympathetic morally upright social superiors would assure the prisoner that he or she was not alone in the world, but that each was cared for by a benevolent, paternal society and that assistance would be given to ameliorate the pressure of environment. Secondly, there was a theory as to method of aid, based on the philosophy of charity urged by the Charity Organisation Society, a major fount of wisdom about charitable projects in the late Victorian era. According to this theory charity must never be given indiscriminately, because such charity debauched or 'pauperised' the recipient, discouraging self-reliance and making no demands upon him or her, rather teaching the lesson that fecklessness, laziness and vice would be subsidised by charity. Charity must only be given after careful investigation of each case and a precise assessment of need and moral desert. Thus the drunken spendthrift should be referred to the state Poor Law, never relieved by charity; the applicant who had worked all his life until injured and unable to support his wife might be helped. However, the charity 'package' put together must be such as to meet the deeper needs of the applicant, in other words to put the applicant in such a position that he or she would be able to help themselves towards a life of independence and self-reliance. So, according to this theory, money doles given to destitute people indiscriminately were anathema, because these created hosts of scroungers and institutionalised dependence and idleness; provision of tools to an ex prisoner, who had foolishly given way to temptation but had hitherto led a blameless life or placement of a female prisoner, who had no family or employment in a labour home, exemplified the correct approach. Lastly, whenever charity was given, it must be adequate to set the recipient squarely in a position to live independently—inadequate charity was baneful in that it pauperised by ensuring failure of self-reliance and therefore despair at failure.

The Gladstone committee had been critical of the local aid societies[1] and Ruggles-Brise at once instituted an enquiry into them by the Rev. G.P. Merrick who was appointed the first visiting chaplain of the commission at the same time. Merrick concluded that the work of the societies at local prisons was badly organised and underfunded, depending mainly on magistrates' donations. Too many societies gave indiscriminate aid and state monitoring of them was ineffective.[2] Their approaches varied immensely, some giving money, others only goods such as clothing, some finding lodgings and employment, others doing neither and they varied also regarding groups to whom help would be given: some refused to help released tramps, others only helped longer sentenced prisoners, some found women prisoners difficult to help. Furthermore, convicts tended to be a problem for these societies. The tactic used by the authorities between the mid nineteenth century and 1910 was to wheedle convicts into accepting assistance by local aid societies by giving the convicts an increased grant—'gratuity'—if they would agree to allow the local aid society of their home area to dispense it. The convicts therefore agreed in order to gain the increase, but on release would demand that they be given their whole gratuity at once, often using 'very strong language': as Merrick's successor noted, 'The men demand the cash with oaths and threats and give endless trouble when goods are given in lieu of money'.[3]

In other words, Merrick concluded, the local societies were, with some honourable exceptions, in need of reconstruction. For the next forty years the prison commissioners and local visiting magistrates became increasingly embattled over the issue of reform of the system.

The strategies attempted by the commissioners were threefold. In the first place Ruggles-Brise deprived them of a role with the special groups such as borstal trainees, convicts and preventive detainees upon whose management so much public attention was focused. So, the Borstal and Central Associations were heralded as highly efficient and expert at their work. The executive staff of these two associations therefore visited all prior to their release and in their own annual reports insisted that the trainees and convicts planned for release with their staff and that the aid given was sufficient to ensure that the inmate had a fair chance. It was argued that accommodation and employment were found when necessary and the conditions of the licenses carefully enforced. So, borstal trainees must report to the office of the Borstal Association on release, report regularly to the supervisor, be hardworking and 'abstain from any violation of the law, shall not associate with persons of bad character and shall lead a sober and industrious life to the satisfaction of the Borstal Association'.[4] Similar conditions were applied in the licenses of preventive detainees. Therefore, the public were assured that these special groups were systematically and purposefully maintained and controlled for lengthy periods after release and that, if they proved recalcitrant, they were returned to institutional control by revocation of license. Outside the London area specially selected associates or supervisors would be chosen to carry out the work, but the pre-release planning was always done by the Borstal and Central Associations.

The second strategy was to use the powers of grant aid and certification to regulate the local prison aid societies. Merrick had drawn up a profile of a good aid society in his report to the commission.[5] Such a society would work closely with other prisoner aid societies. It would keep registers and records. It would employ agents and would consider carefully the needs of all prisoners in the institution, awarding aid differentially. It would pay attention to the theory of charity relief and would know intimately the numerous charitable organizations and institutions within the community and recruit voluntary helpers to give friendship and guidance to ex prisoners. It would itself keep watch over ex prisoners after release and in all its dealings would be flexible according to need and desert but pay particular attention to finding work and accommodation and providing necessities such as food and clothing. Lastly, it would coordinate and establish influence over the independent aid organizations.

This was all very well but, as visiting chaplain of the commission, Merrick had his work cut out to make it stick. For one thing, these societies were exceedingly proud of their ancient traditions, often going back to the 1823 General Gaol Act and deeply distrusted outsiders. Furthermore, the prison commission was on difficult ground for the local visiting magistrates were often highly influential men who would not hesitate to appeal to friends and relatives in government or Parliament against the prison commission and its little group of inspectors and specialists. Memories of the way Du Cane had handled magistrates were fresh in the minds of many of them and they were suspicious of the prison commissioners whose new policies seemed by implication equally dismissive of them. Thirdly, of course, the local governors and chaplains were closely involved in these societies and tended to eulogise their success and efficiency. Colonel Rich, for example, made no secret of his admiration for them and his contempt for 'soft, sloppy sob stuff'.[6] He found local visiting magistrates 'a real good lot of the old stock . . . gentlemen and sportsmen of the best type, but strict and severe as leaders of men have need to be and should be'.[7] In annual reports prison chaplains lauded the work of their own society.

Ruggles-Brise was not a man to be bamboozled by this and he turned to his third strategy, that of manoeuvring them into policing and improving themselves. Here he stumbled upon a hornets' nest.

There had been in existence since 1878 a 'Central Committee' of a body called the Reformatory and Refuge Union (to do with various institutions connected with juvenile offenders and others not under the jurisdiction of the prison commission). This 'Central Committee' had been set up by the Reformatory and Refuge Union to act as a coordinating body to extend the operation of aid societies and to increase their efficiency but it had led a soporific existence ever since. In May 1911 Ruggles-Brise sent a confidential memorandum to this body proposing to abolish 'gratuities' to local prisoners and to use the money as increased grant aid to local societies. This was a sprat to catch a mackerel, for he also proposed a new 'General Council' to coordinate all aid to local prisoners, to be elected by the local societies with rights and duties to regulate their operations.[8]

It was not long before news of this got round and a storm of protest broke out. Some small societies feared that the large influential societies would dominate this council, for example the Surrey and South London society or the Royal Discharged Prisoners' Aid Society, based in London and set up in 1857 to assist convicts before the establishment of the Central Association, thereafter working at Wormwood Scrubs. These larger ones, on the other hand, feared that the smaller ones would have voting rights on such a council equal to their own.[9] All seemed to fear domination by the central state and Ruggles-Brise was warned that 'most societies hold conservative views. Some . . . object to take the trouble to carefully consider whether the money at present available might not be better apportioned'.[10]

Ruggles-Brise was not to be put off for he was convinced that the aid societies were intolerably inefficient and contemptuously noted that aid to some meant 'a cup of tea and a bun' whilst one society had a seventy year old agent on £90 a year who had never found work for anybody.[11] Furthermore, at the back of his mind was the vision of a grand, streamlined system of preventive care in which all the aid to convicts, borstal trainees, preventive detainees and local prisoners would be concentrated[12] and he soon returned to the attack.

At this point a number of influential London aid workers such as Frank Whitbread, the Chairman of the Royal Society, became converted to Ruggles-Brise's view and began to urge reform of the Central Committee whose chairman, Lord Shuttleworth, (also President of the Royal Society) was implicitly exposed to substantial criticism. Tension heightened substantially when a bequest of £20,000 was left to the Central Committee, for the Surrey and South London Treasurer was convinced that the Central Committee was incompetent to use this appropriately.[13] A number of large London Societies, including the Royal Society, formed an alliance to drive out the 'Central Committee' of the Reformatory and Refuge Union and redesign the central coordinating body and they approached the commission in February 1916 to ask Ruggles-Brise's view.[14]

By now Ruggles-Brise was in a difficult position. He had had a long association with Lord Shuttleworth and had carefully tried to avoid public criticism, preferring rather to manoeuvre behind the scenes to strengthen the control of the local societies by a central body. So, he was unwilling to back a coup d'etat against Lord Shuttleworth, although he wanted radical reform of the Central Committee. In February 1916 he therefore wrote guardedly to the Surrey and South London treasurer, admitting his dissatisfaction but not committing himself to any action.[15]

The dispute swelled into a public row during the summer and autumn of 1916 and Lord Shuttleworth now appealed to Ruggles-Brise to support him against foes who, in his view, were trying to destroy the Central Committee.[16] Lord Shuttleworth indeed resigned his Presidency of the Royal Society whose members, he believed, had betrayed him and begged Ruggles-Brise to support a defensive action to the effect that the Central Committee should at least be left alone until after the war.[17] Ruggles-Brise tried without success to calm things down, lamenting that 'a good deal of irritation has been caused by what those imperfectly acquainted with the object of the scheme conceived to be an attempt to humiliate the Central Committee, by proclaiming its inefficiency and unsuitability as a representative body'.[18] In March 1917 Ruggles-Brise was still refusing to side against Lord Shuttleworth, arguing that he could do no less than support the latter's plea for a moratorium on debate 'in view of his work and cooperation with me in the past'.[19] However, feelings were now running high and in early 1918 the London discontents set up the Central Discharged Prisoners' Aid Society which swiftly took over from the old central committee of the Reformatory and Refuge Union. Its functions were defined as advisory, not regulatory, to promote cooperation between local societies, provide a central pool of information for local groups, encourage local societies and consider subjects of plain interest to all involved in prisoners' aid. After the war Ruggles-Brise became president of this and was soon urging to members his vision of a 'National Society for the Prevention of Crime and for the Protection of the Young Offender':[20] in this would be amalgamated all the different supervisory systems for young and older offenders along the lines of certain American states.[21]

In effect, however, Ruggles-Brise had failed, for the new Central Society was little more than a representative gathering of local aid personnel without any mandate to regulate or monitor. Very little changed and during the 1920s the commissioners continued to be privately deeply critical of the failure of the Central Society to improve the quality of prisoners' aid. Waller and Maxwell tended to leave well alone but Harold Scott, chairman between 1932 and 1938, decided to act. He obtained the extension of the remit of the Departmental Committee examining prison industries to cover the ways in which prisoners were helped to find work on discharge. The report of this investigation was laid before parliament in the late spring of 1935.

Scott had already become suspect to the aid societies who believed that he was aiming at centralisation. In November 1933, at a meeting of the Central Society, chairman Frank Whitbread 'announced at once his complete unwillingness to have anything to do with anything that might seem to be inquisitive or dictatorial as regards Discharged Prisoners' Aid Societies'. All suggestions from those favouring Scott's desire for change were met 'with a deep post prandial silence . . . Whitbread said they would stick to their old policy and Taylor (the other mummy) said they were not a directing and governing society'. Scott's informant added that he ought to get the Charity Commission 'to pack away this collection of imperfectly stuffed old bolsters' who should alternatively 'be pushed down a public convenience and the plug pulled'.[22]

The ranks, however, were not firm for some local representatives to the Central Society were accusing it of 'paralytic inertia' which 'must be superseded by an entirely new organisation'.[23] Nevertheless the central and local societies in the main continued to resist any idea of control. As one representative wrote: 'no aid society worth its salt will grant executive powers or would be willing to accept dictation from any central council . . . any more than, say, the London Chamber of Commerce, the Manchester, Liverpool or any other Chamber of Commerce would dream of giving executive powers to the Association of British Chambers of Commerce'.[24]

In fact the local societies had a number of axes to grind. In the first place, closure of prisons in recent years had caused them problems because their business had always been conducted at the local prison, which, in any case, gave a strong identity to each society. Now, with local prisons reduced to less than thirty, many societies, which had lost their prisons, functioned to deal with prisoners from their own county or borough who had been committed to the more distant local prison of, say, the next county and must rely heavily on the cooperation of the society of that prison. Furthermore, local aid workers and others also resented change of use of a local prison. In 1931, for example, the commissioners decided to turn Portsmouth into a preventive detention prison and this was strongly objected to on the grounds that local Portsmouth prisoners would now serve their sentences at Winchester, thus entirely disrupting the local aid society: local people wanted Portsmouth prison to deal with local men and women.[25] Indeed, the new policy of training prisons caused further confusion and the society at Wakefield was overwhelmed by an entirely new set of demands upon it whilst, in general, local societies found that even more of their local prisoners were being sent far away as a result of deliberate policy.

The report of the departmental committee, which included Harold Scott and Margery Fry, was an elegantly phrased condemnation of the local societies.[26] It concluded that a strong National Council should be set up to administer and allocate all state grant to local societies, employ its own officers, coordinate local societies and to 'govern the policy of societies as a whole and to approve their constitution'.[27]

The Departmental Committee members were at once accused of high handedness and disregard of the views of the societies themselves.[28] In mid 1935 these called a special conference and commissioned Frank Whitbread, chairman of the Central Society, to produce a rival report in which a strong attack on prison commission policy was made. Whitbread concluded that for years the local societies had been the victims of prejudice and hostility and that many of their problems were a direct result of prison commission policy.[29] The many excellent voluntary workers who gave up time and effort had, said the rival report, been insulted and demeaned by the departmental committee.

The fury of magistrates generally over this issue has already been described but throughout the 1935 summer the commissioners were more generally warned that, if they tried to absorb the societies into a central system, there would be very serious trouble. On the other hand, opponents of the Central Society continued to castigate it as 'a dead weight of archaic prejudice . . . like a flock of sheep, a meek ignorant following of a chairman (F. Whitbread) who has a great big bee in his bonnet'.[30] Members of Parliament were recruited to resist the commission, now accused of representing 'the deadening hand of centralisation' by one side.[31] On the other some aid workers like Leo Page, Frank Dawtry and Captain Barclay of the Berkshire, West Riding and Bristol societies supported the commission and urged that at least there should be open minded discussion of the Prison Industries Committee report.[32] Yet another report, this time by the Royal Society, admitted the need for improved monitoring and inspection and conceded that some societies did have 'inefficient management and inaccurate accountancy, which are apt to lead to scandals', concluding that, if the Central Society did not take a more controlling role, the state would inevitably do this for them.[33]

The outcome was a compromise between the status quo and central control. Following these disputes the National Association of Discharged Prisoners' Aid Societies was set up to replace the Central Society and to attempt to coordinate local groups. This N.A.D.P.A.S. was to act as an official link between the commission and local societies, advise the commission on allocation of state grants and to act as aftercare agency for those released from Wakefield training prison (at which a specialist welfare officer was appointed). At the same time some of the smaller aid societies formed amalgamations. In Wales, for example, four of these united to form the South Wales and Monmouth society.[34] In 1938 the new National Association assisted the societies at Pentonville, Brixton, Wandsworth and Wormwood Scrubs to amalgamate to form an expanded Royal Society for London's prisons.[35]

There had also been changes in the Borstal Association during the 1930s, for Paterson had concluded that the official supervisors (in London and Liverpool the salaried staff of the Association, elsewhere around three hundred 'associates' mostly probation officers) were too much seen by the borstal trainees as official scrutinisers of their conduct. A network of voluntary 'unofficial friends' was therefore set up in 1935 to supplement their work along the lines of the American Big Brother and Big Sister schemes. These helpers had 'no official status and powers and because of this possess a weapon and an opportunity which it would surely be folly to ignore'.[36] So, the official supervisor would give material aid and administer the license, whilst the volunteer would bring 'personal contact . . . unofficial and fraternal'.[37] These volunteers were given careful instructions on the need to allow friendship to develop patiently, to avoid evangelising or trying to 'trot a lad off to church the first minute you meet', to join in games or visits to the cinema with him and advised: 'don't expect a saint or you might be disappointed and don't expect a sinner or he might . . . don't be shocked if he celebrates liberty. Most of us did when we got demobbed'.[38] It should incidentally be noted that borstal girls had been separated from the Borstal Association in 1928 by Lilian Barker and were supervised by the Aylesbury Association which acted as a an aid society for these and Lilian Barker and her assistants found supervisors for the girls themselves: she retained this role after promotion to assistant commissioner.

The approach of the local aid societies to adult prisoners was often makeshift and at times harshly judgmental. Prisoners did not favour the aid societies in the main and felt that they would be distrusted and would receive moralising criticism. So Harland-Edgecumbe refused to 'face that committee of men who hunger and thirst after righteousness'[39] and James Leigh found them insensitive and grudging. 'We can do nothing for you . . . unless you have friends or relatives who are willing to help you, I am afraid your position on discharge will be difficult'.[40] Leigh felt that the societies were plagued by complacency and hypocrisy and that the representative was 'almost callous in his tactlessness'.[41]

It was widely reported that the societies tended to harass and lecture prisoners brought before them for application. One young man asked for a pair of trousers and was obviously baffled by the stern admonition he received in return, because he was going out to live with a girl and thus 'you have forfeited all claim to my sympathy'.[42] The representative stalked from the cell leaving the bewildered prisoner to ask the warder; 'Yes, but what do he si abaht the trahsers'?[43] Moralising at prisoners was common place in these situations. Thus another was asked what he did on Sundays, the society representative hoping for some account of church attendance: however, 'me and feyther collect rags and bones of a Sunday'.[44]

The theory of charity according to the Charity Organisation Society was seldom applied. Captain Clayton recalled that in his earlier days 'the proceedings used to remind me of some weird auction mart' with prisoners skilled in the ways of these societies, often supported by the more generous members, calling out for the original offer to be increased.[45] Major Blake recalled the arguments between prisoners and aid societies.

| | |
|---|---|
| Prisoner | 'Can I have a new pair of trahsis, Sir? |
| Chairman | What's the matter with your own trousers? |
| Prisoner | They're all wore out, Sir |
| Agent | I'll have a look at them and if they're too bad I can fit him from stock. |
| Prisoner | I'd rather have a new pair, gentlemen |
| Agent | Yes and so would the pawn broker. Next.'[46] |

Doubtless there was improvement during the Paterson era but, frankly, it is difficult to see much as far as the local societies were concerned. Prison visitors were now setting a higher standard of assessment of need and problem and yet, although the aid societies softened their approach some-

what, overall they resisted suggested changes of method and clung to a rapid
fire and in the main uncreative way of responding to the requests for help.

| | |
|---|---|
| Chairman | 'Can you carry a hod of bricks? |
| Prisoner | No. |
| Chairman | Are you going home to your family? |
| Prisoner | Yes Sir. |
| Chairman | Have you any money of your own? |
| Prisoner | Yes Sir but only tuppence |
| Chairman | Very well . . . we will give you a little cash to |
| | help to take you over your first week.Good luck |
| | to you. I hope we shall not see you here again.'[47] |

There were a plethora of religious aftercare organizations outside prisons
which aimed to help the prisoner keep to the narrow way and maintain him
or herself. Some of these ran refuges for women prisoners deemed too
unselfreliant to survive without residential care and protection and the
Borstal and Central Associations made extensive use of these during
Ruggles-Brise's time. But the Salvation Army, Church Army and Church of
England Temperance Society were merely three out of many organisations
setting up shelters, labour homes, refuges, employment centres, workshops,
labour yards and so forth. All the major prison oriented voluntary
organisations, such as the Howard League, were involved in the 'aftercare'
project and women in particular were placed often in the network of hostels
and refuges run by outside organisations all over the country. So, a
succession of borstal girls and female convicts trooped through these
establishments as part of the conditions of their release licenses. E. Chappell
was thus discharged from Aylesbury borstal on 14.12.1911 and went to
Stafford Industrial Home: she remained two years before running away and
was regarded as feeble minded.[48] L. Wilkins was discharged in February
1910, sent to a Home at Fulham but had her license revoked three days
later. In late May 1910 she was back at a Church Army Hostel but refused
to stay and was sent to another hostel. After further defiance she was placed
in service but stole from her employer and ended up in another Home. In
April 1912 she was married and no further record of her kept.[49]

Between 1895 and 1939 there were some new voluntarily led experiments
in aftercare. For example, the Christian Scientist Arnold Hall opened a
restaurant in London in the 1930s, staffed by convicts and ex prisoners and
consulted closely with the Howard League about this.[50] Predictably the
Home Office was not keen, having 'little faith' in Christian Scientists and
'none at all in those of them who also dabble in penology'.[51] The London
Sheriff's fund concentrated on financial help to deserving prisoners' wives
and children and were followed in this by a number of London aid societies

themselves. The Duchess of Marlborough opened an establishment in London where wives might go to work in a laundry and sewing room with a children's creche attached. Just before the Great War a prisoners' wives' aid society was founded by the Church Army in Manchester and in 1917 the National Society for the Prevention of Cruelty to Children was formally recruited to help prisoners' families by the prison commission.[52]

The treatment of prisoners was nevertheless often severe and inquisitional and prisoners and ex prisoners often did their best to wring what advantage they could out of the system, whilst the women tended to abscond frequently from the institutions to which they were sent. The exchanges seemed to vary little with, on the one hand inspection of previous conduct and of moral desert, on the other desire to maximise profit from the system.

| | |
|---|---|
| Ex prisoner | 'If you don't help me tonight I shall do a . . . burglary. I want some clogs and some coppers for food. I haven't had a bite all day' . . . |
| Voluntary Worker | 'Whether you go back to "stir" or not rests with you, Jud. You have had plenty of chances and now . . . you come again for help. But it won't do and I shall not help you tonight'.[53] |

or as reported by Thomas Holmes, secretary of the Howard Association

'What do you want'?
'Oh you are Mr. Holmes. I want you to help me'.
'Why should I help you? I know nothing of you'.
'I have just come out of prison'.
'Well, you are none the better for that'.
'Well, you help men that have been in prison'.
'Sometimes, when I see they are ashamed of having been in'.
'Well, I don't want to get in prison again'.
'How do I know you have been in prison'?
'Why, didn't you speak to us like a man last Sunday'?
'Yes I was at Pentonville last Sunday and I hope I spoke like a man'.
'Ah that you did! And when I heard you I said "I'll see him when I come out. He will be sure to give me half a dollar." '[54]

There remained an archaic anachronistic quality about aftercare of prisoners by local societies between 1895 and 1939 as well as a good deal of complacent self-congratulation. It often seemed that local aid societies were on the side of severity towards and swift judgement of prisoners rather than more careful assessment and sensitivity towards them. This is not to ignore the effort put into this work by some local aid society workers and by many voluntary organizations. The Church of England Temperance Society, for example, maintained fifteen shelters, missions, homes, colonies and labour yards in England in 1923:[55] the Salvation Army or the Church Army were often the only people who would help the destitute and homeless ex prisoner. Yet, as a whole, local discharged prisoners aid societies did not impress prisoners  and the prison commission saw them throughout the period as in need of radical reform.

There was also criticism of the Borstal Association. J.R. Gordon who had served a borstal term was bitter in his condemnation of the association, although he was overall positive about Paterson's borstals. Gordon suggested that borstal boys, in the main, saw the association as unhelpful and condescending and that the accommodation found was of poor quality.[56] He emphasised that trainees needed a sincere and well disposed associate ready to lend an enthusiastic helping hand. Furthermore, some of the archival material does not reveal Wemyss Grant Wilson's attitude to borstal trainees in a particularly encouraging light. He was reproved by the prison commission for his attitude to borstal license revokees and Victor Bailey felt that the Borstal Association tended to concentrate on 'deserving' cases according to charity organisation principles: this in reality meant that those with settled families and homes and those who had been docile in training were the ones who received help whilst the others tended to be inadequately assisted.[57] Admittedly it was hard to find work for the large numbers who were released at a time of high unemployment, but the view of the prison commission itself was that the supervisors were often too busy and too remote from the young men to give adequate time or commitment to the task: this view was shared by some local groups and in 1937 ten philanthropic and religious organisations in Bolton set up a committee to promote 'a sort of elder brotherly contact' to supplement borstal aftercare.[58] All too often the case notes of the Borstal Association contained meagre entries, such as 'has not been reported as reconvicted' or 'satisfactory when last heard of' and by their own account the association found it hard to keep track of many of the trainees.[59] It seems clear that the Aylesbury Association was more dynamic both with borstal girls and women convicts and that Lilian Barker and her small group of helpers worked dedicatedly to arrange extensive help for these: the numbers of course were much smaller than those of the male trainees. However, Barker had great patience with relapse on license. Her biographer remarked, 'I think she cared more for these girls even than those who made easy happy marriages and who never gave her a moment's anxiety'[60] and she and her staff were in frequent contact by letter and visit with the girls on license, using personal contacts to place them in jobs, sending them gifts and visiting them.

The evidence about the Central Association for discharged convicts is somewhat conflicting. The theory was that all preventive detainees and penal servitude prisoners were, like borstal trainees, prepared for their release. The Association also attempted to coordinate a large number of leading voluntary agencies such as the Church Army, Catholic Church, Church of England Temperance Society, Wesleyans, Free Church and Jewish Aid Societies, who were all represented on its council. The actual effectiveness of the system is less certain. Stuart Wood in the 1920s was told that work could not be found for him on release but added that Wemyss Grant Wilson did deal with him kindly during their meetings in prison and that a grant of £10 was made to him.[61] In addition, the evidence of ex convicts to the Labour Research Enquiry was overall that helpful associates were found to advise and assist them after their release.[62]

However, there was criticism of the Central Association. One who had worked for six months for both the Borstal and Central Associations in the late 1930s told the prison commission that often visits to convicts in prison were not made or were peremptory and that the associates were often agents of the local aid societies or part timers at a very low rate of £1 per case per year. In general this man was very critical and he applied his criticisms equally to the Borstal Association. It is of some significance that Paterson minuted to the chairman of the prison commission that he agreed with this overall assessment.[63]

Almost all convicts and many short term prisoners referred to the stress caused by leaving prison. Many became tense, irritable and apprehensive as release approached. Jim Phelan snarled and shouted at prisoners and officers just before release and on leaving Parkhurst stood by the shore at Ryde sobbing unrestrainedly, being thereafter nervous of people and embarrassed at his ignorance of simple everyday matters.[64] Macartney was convinced that people knew him for an ex convict and watched him in the street. He was often close to tears after release and was frightened by the speed of the traffic. He particularly recalled the kindly encouraging reception of the Criminal Record Officer at Scotland Yard where he had to report as part of his license conditions.[65]

One aid worker summed up the feelings of many prisoners to the Labour Research Committee: 'the discharged prisoner is like a child bewildered, everything is strange. He imagines himself to be the cynosure of all eyes. He returns to work shy, lacking every essential of an efficient workman'. To this a Salvation Army officer added that 'loss of contact with the outside world makes men mentally petrified . . . numbed . . . a period of convalescence on release is almost essential. Great allowances have to be made for some months'.[66]

# NOTES

1. Report from the Departmental Committee on Prisons, PP 1895, LVI: 14-15.
2. Report to Her Majesty's Commissioners of Prisons on the Operations of the Discharged Prisoners' Aid Societies by the Rev. G.P. Merrick, PP 1897, XL: 10, 11, 12, 14, 46.
3. Ibid: 54. PRO P Com. 7/404, Memo S.P.H. Statham Chaplain Inspector to PC, no date, early 1911.
4. E. Ruggles-Brise, *The English Prison System* (MacMillan 1921): 242.
5. Report, G.P. Merrick, PP 1897, XL: 100-2.
6. C.E.F. Rich, *Recollections of a Prison Governor* (Hurst & Blackett 1932): 97.
7. Ibid: 28.
8. Gratuities PRO P Com. 7/397, Confidential Memo E. Ruggles-Brise to Central Committee of DPAS, 8 May 1911.
9. PRO P Com. 7/397, PC memo. M.L.Waller, 13 June 1911.
10. PRO P Com. 7/397, Central Committee DPAS to E. Ruggles-Brise, 18 Oct. 1911.
11. PRO P Com. 7/397, Local Prisons Discharged Prisoners Associations, Suggestions for a Central Council, no date.
12. PRO P Com. 7/397, PC Memo to Chairman Central Committee, 25 March 1913.
13. DPAS Central Council 1911-16, PRO P Com. 7/404, W. Negus to PC 1 Feb. 1916.
14. PRO P Com. 7/404, W. Negus to E. Ruggles-Brise, 1 Feb. 1916.
15. PRO P Com. 7/404, E. Ruggles-Brise to W. Negus, 21 Feb. 1916.
16. PRO P Com. 7/405, Lord Shuttleworth to E. Ruggles-Brise, 23 Nov. 1916.
17. PRO P Com. 7/405, Lord Shuttleworth to E. Ruggles-Brise, 27 Feb. 1917.
18. PRO P Com. 7/405, E. Ruggles-Brise to Royal Society, 29 Dec. 1916.
19. PRO P Com. 7/405, E. Ruggles-Brise to F. Whitbread, 3 March 1917.
20. Rehabilitation of Discharged Prisoners, PRO HO 45-21652-405949 /3 Annual Report of Central Discharged Prisoners' Aid Society, March 1919.
21. RCP & DCP yrend 31 March 1919, PP 1919, XXVII, App. 1: 36.
22. Departmental Committee on Prison Industries and Aftercare 1932-7, PRO P Com. 9/183 /17a No signature to H. Scott, 20 Nov. 1933.
23. PRO P Com. 9/183 /17, M. Pinker to A. Maxwell, 18 Nov. 1933.
24. PRO P Com. 9/183 /15a, H.Wood to A. Maxwell, 31 Oct. 1933.
25. Portsmouth Prison and Preventive Detention 1931-1940, PRO HO 45-18498-655767/1. HO Memo re Portsmouth Deputation 30 July 1931 /2 /5 /7.
26. Report of the Departmental Committee on the Employment of Prisoners, Part 2 Employment On Discharge, PP 1934-5, XI.
27. Ibid: 30.
28. Employment of Prisoners, PRO HO 45-24125-651577/26. Cut. H.C. Wood, Letter, *The Times*, 18 June 1935.
29. Ibid. /42 Report of a Special Committee of the DPAS on part 2 of the Salmon Report.
30. PRO P Com. 9/183 / 28 W.H. Blackburn to W.C. Crook, 14 June 1935.
31. Ibid. /35 H.C. Wood, Kent DPAS.
32. Ibid. /35 Report of Proceedings of the Conference of local DPAS, London, 18 July 1935.

33. Ibid. /48 Report of The Royal Society for the Assistance of Discharged Prisoners, 23 Oct. 1935.
34. RCP & DCP for 1936, PP 1937-8, XIV: 43.
35. RCP & DCP for 1938, PP 1939-40, V: 35.
36. PRO P Com. 9/439 / 305. Report of the Borstal Association, 1938: 21, 24.
37. Ibid: 23, 24.
38. PRO P Com. 9/439 / 81 Borstal Voluntary Committee Review, Feb. 1938, printed.
39. F.W. Harland-Edgecumbe, *The Lord High Executioner: An Amazing Account of Prison Life in England and America* (Long 1934): 273.
40. J. Leigh, *My Prison House* (Hutchinson & Co. 1941): 237.
41. Ibid: 238.
42. R.F. Quinton, *Crime and Criminals* (Longman, Green & Co. 1910): 129.
43. Ibid: 130.
44. Ibid: 130.
45. G.F. Clayton, *The Wall is Strong* (Long 1958): 68.
46. W. Blake, *Quod* (Hodder & Stoughton 1927): 218.
47. J.A.F. Watson, *Meet the Prisoner* (Cape 1939): 182.
48. PRO P Com. 7/561, Girls discharged Aylesbury, 1 Jan. 1910-30 Sept. 1913.
49. Ibid.
50. *Justice of the Peace*, 16 Dec. 1933, XCVII: 802, 809.
51. Rehabilitation of Discharged Prisoners 1920-47, PRO HO 45-21652-405949/26, HO Minute, 18 July 1929.
52. PRO P Com. 7/403, Report Preston and Mid Lancs DPAS, 3 Jan. 1911. 1st Annual Report of the Manchester, Salford and District Prisoners' Wives Aid Society, yr end Jan. 1914. Memo PC to all Male Prisons, 5 Feb. 1917.
53. C.E.B. Russell, *Young Gaol Birds* (MacMillan & Co. 1910): 131-2.
54. T. Holmes, *Known to the Police* (Arnold 1908): 95.
55. H.H. Ayscough, *When Mercy Seasons Justice* (Church of England Temperance Society, no date): App. 2.
56. J.W. Gordon, *Borstalians* (Hopkinson 1932): 207-17.
57. PRO P Com 7/516, M.L. Waller to B. Thomson, 5 Jan. 1911. V. Bailey, *Deliquency and Citizenship: Reclaiming the Young Offender* (Clarendon Press 1987): 214.
58. *The Magistrate*, Dec. 1936/Jan. 1937, 4 (LXXI): 1102.
59. S. Hobhouse and A.F. Brockway, (eds) *English Prisons Today* (Longman, Green & Co. 1922): 434.
60. E. Gore, *The Better Fight: The Story of Dame Lilian Barker* (Bles 1965): 198.
61. S. Wood, *Shades of the Prison House: A Personal Memoir* (Williams & Norgate 1932): 332.
62. Hobhouse and Brockway, *English Prisons*: 458.
63. Central Association and Borstal Association 1939, P Com. 9/5. Report dated 6 Jan. 1939, Signature illegible PC Minute, 30 Jan. 1939.
64. J. Phelan, *Jail Journey* (Secker & Warburg 1940): 380-4.
65. W. Macartney, *Walls have Mouths: A Record of Ten Years' Penal Servitude* (Gollancz 1936): 432-3. For fear of traffic, see also Boden, P.H. Ball, *Prison was my Parish* (W. Heinemann 1956): 80.
66. Hobhouse and Brockway, *English Prisons*: 514.

# Conclusion

On August 18th, 1935, the day that Sir Evelyn Ruggles-Brise died, the Eleventh International Penitentiary Congress opened in Berlin. Ruggles-Brise's pronounced international outlook (he had been president of the congress movement between 1910 and 1926) had been continued by the prison commissioners. Paterson had advised colonial and foreign governments about prisons and borstals and toured these and, when he went to America, he had been deeply impressed by much that he saw—dining rooms and libraries 'as beautiful as those of Oxford and Cambridge. Cloisters with Norman arches surround the grassy quadrangle', camps where prisoners 'have the bearing of pioneers . . . a training far more appropriate to their future than the slow and meticulous regime of prison life' and self-governing colonies in Massachusetts with governing bodies of prisoners and so forth.[1] Paterson was critical of many of the local county gaols, but was undoubtedly influenced by the work of Thomas Mott Osborne and his belief in Leagues of Honour in part reflects this. For their part his American contacts liked him although they were somewhat ruffled by his criticisms.[2]

In the 1920s and early 30s there had been much discussion between various agencies about the establishment of an international minimum standard for the treatment of political and criminal prisoners to guarantee them against torture, starvation and so forth in prisons as well as a basic minimum of instruction, maintenance and care. As president of the International Prison Commission, which governed the quinquennial congresses, Ruggles-Brise had been much involved in this, but there were disputes in the late 1920s. The Home Office and prison commission in Britain argued that the congresses and their governing International Prison Commission should be the authority for drawing this up and urging it upon the League of Nations, but the Howard League deemed the former body unsuitable for this and wanted direct appeal to the League of Nations.[3] By 1930, with the involvement of Paterson, Waller and Lord Polwarth, chairman of the Scottish prison commission from 1909 to 1929, a list of rights and duties had been drawn up by the International Prison Commission and was being urged upon the League of Nations.[4] Lengthy negotiations, consultations and referrals followed this recommended guarantee of all kinds of stimulating and regenerative programmes to the prisoners of the world: whether the Japanese in Manchuria or the Italians in Ethiopia took note of it is not recorded, but the disputes about all this rumbled on at the 1930 Congress in Prague, where the Howard League's call for decisive action was noted and there was much general discussion amongst these world wide experts on crime and punishment. Britain sent Paterson and Lord Polwarth and three other official delegates who were accompanied by well over a hundred prison officials, social workers, prison visitors, magistrates and others to mull over and debate with similar groups from all over the world the progress of the optimistic liberal penological project.

Not many of them came to Berlin in 1935. The Howard League would have none of it and in any case the National Socialists did not want them. There had been a row, because some Howard League members had insisted on participating in a mock trial in 1933, to do with the destruction of the Reichstag by fire, and the Nazis felt that they were not friends of the Fatherland. But archbishops as well as Members of Parliament and some Jews were unhappy about the Congress being held in Berlin at all[5] and thus only about twenty British delegates assembled and debated in Berlin, whilst over the sea the body of Sir Evelyn Ruggles-Brise returned to the village church of his childhood home for burial.

The National Socialists had a different view of the prison project and gathered over five hundred of their people to explain it all to the rest. It was, after all, unfortunate that misunderstandings had led to a certain lack of friendliness towards the Reich and here at last was a chance to set the record straight. Dr. Goebbels, in particular, wanted delegates to appreciate the true inward dynamic spirit of the new creed, 'the constructive work of the National Socialist state',[6] and there was plenty of opportunity to tell the Congress about the application of it all to the criminal justice system. Reichsminister for International Penal Policy and Commissioner of Justice, Dr. Hans Frank, patiently took them through it: 'the National Socialist legislator regards the criminal as the result of an already appearing menace to the health of the nation. He teaches eugenic prophylactics' and indeed a 'racially intact' people 'will get rid of the criminal as a healthy body gets rid of the germs of disease'.[7] Frank gently chided the liberal democracies for their misunderstanding: 'we have been . . . judged sometimes in a friendly but more often, unfortunately, in an unfriendly manner by a large number of persons with international interests on account of our penal policy'. He asked delegates to reflect upon the operation of their own systems which allowed the impure and unfit to propagate and prosper.[8] It must be clearly understood, he added, that the 'National Socialist State knows no humanitarian scruples . . . the National Socialist Jurist is a fanatical exponent of the principle of reprisal, yes, of intimidation . . . against the destroyers of the national community ... those who are unworthy of procreation endanger the state'.[9]

So, they heard about the inspiration of the new judges who would mystically incorporate the deepest intuition and will of the Fuhrer and race into their sentencing and who need no longer require any proven crime, merely a suspected personality or type. The Nazis wanted resolutions passed by individual delegates' votes, thus ensuring that their huge delegation would win every vote, but Paterson and Polwarth insisted that each nation should have only one vote and spoke vigorously against the views pro- pounded. Others noted the presence of peculiar observers, 'members of the secret police' who 'sat insolently at the back of committee rooms, smoking cigarettes and chattering whilst speeches were being made'.[10] The Home Office bothered little about it all, for they had long since written off these congresses as 'bewildering and ineffective' talking shops which could safely be ignored.[11]

The last two years of the peace were a time of criticism of the prisons of England, for Macartney's book had been widely read and in both houses of parliament there were anxieties about the survival of ponderous regulated routine. In May 1937 Sir Samuel Hoare became Home Secretary and, at once, began to hammer out a new Criminal Justice Bill, which would be firmly grounded on all the departmental committee recommendations which had mounted up in the 1930s and were awaiting law. So, Hoare now proposed a new form of corrective training for reformable serious offenders, the abolition of corporal punishment and penal servitude, a sentence of preventive detention to stand in its own right for unreformable recidivists, more probation and psychological treatment, non custodial task centres later to be called attendance centres, special institutions for training and assessing adolescent offenders, hostels for younger criminals and so forth. Each idea was debated and wrangled over in press and parliament and the bill went into draught after draught—thirteen by October, 1938. When Hitler was preparing to spring on Austria they were arguing about whether the police should run the task centres and officials were lamenting that the bill 'touches the existing law at innumerable points', likely to 'draw fire' from lawyers, 'prison reformers' and 'welfare workers', and impossible for parliament to pass.[12] Around the time that Czechoslovakia went down the Children's Branch of the Home Office was scathing about a 'retrogressive' bill and bitter about their being ignored during the consultation stages.[13] When the tanks and infantry moved out towards the Polish frontier they were arguing about the abolition of corporal punishment. In the event there was not time for the bill to pass, for in large portions of the European continent armageddon had come to pass.

The prison commission was sent off to Oriel College, Oxford for the war and everybody with less than three months to serve and all borstal boys who had done over six months (three for girls) were sent home, the London prisoners remaining being evacuated to the provincial prisons. This caused a stir, because the release of borstal trainees seemed to some to turn the 'whole borstal system . . . into a farce', with protesters unable to 'conceive what was in the minds of the Prison Commission'.[14] Soon the prisoners who were left were assembling gun turrets for tanks or making military roads or out with farmers working the land, producing cattle, fruit, sugar beet and tomatoes, with some female prisoners making 'dolls and teddy bears which can be dressed and undressed' for evacuee children.[15] As one borstal boy wrote, 'I am working on a farm now about ten miles from (Usk) driving a tractor and looking after cattle . . . the farmer and his wife are very nice people, they remind me a little of you and dad, Mum, the boss is about as big as Dad, is always happy and the missus is always petting the kids like you used to mum, when me and Kenny were kids . . . I realise now if I had done as you and him told me I would probably have been a help instead of a hindrance . . . and a son to be proud of, but I swear you will never regret sticking to me, neither of you'.[16]

In the thousand year Reich the administrators were filling the prisons, concentration camps and gas chambers, impelled by a vision of a world free of the impure, the misshapen, the impaired and the criminal. There the scientists pondered over the constitution of such creatures and experimented upon their bodies in order to push further the boundaries of their science. In their world elimination held centre stage, although they claimed that it was not entirely so. So, they told their slaves at Auschwitz that work makes free and their prisoners that 'work, discipline and benevolence overcome hardness of heart, wash out what is past and lead back home'.[17] The reality, as would become clear, was somewhat different.

In introducing this book I made clear that there has been a sharp divergence of view among modern writers about the history of prisons. Michel Foucault viewed the claims of humanity and progress made by prison disciplinarians during the late eighteenth and early nineteenth centuries with profound suspicion.[18] He distrusted what he saw as the origins of modern penality, the strengthening of carceral institutional control on the basis of apparently promising and benevolent schemes of reclamation. Foucault saw these new structures as witness to the almost irresistible tendency of the institutions of power and of the human sciences to cross fertilise so as to subjugate human personality and to deploy social groups by complex strategies of control and division. He viewed as a major problem with modern prisons their growing tendency to serve as an integrated element of 'the carceral city' with its panoptic 'mechanisms of normalization and wide ranging powers' as well as coercive behavioural treatments and technologies.[19] Foucault saw the decisive shift as commencing in the late eighteenth century and steadily strengthening thereafter. Although Michael Ignatieff laid more emphasis on the humanitarian and reformatory elements of English prisons in the period it cannot really be suggested that his distrust of these institutions was markedly less than that of Foucault. Indeed he stressed their totalitarian nature and the class based system of control upon which he believed them to have been based again stressing that in this period were to be founed the origins of a decisive shift from infliction of bodily pain to mental incursion which has remained part of penality to the present day.[20]

More recently David Garland modified Foucault's thesis. He stressed that there was a second period of change which began in the late nineteenth and early twentieth centuries and marked a departure from the earlier classical principles of measured uniformly administered punishment according to seriousness of crime and the need for deterrence. Between 1895 and 1914 Garland was sure that the English system of criminal disposal embraced a new principle of differential disposition according to positivistic diagnosis of 'condition and the treatment appropriate to it'.[21] He allocated eugenic theory a substantial part in this revolution in penal disposal. Foucault was therefore wrong, he argued, because the processes of 'normalisation, classification, categorisation and discrimination between different criminal types simply did not occur in Britain until after 1895'.[22] Nonetheless, whatever the disagreement between Foucault, and Garland, their thesis has been that the modern penal system tends towards increasing surveillance, measurement of personality, secret administrative dispositions, treatment on the basis of perceived propensity or tendency and Foucault was himself pessimistic about the future of humanity faced with such penetrating and irresistible forces as the modern human sciences and the network of penal, educational, therapeutic and disciplinary institutions grounded on them.

On the face of it the thesis advanced by Foucault and modified by Garland is not difficult to sustain with regard to prisons between 1895 and 1939. It might be urged that prior to 1895 during the Du Cane era the human sciences emphasised the necessity for extreme deterrence and severity whilst retaining all the panopticism and regimentation of the earlier Victorian era and insisting upon the abnormality of prisoners and the necessity for harsh discipline and seclusion from surrounding society. Then at the end of the century the human sciences integrated constitutional and environmental theories of criminality and produced a set of technologies (paternal intervention, charitable philanthropy, differentiation of criminal and mental pathologies) to control, survey, classify and further marginalise prisoners. Thus, it might be said, the Gladstone committee, whilst it retained overall a classical basis for prison discipline in measured punishment, deterrence and moral culpability, also insisted upon such aspects as medical regimes for inebriates, preventive incapacitation of habitual criminals, extended and indeterminate training for young prisoners, more elaborate and efficient means of instruction, stronger systems of control and surveillance through welfare and aftercare measures.

So, according to this view, the Ruggles-Brise era saw the birth (or according to Foucault the rebirth) of a set of welfarist / controlling strategies which burgeoned during the interwar years. The activities of such medical officers as Charles Buckman Goring served to emphasise the complexity of criminal personality and the need for eugenic measures to detect it and control its reproduction. Particular groups were selected for special treatment on the basis of diagnosis by mental scientists (inebriates). Other measures of quarantine were applied to those perceived to be of recidivistic tendency (preventive detainees). The element of indeterminacy was strengthened and the power of administrators increased to advance or retard release date (preventive detention and borstal). Administrative dispositions at all stages of sentence increased and differential management according to classification and stage of sentence became more significant (penal servitude, borstals and the three divisions in local prisons). Surveillance and control was extended by welfare measures both during sentence and after release (Borstal and Convict Visiting and Discharged Prisoners' Aid). Furthermore between 1895 and 1939 an intellectual field was in dispute on which at first eugenists appeared to gain the advantage but were later checked and their thesis integrated with mental hygienism. This dispute signalled ever more strongly the need for the human sciences to develop new categories of method and understanding and to suggest a new interlocking set of specialist penal institutions of control, surveillance and categorisation onto which could be built new facilities as the unending search of the human sciences brought new solutions to light (Grace Pailthorpe's hospital/prison/clinic complex). At the last the prison system might thus reach outside the walls to lock into the welfarist/hygienist project beyond, a project involving the analysis and treatment of the very psycho social interior of the family, the complex hitherto uncharted intellectual and emotional development of the individual (psychoanalysis and lady visitors at Wandsworth and later Wormwood Scrubs boys' prisons). Lastly educational techniques were harnessed to the great reformatory endeavour grounded, as Garland made clear, in the desire to instruct prisoners and borstal trainees in those things which their superiors wished them to know and in attitudes which they wished them to hold.[23]

David Garland himself made it clear that it was necessary to be cautious about the application of the penal/welfare complex which he described as a set of ideas, and its actual application in practice. This is particularly necessary with regard to English prisons between 1895 and 1939. In the first place, as I have made clear repeatedly, the working of penal disciplinary and reformatory projects fell short of the claims made for them. The two state inebriate reformatories proved a fiasco, not least because of the collective resistence of the inebriates, and had to be discontinued. Preventive Detention began with a strong belief that it could rid society of habitual criminals by carceral segregation. In the event judicial distrust of the measure ensured that the project did not thrive and after 1931, when Camp Hill became a borstal, it was never viewed as an effective means by which habitual criminality could be excised from society. Borstal fared better than inebriate reformatories or preventive detention although before 1920 there were great problems in operating the system again in part because of the resistence of the trainees. Certainly as a radically different way of segregating, classifying and defining young offenders borstals would have been viewed with great suspicion by Foucault and certainly they exercised substantial power to interpret and direct conditions of sentences and actual release date in ways which were typical of Foucault's 'carceral city'.

The local and convict prisons, however, clung tenaciously to the concepts of measured punishment, moral culpability, limited deterrence and uniformly administered discipline and showed only a modest inclination to respond either to the eugenics movement or to the mental hygiene movement which superseded it. It has been made clear in chapter ten that there were enthusiasts for psychoanalytical and psychological treatment of prisoners but it is the case that the Prison Commission and its staff, after initial interest, were distrustful of any eugenic or other theorising which might lead to abandonment of *mens rea* as the heart of criminal jurisprudence. Both Horatio Donkin and subsequently Norwood East repeatedly made clear that they resisted all trends towards seeing criminality as the determined outcome of environmental or biological conditions and were cautious about modifying prison discipline to classify or manage prisoners on such a basis. This is not to deny the enthusiasm with which Norwood East supported research in and study of the validity of psychology and psychotherapy in prisons. However, he and almost all prison medical staff were highly conservative in their view of prison discipline. As Norwood East remarked, 'at present . . . we only see through a glass darkly: the future researches of the psychiatric and child guidance and educational expert may give us light and better understanding'.[24] In fact this conservatism was in marked contrast to the remarkable expansion of use of mental hygienist and Freudian approaches outside the prisons.[25]

There is another sense in which the notion of a disciplined, routinising, expanding carceral archipelago does not correspond with trends in English prisons between 1895 and 1939. The plain fact is that far from expanding in size and taking into its grip ever larger numbers of deviants, the prison system shrank to an extent which today seems wholly remarkable. So from around 17,000 daily average of prisoners in 1900 the population of prisoners and borstal trainees had fallen to around 11,000 by 1936.[26] Local prisons themselves reduced in number from fifty six in 1914 to twenty six in 1930.[27]

As earlier made clear Andrew Rutherford pointed to a strong tendency towards reduction of use of imprisonment between 1908 and 1938. He saw Churchill's work as Home Secretary as important in laying the foundations of what Rutherford called a reductionist era. Clearly wider use of probation and the 1914 Criminal Justice Administration Act which obliged courts to consider allowing time to pay fines before committal were, as Rutherford remarked, important in this process and indeed between 1908 and 1938 the total number (excluding remand prisoners) of receptions fell from 205,216 to 40,430 with a dramatic fall in numbers of fine defaulters and substantial falls in civil prisoners and those sentenced to prison as a punishment. Furthermore there was a remarkable reduction in numbers sent to prison for short sentences, an overall substantial reduction in length of sentences of penal servitude and an increase in non custodial sentencing generally.[28] Whatever the explanation the facts call into question the notion of modern carceral systems drawing into their grip increasing numbers of deviants.

Ignatieff dwelled particularly upon the rigid severities of the penitentiary and Foucault clearly disbelieved the claims of prison disciplinarians of the early ninetheenth century that they were founding their endeavour on a concept of universal human value. Certainly, had either of these writers considered prisons in the inter war years they would have paid particular attention to the writings of Jim Phelan and Wilfred Macartney each of whom made it clear that the overall effect of the system was to reduce the humanity of those subjected to it and to mark them out in their own eyes and those of society as pariahs or of inferior value to others. Indeed Phelan and Macartney depicted the emotional, spiritual and mental deterioration which they observed and maintained that this was the inevitable consequence and deliberate purpose of the system.

In answer to this it has initially to be said that the English prison system of the inter war years was humane compared with the carceral systems which took shape in Nazi Germany and the Soviet Union during the inter war years and that Solzhenitzyn's carceral gulag infinitely outstripped in horror anything that was done in England at the same time. Furthermore it is possible to point to penal atrocities routinely carried out in other countries at the same time, whether the collusion of the Alabama authorities with lynching of black men suspected of molesting white girls[29] before the First World War or mass public beheading of Siamese offenders in the 1920s.[30]

In saying this I am not wishing to deny that English prisons were, as many of the testimonies recently collected by Philip Priestley remind us, severe, regimented and disciplinary in the early twentieth century.[31] Not withstanding, provision of the basic necessities of life, freedom from widespread institutionally legitimised violence by staff and an effective recognition that prisoners of the state have the right to some dignity and protection were characteristic of the English prison system between 1895 and 1939. Such features were not typical of many prison systems in the world either then or thereafter.

In that context there is a growing body of modern literature warning mankind about the importance of ensuring the genuine inclusion of the individual perceived by the state as surplus to requirements or potential saboteurs of social and political progress. Michael Ignatieff himself viewed prisoners as occupying a space which lay outside the familiar guarantees and protections of organized society.[32] In a later book, not explicitly connected with prisons, he pointed to the perilous position occupied by one whose only recourse lay in appeal to a notional conception of human rights. He wrote: 'woe betide any man who depends on the abstract humanity of another for his food and protection. Woe betide any person who has no state, no family, no neighbourhood, no community that can stand behind to enforce his claim of need. Lear learns too late that it is power and violence that rule the heath, not obligation'.[33] The point of abandonment to desolation and destruction is developed by Bill Jordan, the widely read political and economic theorist, who has repeatedly warned that, where common interests in humanity and shared faith in universal human value through experience cease to be recognised, swathes of populations may be relegated to an underclass, victims of 'a Leviathan trap ... once the Hobbesian door shuts behind us'.[34] The end of such warnings disregarded is exclusion of millions from participation, dialogue and compassion the worst case example of which is harrowingly depicted by two of the most eminent analysts of the Holocaust in terms of removal by liquidation of a whole race seen as less than human, surplus to requirements or a menace to society or state or party.[35]

It seems to me that Foucault and subsequently Garland did not grasp that the reformatory project was more than a mere outcome of strategies of power crossfertilising with knowledge to justify greater intervention. Doubtless their analysis is in part correct and it would be the height of naivety to deny this. Yet I have tried to show that in the prison system of the early twentieth century there was a genuine, rather than merely rhetorical, belief that English prisoners were possessed of an individual human worth and that there was a plain duty on the part of the state and society to recognise this as a principle enshrined in law and administrative practice flowing from law, conscience and values rather than merely increasing leniency to ensure more subtle and effective control.

Between 1895 and 1921 the Ruggles-Brise era was a reaction, albeit a cautious one, to the Du Cane era which had come close to compromising this principle of entitlement. After 1921 it is clear that leading administrators such as Alexander Paterson or Harold Scott were convinced as a matter of religion, personal experience and intellectual concept, that they had a personal moral responsibility to reduce severity and reclaim the prisoner. Furthermore this conviction was shared by many prison officials even though their philosophies of society varied greatly. It was thus of prime importance to such as Colonel Rich, Major Blake, Lilian Barker or William Llewellin that prisoners should not be abandoned and excluded as sub human saboteurs of the social order but rather treated with fairness and dignity and, if possible, reclaimed. Alongside Foucault's and Garland's emphasis on panoptic surveillance, intrusion, discipline and control therefore it is necessary to set a genuine and sustained intention to punish and protect the prisoner according to a framework of legal obligation and a faith that the individual prisoner shares in the universal worth of men and women.

There remain some lessons to be drawn from this study concerning the history of the reformatory project which might be of relevance for, although at present the project appears an unlikely or even distasteful preoccupation for penological theorists, it seems clear from its ebb and flow in history that one day it will return to English prisons. The lessons of this study may therefore be useful against the day of that return for, as Churchill reminded Parliament in 1938, 'all wisdom is not new wisdom'.[36]

In the first place, all reformists, whether individuals or groups like the Howard League, could achieve little in the prisons without convincing the Prison Commission and Home Office that they were not subversive or destructive. Often this took many years: the Howard League experienced several decades of being seen by the Home Office and Commission as a potentially hostile and disloyal 'bete noir', before being accepted as dutiful, loyal and appropriately critical. Other groups were dismissed as trivial, eccentric but harmless and, like the People's League of Health, eventually allowed to give their lectures provided that the rules were kept. Any group which appeared radical or subversive to the Home Office was excluded from dialogue or participation and suffragist groups were thus given no access. Throughout the entire period 1895-1939 the Home Office maintained elaborate surveillance and banks of filed information about all groups which professed interest in the penal reform movement. The prison commission always referred such groups to the Home Office for vetting when they first encountered them.

Secondly, the archival material of this period leaves no doubt of the careful way in which the Home Office checked and assessed public opinion about crime and punishment. Clerks collected and filed local and national newspaper cuttings, journal and book extracts and all projects were considered against the likely public reaction before anything else. When the Home Office gave support to a new project, the officials there had considered it, not only in terms of financial implications (and the Treasury were a frequent check on prison projects) but also in terms of likely public reaction and accusations of molly coddling criminals.

Thirdly, without the support of the courts new statutory measures tended to come to grief. Judges had to be convinced that these measures were well grounded in English legal principles and, as the history of preventive detention showed, they would not make full use of new provisions if they appeared to judges to contain strange or problematic legal principles. With preventive detention judges were unhappy from the beginning, because it represented double sentencing, it contained a concept of habitual criminality which was problematic in terms of the law of evidence and later many judges considered the double sentence, in any case, to be too severe. They therefore were reluctant to pass it.

However, courts could also undermine new measures if they did not understand them and Ruggles-Brise's three divisions and borstals show this. With the divisions courts failed to understand what was on offer to them and therefore hardly made use of the second division. With borstal sentencers continued to send mischievous or sickly young people to them, despite repeated admonitions that borstal was for the young, strong, persistent criminal headed, otherwise, for a life of recidivism and penal servitude.

Fourthly, the modern reformist needs to reflect that official rhetoric was often a poor guide to what actually happened in prisons. This is not to say that the huge annual reports of the prison commission or the long explanations, given by ministers in answer to backbench questions, con-tained deliberate lies, although sometimes half truths were deliberately presented as wholes. What was deceptive, however, was the overall message that the prison project of reformation and easing of severity was proceeding efficiently and smoothly, a claim which the Home Office and Prison Commission wanted to believe and which the majority of the public wanted to have confirmed. As Jim Phelan would have said, there was a touch of Madame De Luce about that huge and nowadays scarcely consulted array of annual reports and compendious additional detail, hundreds of pages long, produced with meticulous care between 1895 and 1939.

The advocate of a return to reformation might reflect upon the fact that between 1895 and 1939 the success rate of projects was consistently exaggerated by their advocates. Ruggles-Brise and his successors claimed that offenders were being reformed in large numbers and this was not hard to do, given that the prison population was falling so remarkably; yet, as supporters of the separate system found in the 1840s, grand claims to mass rehabilitation by reformatory projects have always been deceptive and have never borne close scrutiny. If we have learned nothing else from the history of the reformatory endeavour, let us at least learn that its claims to achieve huge success rates are suspect and that prison populations rise or fall according to far more complex influences—changing sentencing practice between 1895 and 1939 being one cause of decline in numbers in this period.

The actual provision made and resources granted for reformatory projects were always less than were required to mount effective programmes of rehabilitation. Indeed, at times, the resources and personnel were hugely out of kilter with the ambitions of the Prison Commission; for example, the idea that chaplains would work closely and intimately with individual prisoners could hardly be translated into practice, given the very high number of prisoners to each chaplain. Even the claims made for the borstals in the inter war years need to be treated with care. As their most recent historian has pointed out, despite the exceptions such as Lowdham Grange or staff such as William Llewellin, the system as a whole lacked the resources or the capacity to individualise, differentiate or classify more than super-ficially or indeed even seriously attempt to teach borstal trainees a trade. Rather, most of the borstals dealt with inmates on a collective basis and did little more than try to instil habits of industry and good conduct into trainees.[37]

It might be added that on occasion the Commissioners used reformatory projects as a Trojan Horse carrying within them a plan to reduce severity yet couched in reformatory terms to persuade Home Office, Treasury and general public of the legitimacy of the project in question. So it was clearly Harold Scott's intention to create more humane and relaxed conditions at New Hall Camp yet the experiment was justified on grounds that prisoners would learn self-control and responsibility through group loyalty and greater freedom. Access of outside prison visitors and entertainers was also secured through appeals to the educational and uplifting quality of their contribution to prisoners' lives. This in no way is to suggest that such commissioners as Scott or Paterson were not enthusiastic reformists but it is nonetheless the case that reformatory claims assisted them in their urgent wish to abandon what they saw as the more obvious and harsh remnants of late Victorian severity.

Turning to the prisons as a whole the attitude of the Prison Commission to prison officers is striking. The fact is that they were not seen as major participants in the reformatory project, although lip service was paid to their value. Indeed many prisoners remarked with genuine sympathy upon their oppressed state in Ruggles-Brise's time and during Paterson's period the new borstal posts of tutor and housemaster were never considered suitable for them. It is plain that the relationship between the Commission and prison officers was often problematic between the years 1895-1939, not only because there was frequently resentment and discontent among prison officers, but also because the Commission was failing adequately to exploit its largest resource. Prison officers were with prisoners night and day, and yet their potential as reformatory agents was not seriously recognised. It had been exactly the same in the 1830s and 1840s when the new chaplains and governors were lauded as experts in the separate system, warders as mere operatives of the regulations. Yet, as one officer said to James Leigh about purveyors of new reformatory ideas in the inter war years: 'they can be smart with the staff for years, because they're educated enough to know how far they can go. But us fellows always win in the end'.[38] In this case he was speaking of prisoners setting up groups and fellowships in the Paterson era, but the prison officer was equally well placed to make or break the schemes of the commissioners.

The fact is that the prison project between 1895 and 1939 not only depended upon philosophy and governmental machinery for success but also on the spirit, enthusiasm and courage of personnel. Many of those regarded as most successful by prisoners, for example Blake, Rich or Clayton, were often a thorn in the side of the Commission and Paterson himself was a radical critic of the prison system throughout his life. Prisoners were very clear that the mere bureaucrat, who repetitively operated such things as marks, labour systems, prisoners' aid systems or whatever, were operating at a level which crushed human spirit, initiative and dignity. It was those governors, chaplains and officers who allowed their own enthusiasms free rein who were most remembered by prisoners, although equally cranks or theoretical eccentrics were speedily dismissed by them. However, the governors who made the greatest impact did so by virtue of what prisoners saw as their obvious human decency, fairness and directness. These varied greatly in their general views—Barker and Llewellin were out of the Paterson stable; Rich and Clayton were nostalgic conservatives whilst Major Blake thought that the entire system was going down the drain and would not abide Paterson for any price.

There is one final matter for comment. During the years 1895 to 1939, the ground of dispute about prisons included much that was the same as in the 1780s, 1830s or indeed the 1980s. So, between 1895 and 1939 they wrangled over whether prisons should be painful, deterrent and harsh or reformatory and re-educative. Then, as now, one side insisted that prisoners chose to become predators and should face the full penal consequences of their choice, whilst others pointed to psychological factors and social environment as the mainsprings of crime thus reducing culpability. Then, as with Lord Justice Darling's attitude to 'Ruggles-Brisia', one side accused their opponents of sentimental naivety and, as today, ridiculed those who believed that crime resulted because 'somebody's grandmother three times removed had a breakdown'.[39] Then, as now, hard liners expostulated at the quality of Christmas dinners for prisoners, incidentally substantially improved during the inter war years, and would have agreed with a modern conservative declaring in 1988, 'there's something wrong with our society . . . I saw the Christmas day menu . . . old people outside couldn't afford it . . . they had a band brought in'.[40]

One item, however, did not surface between 1895 and 1939. The debate about management of prisons by private enterprise had been hard fought in Britain around the end of the eighteenth century and emerged again in the late 1980s. However, in the period under consideration, it found no echo, for almost all believed that the state alone should manage prisons to which might be admitted some high minded philanthropic groups. The view that a private contractor would be a more effective prison manager, as well as cheaper, had been advanced by Jeremy Bentham and decisively defeated in 1811 by those who insisted that the duty of moral and spiritual reformation could only safely be entrusted to the state.[41]

Overall in England the inter war years witnessed a significant growth in the liberal ameliorative approach to prisoners. Advocates of this, furthermore, managed to retain their advantage despite such set backs as the Dartmoor riot which, like most prison riots, gave temporary encouragement to their opponents. So, impelled by what Radzinowicz and Hood described as 'the very optimistic approach towards crime and its control which flourished in the period between the two World Wars'[42] in the late 1930s, the commissioners were preparing an assault on the great architectural monoliths bequeathed to them by the Victorians and intending to move further towards camp institutions for men and women. None of this was, of course, at all welcome to those who held opposite views of the purposes of prison but these were spared any further reforms by the outbreak of war. Nonetheless they would have to wait longer than 1945 to gain their ascendancy: the fate of Paterson's heirs, however, is another subject of study.

## NOTES

1. S.K. Ruck (ed), *Paterson on Prisons: Being the Collected Papers of Sir Alexander Paterson* (Muller 1951): 70, 71, 91-3.
2. PRO P Com. 9/80, E.R. Cass General Secretary American Prison Association to A. Paterson, 18 May 1933.

3. Minimum Standards of Treatment 1926-9, PRO P Com. 7/61 / 1 / 1D / 1E.
4. Ninth International Penitentiary Congress 1925, PRO P Com. 7/62, International Penitentiary Congresses 1930-35, PRO HO 45-20458-553922/21, Lord Polwarth to Sec. Gen. League of Nations 28 June 1930.
5. International Penitentiary Congress Berlin 1934-6, P Com. 9/195 /1, /2, /5, /6, /8.
6. International Penitentiary Congresses 1930-35 PRO HO 45-20458-553922/47, Dr Goebbels, *The Constructive Work of The National Socialist State,* printed.
7. Ibid. Printed address, Dr Hans Frank.
8. Ibid.
9. *The Times,* 19 Aug. 1935: 9 col. d.
10. *The Times,* 21 Nov. 1935: 7 col. f.
11. PRO HO 45-20458-553922/47, HO Minute, 17 Oct. 1935.
12. Criminal Justice Bill PRO HO 45-17666-805270/37-30, Sir Granville Ram to Sir A. Maxwell 3 Feb. 1938, Chief Constable Birmingham to HO, 18 Jan. 1938.
13. Criminal Justice Bill PRO HO 45-17667-805270/68-59, Children's Branch HO to Sir A. Maxwell, 19 Sept. 1938.
14. PRO P Com. 9/90, Dr Magrath to PC, no day, Nov. 1939.
15. Industrial Training in Borstals, PRO 45-19688-442964/15, /16 Press statement, 7 Oct. 1943.
16. Ibid. /18 Unnamed borstal boy to parents, no date.
17. H. Scott (ed), *German Prisons in 1934* (Printed HM Prison Maidstone 1936): 81.
18. M. Foucault, *Discipline and Punish: The Birth of the Prison* (Penguin 1979).
19. Ibid: 307, 306.
20. M. Ignatieff, *A Just Measure of Pain: The Penitentiary in the Industrial Revolution* (MacMillan 1978).
21. D. Garland, *Punishment and Welfare* (Gower 1985): 28.
22. Ibid: 32.
23. Ibid: 255-7.
24. RCP & DCP for 1936, PP 1937-8, XIV: 64.
25. N. Rose, *The Psychological Complex: Psychology Politics and Society in England, 1869-1939* (Routledge & Kegan Paul 1985).
26. RCP & DCP 1902, PP 1902, XLVI: 20. RCP & DCP 1936, PP 1937-8, XIV: 15.
27. RCP & DCP 1931-2, PP 1931-2, XII: 34.
28. A. Rutherford, *Prisons and the Process of Justice* (Heinemann 1984): 123-31. L. Radzinowicz, 'The Present Trend of English Penal Policy' *Law Quarterly Review,* April 1939, CCXVIII: 273-88.
29. HO 45-10503-125632, Reforms in Prisons and Police Courts. Howard Association Annual Report, Oct. 1904.
30. J.L. Gillin, *Criminology and Penology* (The Century Company 1935) 246-7.
31. P. Priestley, *Jail Journeys: English Prison Experience, 1918-1990* (Routledge 1989).
32. Ignatieff, *A Just Measure of Pain*: XII.
33. M. Ignatieff, *The Needs of Strangers* (Chatto & Windus 1984): 53.

34. B. Jordan, *The Common Good: Citizenship, Morality and Self Interest* (Blackwell 1989): 183.
35. R.L. Rubenstein and J.K. Roth, *Approaches to Auschwitz: The Legacy of the Holocaust* (John Knox Press 1987).
36. Parl. Deb. 5th Series vol. 339 col. 367, 5 Oct. 1938.
37. V. Bailey, *Deliquency and Citizenship: Reclaiming the Young Offender* (Clarendon Press 1987): 204-5, 217.
38. J. Leigh, *My Prison House* (Hutchinson & Co. 1941): 205.
39. 'What Is Prison For?' *After Dark* series, Chair: Ian Kennedy. Channel 4, 16 April 1988, Terry Dicks M.P.
40. Ibid.
41. W.J. Forsythe, 'Privatization and British Prisons: Past and Future' *Prison Service Journal*, 1989, New Series, 73: 35-7.
42. L. Radzinowicz and R. Hood, *A History of English Criminal Law and its Administration from 1750*, vol. 5, *The Emergence of Penal Policy*, (Stevens & Sons 1986): 778.

# Index